Psychodynamic Perspectives on Asylum Seekers and the Asylum-Seeking Process

Psychodynamic Perspectives on Asylum Seekers and the Asylum-Seeking Process looks at the psychosocial assessment of asylum seekers from three perspectives: forensic, psychodynamic, and political and then attempts to better understand, from a psychodynamic perspective, differences in the historical/motivational routes of asylum seekers themselves.

Barbara Eisold begins in Chapter One by exploring the unique evaluation relationship of psychosocial assessment and the striking will to survive of the asylum seekers that it puts into focus, using a psychodynamic lens. The forensic value of psychosocial assessment and its potential as both a political and a therapeutic tool are then described. Chapter Two describes individuals, who, by background and personal characteristics, shared a profound desire to protest, gravely compromising their survival at home and forcing them to seek asylum elsewhere. Chapter Three discusses women who have suffered female genital mutilation and includes a discussion of the development of strong personal agency in one case. Chapter Four describes abused women from Central America forced to flee from feminicide. The evolution of feminicide is explored, including the development of honor-bound machismo and the wide-spread disregard of law. The hold men have on women is then examined from a psychodynamic perspective.

Psychodynamic Perspectives on Asylum Seekers and the Asylum-Seeking Process will be of great interest to psychoanalysts, psychoanalytic psychotherapists, and all mental health professionals working with asylum seekers.

Barbara K. Eisold has worked as an evaluator of asylum seekers in collaboration with a number of organizations, including Health Rights International, Physicians for Human Rights (PHR) and The Cardozo School of Law, where she is an associate faculty member. She is also a faculty member of the Institute for Contemporary Psychotherapy and maintains a private psychotherapy practice in New York City.

When music is played in a new key, the melody does not change, but the notes that make up the composition do: change in the context of continuity, continuity that perseveres through change. Psychoanalysis in a New Key publishes books that share the aims psychoanalysts have always had, but that approach them differently. The books in the series are not expected to advance any particular theoretical agenda, although to this date most have been written by analysts from the Interpersonal and Relational orientations.

The most important contribution of a psychoanalytic book is the communication of something that nudges the reader's grasp of clinical theory and practice in an unexpected direction. Psychoanalysis in a New Key creates a deliberate focus on innovative and unsettling clinical thinking. Because that kind of thinking is encouraged by exploration of the sometimes surprising contributions to psychoanalysis of ideas and findings from other fields, Psychoanalysis in a New Key particularly encourages interdisciplinary studies. Books in the series have married psychoanalysis with dissociation, trauma theory, sociology, and criminology. The series is open to the consideration of studies examining the relationship between psychoanalysis and any other field—for instance, biology, literary and art criticism, philosophy, systems theory, anthropology, and political theory.

But innovation also takes place within the boundaries of psychoanalysis, and Psychoanalysis in a New Key therefore also presents work that reformulates thought and practice without leaving the precincts of the field. Books in the series focus, for example, on the significance of personal values in psychoanalytic practice, on the complex interrelationship between the analyst's clinical work and personal life, on the consequences for the clinical situation when patient and analyst are from different cultures, and on the need for psychoanalysts to accept the degree to which they knowingly satisfy their own wishes during treatment hours, often to the patient's detriment. A full list of all titles in this series is available at: https://www.routledge.com/series/LEAPNKBS

TITLES IN THIS SERIES INCLUDE:

Vol. 51 *Formulated Experiences: Hidden Realities and Emergent Meanings from Shakespeare to Fromm* Peter L. Rudnytsky

Vol. 50 *The Emergence of Analytic Oneness: Into the Heart of Psychoanalysis* Ofra Eshel

Vol. 49 *Homosexuality, Transsexuality, Psychoanalysis and Traditional Judaism* Edited by Alan Slomowitz and Alison Feit

Vol. 48 *Psychodynamic Perspectives on Asylum Seekers and the Asylum-Seeking Process* Barbara K. Eisold

Vol. 47 *Bearing Witness to the Witness: A Psychoanalytic Perspective on Four Modes of Traumatic Testimony* Dana Amir

Vol. 46 *Travels with the Self: Interpreting Psychology as Cultural History* Philip Cushman

Psychodynamic Perspectives on Asylum Seekers and the Asylum-Seeking Process

Encountering Well-Founded Fear

Barbara K. Eisold

LONDON AND NEW YORK

First published 2019
by Routledge
2 Park Square, Milton Park, Abingdon, Oxon OX14 4RN

and by Routledge
52 Vanderbilt Avenue, New York, NY 10017

Routledge is an imprint of the Taylor & Francis Group, an informa business

© 2019 Barbara K. Eisold

The right of Barbara K. Eisold to be identified as author of this work has been asserted by her in accordance with sections 77 and 78 of the Copyright, Designs and Patents Act 1988.

All rights reserved. No part of this book may be reprinted or reproduced or utilised in any form or by any electronic, mechanical, or other means, now known or hereafter invented, including photocopying and recording, or in any information storage or retrieval system, without permission in writing from the publishers.

Trademark notice: Product or corporate names may be trademarks or registered trademarks, and are used only for identification and explanation without intent to infringe.

British Library Cataloguing in Publication Data
A catalogue record for this book is available from the British Library

Library of Congress Cataloging in Publication Data
Names: Eisold, Barbara K., author.
Title: Psychodynamic perspectives on asylum seekers and the asylum-seeking process : encountering well-founded fear / Barbara K. Eisold.
Description: New York : Routledge, 2019. | Includes bibliographical references and index.
Identifiers: LCCN 2018042346 (print) | LCCN 2018058019 (ebook) | ISBN 9780429424793 (Master) | ISBN 9780429756061 (ePub) | ISBN 9780429756078 (Web PDF) | ISBN 9780429756054 (Mobi/Kindle) | ISBN 9781138354418 (hbk : alk. paper) | ISBN 9781138354456 (pbk : alk. paper) | ISBN 9780429424793 (ebk)
Subjects: LCSH: Women refugees—Case studies. | Political refugees—Case studies.
Classification: LCC HV640 (ebook) | LCC HV640 E37 2019 (print) | DDC 325/.21019—dc23
LC record available at https://lccn.loc.gov/2018042346

ISBN: 978-1-138-35441-8 (hbk)
ISBN: 978-1-138-35445-6 (pbk)
ISBN: 978-0-429-42479-3 (ebk)

Typeset in Times
by Swales & Willis Ltd, Exeter, Devon, UK

Printed and bound in Great Britain by
TJ International Ltd, Padstow, Cornwall

To Kenneth Eisold with love and special thanks for your enthusiastic encouragement of this whole project.
And to all the asylum seekers who have shared your stories with me: I have felt so privileged to be there to listen as you spoke!

Contents

	List of tables	viii
	List of long cases	ix
	Acknowledgements	x
	Introduction	xii
1	The nature of psychosocial asylum evaluations: Implications for client and clinician	1
2	Heroic Asylum seekers from around the world	40
3	Female genital mutilation and the wish for "life": Cultural considerations in the development of personal agency	68
4	Central American women on the run: Feminicide and its history	92
	Afterword	131
	Appendix I: Asylum law in brief	133
	Appendix II: Imprisoning asylum seekers	138
	Appendix III: Outline: Prospective affidavit of a mental health professional in support of an asylum seeker	141
	Appendix IV: Female genital mutilation: facts and figures	145
	Appendix V: Background information: My clients/other women with FGM	147
	Index	150

Tables

2.1 *Heroic asylum seekers: Personal data* 43
3.1 *FGM asylee: Background characteristics* 70

Long Cases

Chapter One
Mr. M — 11
Mr. D — 12
Ms. Therese — 19

Chapter Two
Mr. I — 47
Ms. B — 48

Chapter Three
Ms. A — 71

Chapter Four
Rosa — 94
Elena — 113

Acknowledgements

To list all those to whom I feel I owe thanks is difficult. The list is long and reaches far back! Most immediately I am extremely grateful to those who read my manuscript, all or in part, any piece of it at any stage, and gave me honest feedback. First among these is my very good friend attorney Victoria Schonfeld, who read everything and gave me kind, thoughtful, and enormously useful feedback from a personal and legal perspective. Others who helped are: Drs. Ghislaine Boulanger, Philip Boxer, Rachel Cohen, Kenneth Eisold, Judith Rustin, Fran Geteles-Shapiro, and Mark Zern.

In regard to immigration and the implications of asylum rights, especially about human rights law in general, I am grateful to those who have helped me learn about the subject. This is a recent area of interest for me and I had no idea how much I needed to know in order to understand it at all. In respect of human rights, I am especially grateful to the late Sheri P. Rosenberg, an associate professor at the Benjamin N. Cardozo School of Law. Elaborating on human rights work done at Cardozo by Richard Weisberg, Sheri set up what she called the Human Rights and Atrocity Prevention Clinic at the school. This included the Refugee Representation Project for Asylum Seekers. I was lucky enough to have been part of the latter project from its beginning and to work closely with Sheri and her assistant, Teresa Woods, for a number of years. This work, which became a wellspring of information for me, would have continued had it not been for Sheri's untimely (and tragic) death from cancer, at age 48, in 2015.

I am also grateful to T. Alexander Aleinikoff, former Deputy Director of UNHCR, presently Director of the Zolberg Institute of Migration and Mobility at the New School of Social Research, for the resources he has made available on the subject of migration, including a course entitled Boundaries and Belonging, from which I learned much.

I am also grateful to the staff at Physicians for Human Rights, past and present, especially in regard to its availability when it has come to the questions that have come up for me in working with asylum seekers.

My thanks also go to Donnel Stern, the editor of the series in which this book is published, who encouraged me to write it and then connected me with people at Routledge, who seamlessly lent me their support. Without his immediate response to my question: "is a book on asylum a reasonable book to do?" I do not think I would have proceeded.

Without the asylum seekers who shared their stories with me this book would never have come to be. I thank them from the bottom of my heart for showing me again and again, how very ingenious, determined, and courageous human beings can be. I am astonished at how many of their stories I remember and how frequently these stories come to mind. Above all, I feel honored to have been able to participate, even briefly, in their respective journeys away from horrors unimaginable to the United States.

Finally, I am grateful to my husband, Kenneth, who supported me from the very beginning as I undertook this project, in spite of the fact that it has ruthlessly taken me away from him and tied me down when he would rather I had been more free.

Introduction

"An alliance with atrocity is part of the burden of modernity." Delbo, 1973, quoted in Des Pres, 2003, p.154.

I am a psychodynamically trained psychotherapist. On most days at work I see people one or sometimes two at a time, hour after hour, week by week, year after year. I love the work, but the therapy process is slow and the result not always clear, even once the process has been terminated. It is also quite isolating. I and the person I am seeing sit in my office by ourselves. Then, when the last person leaves, there is no water cooler around which to chat with fellow workers. As an antidote to this situation, I have always spent some hours each month using my clinical skills as a volunteer for one organization or another. Most recently (beginning in 2002) this has been with organizations that do asylum work.[1,2]

This book has been written primarily for people like myself, people who have been moved by the present immigration crisis and are interviewing and evaluating individuals who are seeking political asylum or other legally sound routes to residence in the United States. Needless to say, there are an increasing number of such people. According to the United Nations High Commissioner for Refugees (UNHCR), there are presently 65.6 million forcibly displaced persons in the world (more than ever before), 22.5 million of whom are refugees, 2.8 million of whom are seeking asylum worldwide.[3,4] Although the United States admitted close to 85,000 refugees in 2016, more than ever before, according to the Pew Research Center,[5] to the chagrin of many, since January 2017, the willingness of the United States to open its doors to all immigrants has decreased enormously.[6]

Before describing asylum seekers and the process of evaluating them, however, I want to underscore the fact that the vast majority of people who are displaced are not refugees/asylum seekers at all. These are people who have been forced to leave home because of events (climate change, natural disasters, forced dispossession, in some cases gang-related affairs) that do not meet the United Nations definition of a refugee. Some are in, some outside of their own countries. Having no place to go, they have been detained, forced to live in camps or prisons, for indeterminate lengths of time, sometimes for generations. In these camps their needs are not well cared for and the length of time they will remain is unclear. They cannot return home because the conflict or situation that caused their flight is still ongoing. Who will take responsibility for them and how they will be cared for over the long term is still uncertain. In order to address this problem, in September, 2016, world leaders met at the United Nations to adopt The New York Declaration for Refugees and Migrants,[7] a document in which many nations committed themselves to the protection of migrants and refugees in a host of different ways. This was the first step, to be followed by a Global Initiative, an international conference to take place in fall, 2018, to plan further. A year after the New York Declaration, however, little had changed.[8] This despite the fact that, according to T. Alexander Aleinikoff, previously Deputy High Commissioner of the United Nations High Commission for Refugees (UNHCR), the number of migrants and refugees is not so huge that other countries could not take them in, were they willing to do so.[9] Yet boundaries in potential host countries are increasingly being closed. In this context, asylum seekers already in a host country and living on their own are an oddly privileged group.

This is the case of the 500,000–600,000 asylum seekers already in the United States who are waiting to have their pleas heard by an asylum official. Recently, in 2017, asylum officers have, according to Reuters,[10] been given wider discretion to deny the claims of such people. Perhaps, in response to government sanctions against refugees, and because of the number of asylum applicants in need of evaluation, medical facilities, psychology departments, and related organizations are becoming more involved. There are more people interested in this work in such places than ever before.

My approach in this book combines application and theory, the latter drawn largely from my psychotherapeutic background. Chapter One addresses the task of interviewing asylum seekers and writing affidavits and the implications for a mental health professional of participating in this work. The chapters that follow are based on reflections about the people I have interviewed, rather than about the implications of the rights to which they have laid claim. Before I begin, therefore, a few words directed at understanding the history of human rights, out of which the right to make an asylum claim has emerged, seems appropriate.

Human rights, as the concept is presently understood, are based on a set of values, reflected most concretely today in laws designed "to protect people from government abuse and neglect," to quote Director of Human Rights Watch, Ken Roth (2017). However, this has not always been the case. In fact, the idea of human rights for all is relatively new in human history. It is an idea that has been slow to take hold and is thus very fragile.

In 1951, in *The Origins of Totalitarianism*, Hannah Arendt described the manner in which World War I and the years that followed led to waves of migration as people, unmoored by inflation, unemployment, and civil wars, struggled to find a place in which to settle and live safely. What they found, however, as they roamed from one nation-state to another, was that the rights they had been guaranteed at home, rights upon which nineteenth-century revolutions and politics had been based, vanished as soon as they left their home countries. Legal rights, in other words, were tied to the law of the land, the land in which each individual held citizenship: "Once they left their homeland they remained homeless, once they left their state they became stateless, once they had been deprived of their human rights they were rightless, the scum of the earth," Arendt wrote (1951, p. 266). Accordingly, human rights, as then defined, were very different from what we, today, call human rights. Ours today, as lawyer/historian Samuel Moyn defines them, consist of "a set of global political norms providing the creed of a transnational social movement that involves as a central concept the detachment of rights from the nation-state" (2010). These rights, he tells us (2014/2017), were "born yesterday."[11]

Indeed, still following Moyn (2010; 2014), it was Franklin Roosevelt who virtually coined the term "human rights" in 1943, setting in motion events that eventually emerged as the Universal Declaration of Human Rights, in 1948,[12] a document sponsored by the United Nations. However, the idea of human rights for everyone, based on personhood alone, did not then take up residence in the popular imagination. No particularly widespread popular movement sprang up around it. Essentially, the idea existed in United Nations related international organizations only. It was not until the 1970's that human rights "crystallized in the moral consciousness of people," essentially after other ideologies (especially Communism) had failed (Moyn, 2014/2017, p. 136). Moyn credits international NGOs, Amnesty International especially,[13] for popularizing the concept of a new world in which individual protection against the state was possible for all. This, he tells us, had a "utopian dimension:" it included "the image of another, better world of dignity and respect . . . the god that did not fail while other political ideologies did . . . [it was] widely understood as a moral alternative to bankrupt political utopias" (2010, p. 4–5).

However, also according to Moyn (2014/2017), the human rights movement was never sufficiently politicized, never mobilized at the grassroots level. "No casebook of international law contains a section on human rights as a global movement. Instead human rights norms are norms to be enforced by judges" (p. 142), he tells us. In sovereign situations in which judges can use laws that protect human rights, they do so only very specifically, "in domestic polities that give them a role, or regional courts gathering together nations that have already agreed to cede to some sovereign prerogatives." (p. 13). In order to have true moral power in the arena of human rights, Moyn believes, a judge or the legal system needs political alliance. This kind of alliance has never emerged.

In asylum courts in the United States, however, judges can/do assume a specific role in which they can (at their discretion, let it be said) make use of immigration laws[14] that protect the human rights of individuals who otherwise might well be tortured and killed should they be forced to return home. This is still the case, in spite of the fact that, in the last twenty years, these laws have been sorely curtailed,[15] indicating less open, more restrictive values, the result of fear, fear of the other, embodied in the immigrant and the asylum seeker. Today, increasingly, since the Oklahoma bombings in 1996, the policies of the United States government reflect far less openness to immigrants and asylum seekers who have had their human rights violated than was previously the case.

New restrictions have led to increases in racial profiling, border killings, and denial of due process rights. Often asylum seekers are incarcerated and denied the bond hearings to which they are legally entitled, which are the hearings that determine whether incarceration is necessary at all, while they wait for a hearing date. Conditions in detention facilities, moreover, are often inhumane.[16]

Given all this, a licensed mental health professional still has an opportunity, small as it may be, to help to preserve the new and fragile idea of human rights. A thorough psychological evaluation of an asylum seeker can influence the discretionary decision of an asylum referee, in regard to whether the individual before him/her is truly an individual whose human rights have been threatened at home and who thus legally deserves asylum.

Asylum seekers themselves come from a variety of punishing backgrounds. Generally, in my experience, if they have been imprisoned in their home countries, it has been for days or weeks, rather than for months or years at a time. Some have done two, three, four short prison stints and then been released because a family member has intervened and bribed a guard. Finally, threatened with death, they flee and seek asylum elsewhere. Others (as in the case, for example, of women who have suffered female genital mutilation) arrive in the United States victimized by brutalizing social customs at home, and apply for asylum, hoping either to save themselves or their children from more of the same. Some are fleeing life-threatening circumstances (war, tribal rivalries, political demagogy, gang violence, etc.) over which they have no control. Each of these individuals has survived atrocities. Their fear of returning home is "well-founded" indeed.

Over the years, it has become increasingly clear to me, as I have completed evaluations, that it is the will to survive of each of my clients that has most interested me. Every time I interview an asylee, I wonder, how that person managed to live through her[17] ordeal and could I have done the same? More often than not the answer to the latter question is, "no." The stories my clients have told me have often been unimaginable. Take, for example, the highly regarded, self-respecting middle-aged woman, from an African country who I interviewed. She has two graduate degrees and two grown daughters; she is fluent in English, French, and two African languages. Years earlier, when her husband had tried to take a second wife,[18] she had objected so strenuously that he had to abandon the project. A very hard worker at home (she was the main wage earner in her family, as well as her mother's only support), she had not been political at all, but on one exceptional occasion, had been convinced by a friend to attend a political rally, which was held in a huge sports stadium.[19] Much to her surprise, mid-rally, the stadium was surrounded by government forces and the exits locked. Shots rang out. Many people were killed at random. Others were taken prisoner. She, in the latter group, was taken with a number of other women to an abandoned house, and held there for days. Their captors were uneducated enlistees from the countryside, all of one ethno/linguistic group, who repeatedly raped and barely fed their prisoners. Some were also forced to witness the torture and murder of others. Any tiny misstep led to death. Helping one another too obviously was forbidden.

How did this woman survive? Indeed (remarkable to me), almost without thinking, she immediately began pretending to be a simple country girl with no education, illiterate, able to speak only the language of her captors, for she quickly understood that death would come if she spoke any language other than theirs. Her inexperienced captors believed her ruse! Then she befriended one of them. He became especially interested in the FGM procedure she had undergone in childhood, which had gone awry. Her genital looked odd to him. It interested him intensely. He had others take a look at it. She tolerated this, seemingly without shame, befriending him all the while. During her interview, we explored her feelings about this man at some length. She had liked him, she told me, but "he raped me anyway!" The rape was traumatic for her, a gravely personal assault. Nevertheless, she managed to stay calm. Eventually, by virtue of the generosity of a relative[20] whom she contacted through the guard, she bought her freedom and survived. Once she was free, she left her country as soon as she could, came to the United States and applied for political asylum. The relative, meanwhile, who remained behind, was later killed by the same government force that had captured her, perhaps because he had provided the funds for her release, she thought. We discussed her feelings about this as well. She felt guilt, but had come to terms with these feelings, she said. When I asked what force had pushed her to survive, she told me that she is her mother's only living child.[21] She had had to survive for the sake of her mother, she said. Her own (grown) daughters needed her too. Needless to say, her extraordinary resilience, evident in her ability to keep fear at bay as she focused on the practical matter of escape, did not keep her from having been traumatized.[22] She had multiple symptoms of trauma and many physical maladies as well. Her will to keep going was still intact, nevertheless.

In the chapters below, I introduce some of the other extraordinary asylum seekers I have been privileged to meet. In presenting them, I intend to make clear that, although it may be possible to think of asylum seekers as members of specific groups, the actual route to asylum is unique for each person. Trauma is also unique to each individual who experiences it.[23] The diagnosis, post-traumatic stress disorder (PTSD), never covers the more intimate details of an asylee's experience. Moreover, there are individuals whose symptoms are not described in the Diagnostic and Statistical Manual (DSM)[24] as PTSD, who have suffered severely nevertheless. Finally, although there are some individuals who experience trauma for the first time as adults, many others have experienced trauma vicariously, if not directly, as children or adults, in the normal course of their lives. The relationship between trauma experienced in childhood and trauma experienced as an adult is poorly understood. Trauma raises many questions which it is beyond the cope of this book to explore.

In Chapter One, the nature of the psychosocial evaluation is described, including a discussion of its forensic goals, its political implications, and its potential as an important psychological experience for both the asylee and the psychologist,[25] given the pressured nuances of the "field" (Lewin, 1936) in which it takes place. The chapter also addresses other issues such as the inevitability of vicarious traumatization for the evaluator, the contributions of interpreters, and the implications of the required collaboration with attorneys. Although the nature of this work is immediately practical, it has more complex implications as well.

Chapters Two, Three, and Four will be devoted to a description of three respective asylum seeking groups, as follows:

Chapter Two describes a group of highly intelligent,[26] multi-national individuals, (seven men, four women) who I have designated as heroic because, despite the fact that they might have moved elsewhere, away from the egregious politics at home, they decided to remain at home and to resist. Indeed, in listening to their stories, it seemed clear to me that they had been chosen as the next in line in families with long-term, multi-generational traditions of resistance. Almost in training for this, as children or adolescents, these individuals had been routinely exposed to the trauma of older relatives. Thus they grew up with models of endurance (Luthar, 2003). In part because of this, once they became resisters themselves, they were able to endure repeated threats to their wellbeing and actual incidents of torture at the hands of their oppressors. This continued until finally they were ominously threatened with death. Only then were they able to change course and flee. Unlike two other resister groups described in the literature,[27] these heroic asylum seekers relinquished the thrill of the fight and took flight in order to plant roots elsewhere for themselves and also for their families. Survival was their goal. To insure its success they had planned a future course of action with great care.[28] In order to better understand them, the complex motivation behind their behavior is considered from a psychodynamic perspective. Brief follow-up information is then presented in regard to their adjustment to life in the United States, which, in contrast to their success as resisters, has not always been successful.

In Chapter Three, women I have interviewed who had suffered female genital mutilation (FGM) are presented, one in considerable detail. This woman, subjected to the most traumatic form of FGM[29] as a child, had, as an adolescent, been forced to marry an abusive man, considerably her senior, whom tradition required her to obey. Nevertheless, in spite of the negative effects of FGM and of endless spousal abuse, this woman was able to develop a strong sense of personal agency which emerged from her desire, as she put it "to have a life." For her, having a life meant having the right to keep her own earnings, forbidden in a culture in which all income presumably belongs to the man. In addition, she wanted to have friends of her own choosing, without the fear of shaming her family. It is suggested (following Jessica Benjamin, 1995; 2004) that this woman achieved agency and her personal goals by subordinating herself to the will of men, first to her stepfather (who ordered her marriage), then to her brutalizing husband (at least until they moved to the United States), and finally to Allah, the ultimate in masculine power in her culture, whose supporting voice she hears regularly at night. With this last support, appropriate in her culture, she was able to achieve personal agency, which not only led her to independence of mind, but eventually to political asylum as well.

Chapter Four, built around interview material, describes a group of women and men from Central America and Mexico. The women, in order to escape feminicido, the violence done to them by men, were designated as "Women on the Run"[30] by Anthony Guterres (2015),[31] then director of UNHCR. The chapter contends that the emergence of femicide (feminicide; feminismo), prevalent in that part of the world, is an outcome of a series of devastating invasions, first by the Spanish, then by the United States, which have led to the repeated humiliation of men, who have come of age in land-based, patriarchal, honor-bound societies. Starting in Mayan times, these successive invasions and their results are traced, with special reference to the development of machismo, a masculine identity seemingly forged to assist men in the transition from an identity integral to owning and working the land to identities loosely attached to other less satisfying, less secure present-day endeavors. This multi-faceted situation, in addition to the failure of present-day early educational systems, poverty, and an overarching unwillingness to respect national and international law, laws that exist to protect women (the "Moral Third," to quote psychoanalyst Jessica Benjamin (2018), are cited as crucial to the creation of feminismo. Without a widely respected container (in this case the law), a large number of men seem to be led by personal feelings of humiliation and helpless rage (Fromm, 1988) which they then turn upon their women.

Women, meanwhile, (using case material) are portrayed as taking up a submissive (*marianista*) role, identified with the Virgin Mary and supported by the Church. In addition, they are described as dependent on their men for a host of practical and less conscious psychological reasons, which together lead to a confusing separation path. Those who take it, often guided by the lives of their children, must contend with the open resistance not only of men, but also of other women.

An afterword will conclude the book.

Notes

1 The organizations for which I have volunteered have included: Doctors of the World (now HealthRight International), The American Friends Service Committee (AFSC), Human Rights First (HRF), Physicians for Human Rights (PHR), and Cardozo Law School.

2 It should be noted that many psychologists, often specialists in forensic psychology, are regularly employed to evaluate asylum seekers and do not work as volunteers. They are paid by the client or by the organization that has requested the evaluation. They often are employed to complete different kinds of evaluations of immigrants in a variety of different legally defined situations. Some of these are described in Appendix I.
3 An asylum seeker is an individual present in a country not her own who has a "well-founded fear" of returning home for one of five reasons discussed in Chapter One. A refugee has the same kind of fear but is applying for asylum from outside the country to which she wants to go. Many other immigrants do not meet this criteria but must leave home for other reasons. According to UNHCR there are more people living as refugees now than was the case after World War II, when there were 65.6 million. (at: http://www.npr.org/sections/goatsandsoda/2017/06/20/533634405/five-surprising-facts-about-the-refugee-crisis). And see also http://www.pewresearch.org/fact-tank/2017/01/30/key-facts-about-refugees-to-the-u-s/.

For a graph of how many refugees admitted in each year by the United States credible fear test: https://www.usnews.com/news/top-news/articles/2017-02-18/trump-administration-drafts-plan-to-raise-asylum-bar-speed-deportations.
4 The CIA lists these statistics, including country by country numbers, at: https://www.cia.gov/library/publications/the-world-factbook/fields/2194.html.
5 See Pew research center graph at: http://www.pewresearch.org/fact-tank/2016/10/05/u-s-admits-record-number-of-muslim-refugees-in-2016/.
6 The Trump administration ruled that only 50,000 refugees will be admitted in 2017, thus reducing by half the number the Obama administration had wished to accept. See http://www.migrationpolicy.org/article/refugees-and-asylees-united-states for more on this.
7 Described in greater detail at: http://www.un.org/en/development/desa/population/migration/generalassembly/docs/globalcompact/A_RES_71_1.pdf.
8 See report from Oxford Refugee Study Center at: https://www.rsc.ox.ac.uk/news/new-york-declaration-on-refugees-a-one-year-report-card-by-jeff-crisp.
9 Aleinikoff describes this situation on an interesting podcast which can be heard at: https://itunes.apple.com/us/podcast/displaced/id1368638855?mt=2.
10 At: https://www.usnews.com/news/top-news/articles/2017-02-18/trump-administration-drafts-plan-to-raise-asylum-bar-speed-deportations.
11 There is some debate about the date at which human rights, as a legal concept superseding nationalism began. Attorney Jennifer Martinez (2014), for example, believes that human rights as a legal concept originated in international law forbidding the slave trade. I find Samuel Moyn's argument more compelling, however, because he also includes in his discussion the manner in which the idea took hold outside of certain legal

circles as a utopian ideal, worldwide. For more detailed discussion of this topic, please see his work itself.
12 See more about this at: http://www.un.org/en/universal-declaration-human-rights/index.html.
13 Amnesty International won a Nobel Peace Prize in 1977.
14 Immigration law in the United States has a long history, which will not be discussed in this book. There are numerous books, written from various points of view on this subject, including: Carens (2015); Aleinikoff (2002).
15 More on this can be found at Human Rights Watch: https://www.hrw.org/news/2016/04/25/us-20-years-immigrant-abuses.
16 For more on this see Appendix II: Imprisoning asylum seekers.
17 I have not kept perfect account of how many women as compared with men I have evaluated, but the majority have been women. For this reason, when talking about asylum seekers, I will use the pronoun, "she" throughout the text, unless the protagonist was male.
18 Muslim men are allowed four wives.
19 More about this famous case is available at: https://www.hrw.org/report/2009/12/17/bloody-monday/september-28-massacre-and-rapes-security-forces-guinea.
20 It is the custom, in some African countries, to help those friends and family in need, regardless of consequences to oneself (personal communication, Jean Pierre Kamwa).
21 In many parts of Africa and other parts of the world, it is understood that adult children will support their parents in old age.
22 An account similar to this one, of a woman who became determined to stay focused on survival as she contended with repeated rapes, is available in the autobiographical account *A Woman in Berlin: Eight Weeks in A Conquered City* (Anonymous, 2000). The author describes her feelings as she faced repeated rapes when Berlin was liberated by the Russians after World War II. After the second rape, she describes an out-of-body experience: "It was as if I were flat on my bed and seeing myself lying there when a luminous white being rose from my body, a kind of angel . . . that floated high into the air . . . my true self simply leaving my body behind, my poor, besmirched, abused body." (p. 61). Then later: "I make up my mind. I have to find a single wolf to keep away the pack . . . I grin to myself in secret, feel as if I am performing on a stage. I couldn't care less about the lot of them! I've never been so removed from myself, so alienated. All my feelings seem dead, except the drive to live. They shall not destroy me." (pp. 64–66).
23 See Chapter One for more detail and references in regard to this subject matter.
24 This document, published by the American Psychiatric Association, is revised every few years. The fifth and most recent edition is available in book form from Amazon and other book sellers. A parallel document, the International Classification of Diseases (ICD), is similarly revised. The latest version of the latter is at: https://www.cdc.gov/nchs/icd/icd10cm.htm.

25 Throughout this book, I have referred to the mental health professional engaged in asylum works as a psychologist. This shorthand represents all licensed mental health professionals: social workers, psychiatrists, psychiatric nurses, and various other licensed mental health practitioners in their respective states. Indeed, an affidavit completed by any individual licensed as a mental health professional is accepted by immigration court as evidence of abuse.

26 According to one source (Randall & Lutz, 1991), "it is often the best adjusted who can leave their countries" in order to seek political asylum (p. 7). In fact, not all people who leave home because they believe they must leave with the intention of becoming asylum seekers. For others, the process takes many years, sometimes because they have been misled by attorneys. See Chapter Four for more on this.

27 Group 1, described as rebels who stayed in WWII: Marton, 1974; Bar-Zohar, 2001; Oliner & Oliner, 1988; Klempner, 2006. Group 2, described by Vamik Volkan (1998; 2006) as motivated to stay by their own "traumatized self-realization" (1998, p. 4).

28 A recent article in the *New York Times* (Searcey & Barry, 2017) tells the story of the Anne family in Senegal. The parents sent off one son after the other, beginning with the eldest, along the "deadliest route" to Europe, according to this article, because "if they would make it, it would really have changed things for us," said their mother (p. 1). As the article records, the two sons did not make it. Unlike the more carefully chosen children I describe, they seemed to have left propelled by desperation, without sufficient preparation.

29 FGM, depending on its severity, can be the cause of life-long infection, pain and dyspareunia, and difficulty with child-bearing. Perhaps above all, it can have negative effects on emotional well-being. See appendix B in chapter three for a description of degrees of severity of FGM.

30 A working paper with this name, published by UNHCR in 2015, to describe the plight of women from Mexico and Central America, is at: http://www.unhcr.org/en-us/publications/operations/5630f24c6/women-run.html. Guterres is now Chair of the United Nations.

31 Related published pieces of my own (Eisold, 2016) can be found in the references.

References

Aleinikoff, T. A. (2002). *Semblances of Sovereignty*. Cambridge, MA: Harvard University Press.

Anonymous. (2000). *A Woman in Berlin*. New York, NY: Virago.

Arendt, H. (1951). The decline of the nation-state and the end of the rights of man. In *The Origins of Totalitarianism* (pp. 268–298). New York, NY: Harcourt Brace & Co.

Bar-Zohar, M. (2001). *Beyond Hitler's Grasp: The Heroic Rescue of Bulgaria's Jews*. New York, NY: Adams Media Corp.
Benjamin, J. (1995) Sameness and difference: Toward an "overinclusive" model of gender development. *Psychoanalytic Inquiry*. 15: 125–142.
Benjamin, J. (2004). Deconstructing femininity: Understanding "passivity" and the daughter position. *Annual of Psychoanalysis*. 32: 45–57.
Benjamin, J. (2018). How therapy with victims of political trauma repairs the third – Commentary on Gómez and Kovalskys's work in the context of post-dictatorship Chile. *Psychoanalytic Dialogues*. 28: 115–121.
Carens, J. (2015). *The Ethics of Immigration*. New York: Oxford University Press.
Des Pres, T. (1980) *The Survivor: An Anatomy of Life in the Death Camps*. New York, NY: Oxford University Press.
Eisold, B. K. (2016). Female genital mutilation and its aftermath in a woman who wished to "Have a life." Submission as a route to personal agency. *International Journal of Psychoanalytic Studies*. 13: 279–304.
Fromm, E. (1988). *Man for Himself*. New York, NY: Fawcett.
Guterres, A. (2015). Women on the run. *Retrieved from:* http://www.unhcr.org/en-us/about-us/background/56fc31864/women-on-the-run-full-report.html.
Klempner, M. (2006). *The Heart Has Reasons: Holocaust Rescuers and Their Stories*. Cleveland, OH: Pilgrim Press.
Lewin, K. (1936). *Principles of Topological Psychology*. York, PA: Maple Press.
Luthar, S. S. (Ed.). (2003). *Resilience and Vulnerability: Adaptation in the Context of Childhood Adversities*. New York, NY: Cambridge University Press.
Martinez, J. S. (2014). *The Slave Trade and the Origins of Human Rights Law*. New York, NY: Oxford University Press.
Marton, S. (1974). *Wallenberg: Missing Hero*. New York, NY: Arcade.
Moyn, S. (2010). *The Last Utopia*. Cambridge, MA: Harvard University Press.
Moyn, S. (2017). *Human Rights and the Uses of History*. New York, NY: Maple Press. (Original work published 2014).
Oliner, S. P. & Oliner P. (1988) *The Altruistic Personality: Rescuers of Jews in Nazi Germany*. New York, NY: Free Press.
Randall, G. R. & Lutz, E. L. (1991). *Serving Survivors of Torture*. AAAS publication Number 91–42S.
Roth, K. (2017). The dangerous rise of populism: Global attacks on human rights values. *Retrieved from:* https://www.hrw.org/world-report/2017/country-chapters/dangerous-rise-of-populism.
Searcey, D. & Barry, J. Y. (2017). Why migrants keep risking all on the deadliest route. *New York Times*. Retrieved from: https://www.nytimes.com/2017/06/22/

world/africa/migrants-mediterranean-italy-libyadeaths.html?rref=collection%2Ftimestopic%2FSenegal&action=click&contentCollection=world&region=stream&module=stream_unit&version=search&contentPlacement=1&pgtype=collection.

Volkan, V. E. E. (1998). *Blood Lines: From Ethnic Pride to Ethnic Terrorism.* New York, NY: Basic Books.

Volkan, V. E. E. (2006). *Killing in the Name of Identity: A Study of Blood Conflicts.* Charlottesville, VA: Pitchstone.

Chapter 1

The nature of psychosocial asylum evaluations[1]

Implications for client and clinician

Introduction

Who are asylum seekers?

Asylum seekers come from all over the world. They do not necessarily share common backgrounds or beliefs. They are living in a country not their own—for the purposes of this book, in the United States.[2] Usually (but not always), in their rush to depart, they have left identifying papers behind. Without these they have no valid immigration status. Once here, they petition for legal protection to remain, based on their "well-founded fear"[3] of persecution in their country of origin. The five "protected" grounds for which they may claim to be persecuted are: their race, religion, nationality, membership of a particular social group, or their political opinion. Under the principle of "non-refoulement," (non-return)[4] they cannot be sent home unless they fail to demonstrate a valid reason to remain. Despite the fact that each case is unique, each applicant must present some evidence, "'direct or circumstantial,'"[5] that she was persecuted for at least one of the five "protected grounds" listed above.[6]

Once they have arrived in the United States, asylum seekers follow different paths through the complexities of our legal system, depending, first of all, upon whether they came with or without valid immigration papers. A student visa is an example of valid immigration status. In Appendix I, I have briefly outlined the various legal categories under which seekers can apply for asylum, depending on their differing claims. Every asylum seeker, however, must present her claim before a representative of the law. Often the first of these representatives is an asylum officer, not a federal judge. These individuals are graduates of a required training course.[7] Only after the petitioner has failed with the asylum officer, is she referred to a judge. Each of these individuals faces different dilemmas in assessing a claim.[8] A psychosocial evaluation is frequently submitted to the official, either judge or asylum officer, because it is accepted as evidence in support of an asylum claim.

The psychosocial assessment process: legal benefits and beyond

Forensic goals

My services to asylum seekers are sought by an attorney.[9] Although some asylum seekers do not secure the assistance of an attorney to help them through the process of applying for asylum, those who do have a much greater chance of success.[10] An attorney will not only represent them, as necessary, in court, but will request the necessary supporting documents. Many asylees are able to find an attorney who will work pro-bono.[11] Whether paid or not, the attorney will be the star of the court presentation. All other contributors (psychologist, medical doctor, country experts, etc.) are secondary figures.

More and more frequently, a psychosocial evaluation is requested by an attorney because, as described above, the court considers psychological symptoms, especially PTSD, to be evidence that an applicant's "well-founded fear" is the outcome of concrete events —traumatic ones—which were caused when the individual was persecuted elsewhere.[12] In fact, according to Vaisman-Tzachor (2014, p. 4) "the psychological evaluation is [often] . . . the only viable evidentiary vehicle by which to demonstrate the veracity of persecution." Thus, along with other advantages that may accrue from such an evaluation, the main one is its acceptance as corroboration of the client's story.

As a health professional offering pro-bono assistance to an asylee,[13] attorneys find me through an agency. There are a number of such agencies.[14] Most recently, the agency from which I have been receiving referrals is Physicians for Human Rights (PHR), in New York City.[15,16]

The primary goal, in completing an evaluation remains essentially unchanged for the psychologist/mental health professional, regardless of the nature of the case. That goal is to describe in detail the client's experience of persecution/torture and its effects, as these occurred at home and as they continue to be experienced. To do this well, however, it behooves the evaluator also to learn about the applicant's well-being before she was persecuted, for the sake of comparing the past to the present. Thus the interview should also include a brief account of the client's past history, both personal and professional.

Before completing an evaluation, it is useful to understand the nature of the client's legal claim, whether it is an affirmative or defensive asylum claim or a claim for withholding from removal under an alternative legal form (see Appendix I for help here), because the nature of the claim often has some bearing on the subject matter that should be covered in the interview. For example, I recently evaluated a seventeen year old girl, still a child (that is, a person under the age of eighteen) from the legal standpoint. She was applying for asylum as an individual with Special Immigrant Juvenile status, for which she was eligible because—as required—her parents had abandoned her before she was five. However, she was also applying as a victim of persecution. She met the legal requirements for the latter because she had witnessed the murder of a friend and then had been kidnapped herself and threatened at gunpoint by the murdering gang.[17] Special Immigrant Juvenile status and persecution are not only separate claims, from a legal standpoint, but they also have separate emotional effects. Thus each needed to be covered separately in my interview.

It is also important to be sensitive to the fact that marginalization of different groups has different effects, first because of the age at which the marginalization begins and then because of the location in which it took place. A gay man who has been marginalized by both his family and his culture (Pepper, 2005; Reading & Rubin, 2011) will probably have suffered longer and in different ways in some countries than a man who has been punished for the political affiliations he developed as an adult. An individual from a certain part of the world, Africa, for example, may have particular culturally ingrained difficulties in representing herself (Smith, Stuart, & Gangsei, 2015). A person who has suffered multiple traumas (Herman, 2004) will have a wide range of symptoms, which may differ from symptoms resulting from trauma that began in adulthood (Boulanger, 2007). For those who come from cultures in which speaking about one's feelings is frowned upon and discouraged (Blackwell, 2005), telling their personal stories may be difficult. The uniqueness of each case should determine the content of the interview and the manner in which trauma is explored.

Depending on its unique characteristics, the attorney in charge may ask the psychologist to emphasize certain details in regard to some aspect of a given case. For example, in cases in which the asylee is applying beyond the one year deadline, the psychologist may be asked to explain the circumstances which have determined this delay. Much less frequently, when the client has been psychotic, the psychologist may be asked to describe where and how her contact with reality might have affected her perceptions, especially of persecution.

Finally, although not specifically important to forensic needs, I deem it important to describe the circumstances in which my interview has taken place, whether in my personal office (usual) or in another setting, especially if that other setting is a prison. When the latter is the case, I try to describe the surroundings in some detail, emphasizing its effects on the applicant's wellbeing. Imprisoning an asylee deprives that person of her rights under the law, according to the original Geneva Conventions. Recently, however, the UNHCR has set new detention guidelines[18] because, in fact, so many countries, pressed by increasing numbers of immigrants, are detaining asylum seekers along with immigrants with other claims. The United States is a grave offender in this regard. In describing the effects of this treatment on the petitioner, in my affidavit, I can underscore the fact that her rights are being abused. Please see Appendix II for more about this.

General set-up and procedure

Before meeting an asylee, I request all the data the attorney has collected. In order to proceed, I need to read either a moderately detailed written interview of the asylee or her personal affidavit. In reading either of these, I learn her history. In the margins I note my own questions about relevant aspects of the individual's life which have not been covered before. I will use these questions to try to elicit a less rehearsed narrative than the one the asylee has told before, for by the time she gets to me, she will have already told her story a few times, to one attorney or another. Often, as a result, an asylee will have memorized much of her presentation or have developed a mode in which she describes it. One person I interviewed, for example, told her (absolutely hair-raising) story in a singsong, rhythmic manner. She put the extra details we arrived at during our interview into this rhythm as well. This may have helped to protect her from what, I learned later, had been life-disrupting despair. Another interviewee began crying as soon as she sat down. She cried, seemingly on cue, at various points in her story, until we got into new, unexplored territory. At that point, to my surprise, the crying stopped abruptly. She looked alert and seemed to be searching her mind for new details, apparently more interested in discovering these than in impressing me with her pain. Fresh, more authentic details, I believe, are not only convincing to the court, but help the client herself to better grasp the totality of her experience.

Often the surprises that emerge in these interviews are deeply touching. One woman, for example, told about the birth of a child she had had at the age of thirteen, the result of a rape, and of the terrible death of this child at the hands of uneducated relatives who had subjected him to a skull-forming ritual, which killed him. A middle-aged man—brilliant, an academic—described the deep depression into which he fell after his father died, the victim of a car crash, set up, he thought, by the political opposition. Neither the death of the woman's son nor of the man's father had been mentioned at all in their own affidavits, based on material collected by their attorneys at an earlier date.

When the client arrives, I seat her facing me. If there is an interpreter, I seat that person behind the client to her right. Although the presence of an interpreter inevitably creates a three-person event,[19] I want the asylee to understand that, as much as possible, the interview we are about to undertake (and co-create) is between her and me, not between her and the interpreter, who in all likelihood she will have met before, in the office of her attorney. In addition to a bathroom, I offer something to drink (water, juice, soda, coffee) and usually some small sort of sustenance before we begin. Thus far, no one has ever accepted any of these before we begin, except water. At the end, however, clients often seem to welcome a bit of both food and drink.[20]

I begin the interview by asking the applicant if she knows why she has been sent to see me. Usually the answer is vague; she may know that I am a psychologist, but what that has to do with her is unclear, maybe even a bit frightening. I explain that, as a psychologist, I will be asking her about the feelings she experienced, first at home, when she was persecuted, and then later, as a result of the persecution. I acknowledge that the interview may well be painful. I explain (looking at her hard, hoping to share my own feelings of incredulity about this) that I do this because her asylum officer (or judge) will consider her feelings to be proof that she has suffered! I try to make clear that I want to hear whatever she has to say about the things she has been through and about her feelings now, as a result.[21] I underscore the fact that all of these feelings are normal. This information may be reassuring to an asylee, who may have wondered if she had gone crazy, given not only the presence of nightmares and flashbacks, but the presence of the uncomfortable conviction that the person she was before her escape has disappeared.[22] I add that I intend to present her as positively as I can to the asylum official, as a person desirable as their neighbor and a co-citizen in the United States. In my experience, asylum seekers want to collaborate with this agenda. Thus, not only have I presented my goals, but I have also received permission to do a difficult interview (which is ethical) and so we begin.[23]

There are a variety of approaches to client assessment.[24] Some clinicians, myself included, simply observe the client closely while doing an in-depth interview, which will cover some or all of the following: the client's pre- and post-trauma past, with special reference to her relationships in childhood, relationships with children (if there are any), parents, siblings, education, family functioning, social network,[25] cognitive style, gaps in memory, inconsistencies in previous statements, apparent contact with reality, physical and psychological symptoms, etc. Here my training as a psychodynamically oriented clinician is useful. It has given me confidence in my ability to organize and structure goals focusing on, among other things, emotions and the survival of the self. I am also more or less at ease learning about defensiveness, pain, the often shame-inducing relationship (should there have been one) between the torturer(s) and the asylee, the shame induced by the perception of oneself as a victim. I keep in mind that, above all, it is necessary to establish the client's credibility. She will need this in order to be granted her plea.

Other evaluators include in their interview either formal testing or a questionnaire developed specifically for this purpose.[26] Some meet more than once, some just once with the client. Interviews can last many hours or just a few, depending on both the manner in which the clinician proceeds and the complexity of the client's story. At this point, my own interviews last approximately two to three hours. In some cases I have seen a client multiple times. In one case, for example, the asylee had been trafficked for sexual purposes. But she was deeply ashamed about this. Thus it took many interviews (and a number of different stories) before finally one of her attorneys figured out what had happened to her. I saw this woman myself three times. Each time, as more information was revealed, my interview included slightly different questions. It's not always easy to get the questions right the first time.

As the interview concludes, I get out the list of DSM V symptoms for PTSD, depression, and anxiety (printed out and clipped inside a folder for easy access) and ask about those not already covered in the interview.[27] Some symptoms may not be relevant. Anxiety may be covered by symptoms of PTSD. In my write up, the DSM will be the basis of my conclusion. In the conclusion, after a brief summary of the main facts about the client's life, plus a brief description of her apparent contact with reality, appearance, willingness to establish eye contact, I write into my report (copy and edit) the list of PTSD symptoms and then specify which of them the client is exhibiting. It is such a set of symptoms that the court will accept as evidence.

At times, the symptoms clients exhibit do not neatly fit the criteria for DSM diagnoses. Leanh Nguyen (2011) tells us that "if you don't 'have' PTSD or Major Depression, you are not a credible torture victim and you are less likely to get asylum or a damage award." Actually, I have not found it difficult to describe the DSM criteria as unlike a particular client's experience and then to delineate the symptoms the client does exhibit in convincing terms. Judges seem to accept this as well.[28]

At the end of the interview, I tell the client that I will send both her and her attorney a copy of my write up[29] by email. If she cannot read English, I suggest that she ask the interpreter for help. I tell her that I want to be certain that my report is accurate. For obvious reasons, clients desire their documents to represent their experience correctly and are grateful to be included in the process of making sure that is so.

The potential political implications of the health professional's affidavit

When I first began working with asylum seekers, I was motivated largely by the desire to help people whose human rights had been threatened in their home countries. However, as I have become more engaged in the work, its political implications have become more apparent to me. After all, my affidavit is designed to inform the decision of a judge, which, in asylum cases, is always a discretionary decision. This legal (life-changing) decision, in other words, is going to be influenced by my report.

In completing a forensic assessment, it is assumed that the psychologist will be as objectively rational as possible in describing the kind and degree of symptoms the client has experienced as a result of persecution. The judge's discretionary decision, in turn, is also based on the assumption of his or her rationality. Our laws, attorney Anne Dailey tells us (2017), are based on Oliver Wendell Holmes' assumption of man as a rational being. However, according to her, this assumption entirely fails to acknowledge the existence of the unconscious. Given the unconscious (and maybe aspects of conscious thought as well) the judges' decisions in asylum cases are likely to be influenced by all sorts of irrational factors, for example, by the compassion they (hopefully) feel for the asylee, and/or by their prejudice against immigrants, by their own total experience of life, perhaps as immigrants themselves, etc.

The psychologist, needless to say, is also an irrational being. In agreeing to complete as objective an asylum evaluation as possible, (s)he may, unwittingly perhaps, side either with or against the laws that grant asylum and with or against the applicant. Indeed, according to Engstrom, Hernandez, and Gangsei (2008), "professionals in the mental health field ... agree that academics and practitioners in the social sciences cannot be neutral" when at work in a context in which the applicant has suffered from politically induced trauma.

I, for one, am on the side of the laws which grant asylum. I also believe in the original mission of the United States, as a nation of/for immigrants, who came here largely for life, liberty, and the pursuit of happiness, without the threat of persecution or torture. In addition, most of the asylum seekers I have evaluated have generally been attractive, intelligent, often extraordinarily so,[30] as well as the best educated members of their families. Many have also survived circumstances which are unimaginable to me. Thus, generally, in the document I write, which will emerge out of the narrative we co-create (Eisenman, Bergner, & Cohen, 2000) I will try to present the applicant as a highly desirable individual, as a person with fine potential as my neighbor, as my equal under the law of the United States. I see this as a political undertaking. Other evaluators have other goals which also have political implications. For example, Leanh Nguyen, long a psychologist at The Program for Survivors of Torture at Bellevue

Hospital in NYC, writes that "what matters to me is daring to see what has survived and to show how dehumanization has taken effect" (2012). To show dehumanization is to show an essential aspect of genocide, a politically motivated plague, especially prevalent in the past hundred years.

Then, there are the political implications of the fact that our national boundaries exclude others, often desperate others. Here I am grateful to the writings of political ethicist J. H. Carens (2015). He believes that there is a "linkage between freedom of movement and equality of opportunity" (p. 228). In modern democratic states, he tells us, our principles presumably commit us to the idea that we are all equal in moral worth. This implies as well some commitment to equality of opportunity for all. But, according to him:

> The gap between principle and policy [in this regard] is particularly wide when the focus is on refugees ... The control that democratic states exercise over the immigrant plays a crucial role in maintaining unjust global inequalities and in limiting human freedom unjustly.
>
> (p. 229)

I find this notion compelling. Its implications are complex and way beyond the scope of this book. Lately, however, in completing asylum affidavits, I have found myself thinking that, at the same time as I am guided by law in helping to pave the way for an asylum seeker to enter the United States, I am also confronting its exclusionary nature. In the United States of late our immigration law has become especially exclusionary. Some European countries are less so and thus have recently taken in millions.[31] We, in the United States, have admitted only a few thousand.[32] Clearly, we have ample space and resources for more. I understand a successful asylum claim as helpful in confronting our very own exclusions.

The nature of the affective relationship between applicant and evaluator: transferential and counter-transferential issues

The relationship between asylee and evaluator has many multi-determined affective aspects, which carry the potential for positive (and/or negative) outcomes for both participants. For the asylee, along with its forensic benefits, testifying can be a step in the direction of making sense of what happened to her.[33] However, "secondary injury" can occur, according to Symonds (2010), in those cases in which her suffering goes unacknowledged. For the psychologist, the interview can be a learning opportunity, especially in regard to the practice of what Engstrom, Hernandez, & Gangsei (2008) have described as "vicarious resilience."

As background to an understanding of the interaction between asylee and interviewer, I have found the concept of the "field," (Lewin, 1936) to be useful because it is focused on the on-going nature of in-the-moment interpersonal interactions. These are especially highlighted in an interview with an asylee because it takes place during a short period of time and will have long-term, extraordinarily life-changing implications.

Kurt Lewin's notion of field theory is based on what he called "the life space," (1936, p.12). This "space," or "field," he thought, is made up of here-and-now states of being which together comprise "the totality of facts which determine the behavior of an individual at a certain moment." (p. 13). These "facts" alter kaleidoscopically from moment to moment, in the here and now, creating new possibilities as they change. They are influenced by both inter and intra personal events.

Lewin's understanding of field is as "a continuous, inevitable, social aspect of human living . . . [an] omnipresent, concrete, empirical reality," as psychoanalyst Donnel Stern (2013a, p. 489) has recently put it. Indeed, two recent articles by Stern (2013a; 2013b) outline the evolution of field theory in the United States, as understood by psychoanalysts both in the United States, in interpersonal and relational psychoanalysis (IRP), and in South America and Italy in Bionian field theory (BFT). It is not my intention to review this work in any depth here, but instead to pull from it the bits that I find useful in better articulating some of the elements of the extraordinarily intense interactions I have experienced with asylum seekers.

To begin with, there is the very here-and-now nature of both field theory and an asylum interview. Unlike an ongoing therapeutic relationship, in which the goal from the beginning is not always clear and often there is no predetermined end date, psychologist and asylee exist in a relationship which, in most cases, will end only hours after it begins. This relationship also has a very clear, concrete goal: to present information to a judge, which will assist the client in her plea for asylum. In achieving this goal, the client is essentially pleading with all those who will help, myself, the evaluator, included. Given this, she will have numerous, multi-leveled transferential feelings in regard to me. She will perhaps see me as a woman, an elderly citizen, an authority figure, a white person representative of white people in what may have been her colonial past, a psychologist with unclear capacities for insight, etc. These must create for her a relationship which is experienced as unequal. Perhaps most salient for her, however, is my connection to her attorney, the person who has sent her to me and who is on her side.[34]

As a consequence of this last point, the asylee and I also share a powerful positive bond because we are both appealing to the law on her behalf. Thus, at its beginning and, to some extent, throughout the entire interview, the relational/cultural "third" (Gerson, 2009) that is created between us consists of the buzzing, ever altering connection we create in "life space," first out of the asylee's fantasies, hopes (and fears), and my fantasies, interest/desire to help, and then out of our common understanding that there is a language called law that exists beyond the two of us, to which we are both appealing. The law, to put it mildly, is a "third" in the room.[35]

However, as the interview proceeds and the asylee's trust in my intentions grows, I often experience a shift, which seems to push the law to the side, away from central focus, and puts the asylee's experience front and center. Sometimes this happens as the result of an unexpected event, sometimes because the client simply becomes engrossed in knowing more about herself, or desires to share, to create again a narrative to explain the terrible things that have happened to her, or because she responds to my desire to hear details, and/or for other reasons or combination of reasons. The press of the time boundary probably encourages this. When it occurs, self-understanding seems to become the goal: the asylee seems to want to sharpen or clarify her life experience, to gain greater conscious control over it. Sharing this way also seems to be empowering in some ways; it connects past and present, helps explain things. Here are two examples.

Example 1: Mr. M, a highly intelligent, middle-aged academic from the Middle East, came early to his interview during which he was ridiculously formal and respectful of me, the female psychologist. His wife, I learned, had accompanied him to the United States, but speaks no English, is not taking language classes, wears a hijab, and rarely leaves the house. The dictator in his home country, he reported, complicated his life, first as a child, in regard to schooling, then as a university student, by imprisoning him, after which he was forced to serve in the army.

Finally, having survived all this, the work he chose, eventually became impossible because of the subversion of hostile government forces. He was utterly committed to this work nevertheless. To him, it represents the preservation of the culture from which he came. Early in our meeting, it was clear to me that Mr. M's life story and the work he chose are not only uniquely fascinating, but directly relate to the political troubles at home. His fury at his government seemed appropriate, since they diminished the meaning of this work, disparaging its importance to his people. Gradually, however, with apparent difficulty, he acknowledged past periods of black cynicism and despair, which included heavy smoking and heavy alcohol use. However, he denied any experience of torture of any kind. No one had humiliated him in this way, it seemed.

Then, suddenly, the door outside my office, leading from the waiting room to the street, slammed loudly, as someone from the office suite left. Mr. M jumped in his seat. A grimaced look of fear passed over his face. Gradually he calmed down. I asked what had happened. Slowly then he told me that the noise was like the sound of slamming doors in prison. He was put there as a university student, for no reason at all, he said; he had done nothing. The state, he continued, just imprisoned students at will. In the overcrowded cell in which they placed him, he could hear people screaming in other rooms. As for him, they tied his hands behind his back and hung him from the ceiling. He lost consciousness quickly. Just because they could, he said, they did this. His cousin, imprisoned in another room, emerged crippled for life. None of this had appeared in the information I had received from his attorney. In reviewing his life experience, he told me, this was the first of what had seemed to him an endless number of painful experiences which changed the course of his life, sometimes for years at a time. It was the senselessness of it all, he thought, that most depressed him. If it had not been for his work, he would have given up.

Example 2: I interview Mr. D, a young man from an African country, an exceedingly handsome, shy, soft-spoken, extremely modest individual, the eldest son in an educated family, married to a woman, now pregnant with his child, whom he met here. Our interview begins slowly. He gives me details, bit by bit, perhaps afraid of shocking me. Just after he was born, he tells me, his father moved the family out of his native country, to escape the warfare that was happening there. His mother is wonderful, he adds; he adores her. A teacher, she cared for him and his brothers, as well as for her students, adapting no matter where they went. Gradually, as his story continues, it seems to me that he was his parents' favorite child, not only because of his intelligence, but because of the gentle care he lavished on them in return for their love. I tell him this. It seems a new idea to him. Clearly, he likes it. The warmth in the room seems to increase.

After the war, Mr. D continued, he had returned to his home country to go to university, where, having done well, he launched himself on what he hoped would become a highly successful career. He is fluent in French, English, the language of his country, and two or three computer languages, and was using all of these at work. However, he was also using his computer skills to help an opposing political party. This continued for a couple of years until, one day, out of the blue, he was picked up by the police in the street, on the way home, and jailed. The jailing was a complete shock to him. He had been under the impression that there had been nothing wrong with undertaking the political work of which they had accused him. Under his country's new constitution, he knew it was permissible. Nevertheless, he was held for twenty-four hours, questioned excessively, told to desist, and then sent home. He continued the political work anyway. Not surprisingly, he was soon picked up again and jailed a second time, this time in a tiny cell, with no food, no toilet facilities, no window . . . and torture. A man had beaten him, repeatedly, over a couple of days, hoping to extract the names of other party members. Then he was let go and told to desist or they would kill him. He had revealed nothing, but the experience had been terrible for him. He could not understand why. Why, after all the country had been through, did the torturer want to treat him so?[36] Incomprehensible, he thought.

A few years before, Mr. D had adopted three siblings, orphaned in the terrible warfare that had taken place. He was particularly attached to the eldest of these, a boy, his "son," he thought, with whom he shared computer skills. As we spoke, more and more details emerged about this son, about how terribly guilty he felt abandoning this boy. Suddenly he was in tears. His wife knew about this boy, he said, but he had not told his lawyers. As we talked, it became clear that his sadness and guilt about abandoning the boy made it difficult for him to deal with the symptoms of PTSD, induced by the beatings he had endured. In some way, he thought, the beatings were deserved because he had abandoned the boy. Indeed to contend with these feelings my client and I met a few times after the completion of my affidavit because he asked to do so. Eventually, employed, having become the father of three boys, he has been awarded the right to remain in the United States. He has been infrequently in touch with me since.

In each of the two situations described above, a change took place, mid-interview, in which, suddenly, aspects of the asylee's suffering were revealed that seemed not to have been revealed quite so clearly before. In each situation, the asylee seemed to need to take advantage of the opportunity our interview provided in order to reveal these aspects. These changes, which occurred in our relational "field," seem to have been examples of the effect on the asylee of having felt "witnessed," a term much used, especially by psychotherapists (for example: Felman & Laub, 1992; Caruth, 1995; Gerson, 2009; Reis, 2009; Ullman, 2011; Boulanger, 2012; Nguyen, 2012; Peskin, 2012; Ornstein, 2003). Witnessing is important as an aspect of the relational field between asylee and interviewer. Thus a word on this subject seems appropriate here before proceeding.

Witnessing, first identified as such by Dori Laub in 1992, has more recently been defined by psychoanalyst Warren Poland as the experience of "being gotten, being understood" (2016, p. 7). Donnel Stern (2012), in turn, describes witnessing as "the act of concentrated empathic listening on the part of one person to the traumatic story of another." Assuming that most individuals have experienced some form of trauma, small or large, witnessing is an essential aspect of psychotherapy, both Stern and Poland think, and of other interpersonal exchanges as well.

To my mind, witnessing has considerably wider implications when the experience the victim has undergone has often been so demolishing that she is left without words to describe it. This mode of experience, which cannot be symbolized, was called *"le réel"* (the real) by Lacan (1982; see also Boulanger, 2007; Stern, 2012). The "real," in this sense, is a confrontation with destruction or death, which "shatters forms, numbs the mind;" it is a radical break with the known world (Caruth, 1995). It is "a dimension in this life ... where there is no meaning, no mutuality" (Nguyen, 2012, p. 311). It exists. There are no symbols to describe it. For some, it is so unthinkable, that there is a press to deny it, to hope that it was a dream, in order simply to make it disappear.

At the same time, however, there is an internal "imperative" (Gerson, 2009) to recount it, to report it, to bear witness to the fact that it occurred

(Langer, 2003) because, in doing so, one creates a narrative, one communicates, thereby connecting past life (Modell, 1994; Stern, 2012) to life here and now. Witnessing helps in situations that have deprived an individual of the feeling of belonging. For some, morality enters the picture at this point. Psychoanalyst, Ghislaine Boulanger, for example, believes that, beyond the professional obligation to listen, psychotherapists are "morally obligated to bear witness when an external event has caused such a profound disruption in the other's sense of self . . . that a witness is necessary to validate the extent of the distress" (2012, p. 318). Philosopher, Avishai Margalit (2002) describes what he calls the "moral witness" as someone who has a collective social function because she has (whether by choice or not) been witness to the effects of man-made suffering/evil and has then also put herself at risk.[37] Chana Ullman (2011) believes that witnessing brings to light previously denied aspects of experience which occurs when individuals deny or dissociate the effect of events related to the trauma imposed on them by virtue of events in the history of their country.[38]

For me there is nothing moral about listening to an asylee. However, the experience is certainly different from the experience of listening to accounts of trauma in which abuse of power is absent, such as, for example, when someone has lived through a terrible storm or a bad car accident. There is implicitly more horror in the former situation than in the latter because it is a relationship between two people that is involved, rather than a relationship with an impersonal, external, chance event. As such, the traumatic experience also has a different effect on the victim, who must account, not only for abuse to her physical integrity, but also for abuse to her sense of self. This causes changes in her understanding of the relational world; it destroys the "images" of the world she has known (Caruth, 1995). I feel more compelled to listen to these stories than to stories describing trauma caused by accidents. Perhaps I feel compelled because there is some blurring of boundaries between myself and the survivor, which automatically results from the awe/disbelief/shock of my response to her account. I do not try to interpret. I have no ambition to alter her memories (Reis, 2009). This, I believe, is not a moral response perhaps because I do not feel that I am at risk. It is my choice to be there. For me, in my internal "life space," the effect of the narrative that the asylee and I have co-created seems to grow and to absorb me increasingly as time goes by.

It was Edgar Levinson who, according to Stern (2013a), was the first IRP analyst to underscore the analyst's:

"transformation" by the field. ... The analyst was understood to be involved in just the same way with the patient as the patient was with the analyst, including the same lack of awareness of a substantial portion of this involvement. There was a leveling, a democratization of the human aspect of analytic relatedness.

(p. 490)

An asylum evaluation is not an analysis. However, my experience of each interview is that it takes hold and includes me; it requires an increasingly larger portion of my involvement. Often, for a period during each interview I become so absorbed that I am not reflecting much on its nature. When this happens I feel tension. Sometimes I feel nauseous. I inevitably lose some of the exchange when this occurs: I do not take it all in. Because, with experience, I now know that this is likely to happen in an asylum interview, I often feel dread before one begins. I know that I will feel compelled to accompany the client on whatever journey she takes, that I will be unable to stand very far outside of it. I do not look forward to this experience. But, once it is over, I frequently feel enlivened by it. On some level I privately rejoice because the person I have interviewed dared to survive. This means that I can survive as well. In addition, often I hear about the individual's incredible resourcefulness in dealing with the trauma she endured. I learn that, when she arrived here, she was able to contend bravely with the inevitable feelings of separation and loneliness that accompany immigration (Ainslee et al., 2013). All of these factors bolster me in some way, contribute to my feeling of strength. I have liked this feeling enough to want to repeat it many times. This is what Engstrom, Hernandez, and Gangsei (2008) have called "vicarious resilience" (p. 13), a strengthening experience, the result of listening to survivor stories. According to this, the feeling creates great satisfaction in the evaluator. My own "vicarious resilience" renews my faith in the force within each of us to survive. I feel honored by the asylee's willingness to share her story with me. For me the experience is a leveling one, as Edgar Levinson describes. All of this is countertransference.

The almost always retraumatizing nature of the psycho-social assessment interview: Implications for both client and clinician

In considering retraumatization, it is probably correct to claim that examination of unconscious processes began with the study of memories which emerged as a result of retraumatization. In 1895 Breuer and Freud, for example, described "psychical trauma—or more precisely the memory of the trauma" as acting "like a foreign body which long after its entry must continue to be regarded as an agent that is still at work." (Freud, 1895/1950, p. 6).

Since then, retraumatization as a concept has been understood by different people in different ways. According to one source (Duckworth & Follette, 2012), it is looked at askance as a "sociopolitical" construction among those who are skeptical about the foundation of any diagnosis related to traumatic stress. Others believe its theoretical/conceptual bases have not been sufficiently investigated (Schock, Rosner, & Knaevelsrud, 2013).

For my purposes here, I use the term retraumatization to describe distress that occurs when the trauma narrative is retold. This is its most restricted use, according to Duckworth & Follette (2012).

Considering the limited nature of the psychosocial assessment interview I conduct, in which the asylee, often poorly prepared and under time pressure, is obliged to provide details of the traumatic events that led to her escape from home, some manner of retraumatization is almost inevitable. This is especially the case because survivors often have little time in which to process the pain and shame caused by the trauma before they are confronted with an interview. Thus it is not surprising that Schock, Rosner, and Knaevelsrud (2015)[39] found significant increases in post-traumatic intrusion experiences[40] in forty traumatized refugees, after they had completed their asylum interview, as compared to ten traumatized refugees who had not yet completed an interview. In addition, after the interview, these same individuals were significantly less able to avoid thinking of the trauma-causing events. In those cases in which they felt helpless to defend themselves, and worried that the outcome of their hearing might not be in their favor, their symptoms elevated considerably.

This and other accounts underscore the fact that the particulars of the recall situation have an effect on the severity of symptoms induced. Schoen (2017), for example, describes completing an evaluation of an inmate in the prison at Guantanamo Bay. This man had been imprisoned at Guantanamo for seven years, and was brought to his interview in shackles. His hopelessness about ever being released may well have increased his symptoms, Schoen reports. In contrast, a group of torture victims in

Sierra Leone who testified about their war experiences before a war crimes commission, reported primarily positive feelings once their testimony was complete. Symptoms of PTSD were apparently absent once the act of testifying had been completed (Stepakoff, Reynolds, & Charters, 2015). The fact that they had unburdened themselves of, among other things, their anger, seemed to reduce the intrusive symptoms of PTSD that they had previously been experiencing, according to these authors.

Thus in interviewing an asylee, the need for empathy cannot be stressed enough (Agosta, 2015). Control, empathy, and respect are advised in undertaking this work (Mailloux, 2014). Some education about the culture from which the client comes, especially with an eye to potential areas of sensitivity in regard to bases for self-esteem may help in lessening the psychologist's ignorance.[41] Attempts to compensate, in this way, for the poor training so many of us have received in what Prilleltensky (1997) calls the "diversity agenda" may help the interviewer to gain a little understanding of a person from a different culture. In this way, evaluators may be able to reduce the degree to which an asylum interview will cause the client pain.

Retraumatization, however, can also have its advantages, some of which were described above. Indeed, secrecy about traumatic experience creates loneliness and wears you down." [A]long with hiding, [it can] confirm a sense of badness," according to Steven Kuchuck (2008, p. 420). This feeling is common among asylum seekers who often harbor guilt about some aspect of the experience they have endured. "[T]he listener . . . the advocate—is crucial to the factualization and symbolization of the traumatic event," Leanh Nguyen tells us (2011, p. 33). Reliving it has the potential to open up "the possibility of a . . . more complex, flexible emotional, life" (Stolorow, Orange, and Atwood, 2001, p. 47) than might have been possible were they to bury their feelings. Indeed, in keeping with this, I have been surprised at how many asylees seem eager to tell their story. Frequently, once the telling comes to an end, I have been told that, yes, because of the retelling, the individual expects nightmares again for a while or will have greater difficulty falling asleep. I have also been told that every retelling makes it easier to go on. Asylees have thanked me for helping them to "better understand my family;" I have been hugged spontaneously by interviewees in tears. Once I was actually sought out by an asylee from Central America, who was in a prison, someone I had not been assigned to evaluate at all, a woman who simply wanted someone to listen to her story because, she said, she had questions and wanted help with them. Here is an account of what she said:

She, Ms. Therese, a mother of three, an attractive woman with an intense, dark-eyed gaze, had become a widow some months before when the Mara (gang) had shot her husband at his job in a jewelry store. The killing was witnessed by their thirteen-year-old daughter who happened to be visiting her father at the time. A few days after the murder, the Mara went to Therese's house unannounced, on an afternoon when the thirteen-year old daughter was not home. They demanded to know where she was. As a witness to her father's murder, the rule of the gang was that she too must die. Ms. Therese could not tell them where to find her. She did not know. So instead they bound and gagged her elder (eighteen-year-old) daughter, herself, and her nine-year-old son, and then raped the mother and daughter (a virgin) in separate rooms, forcing the son to look on. Threatening to kill them all when they returned, they then departed.

In the days immediately following, the thirteen year old wisely never came home; she had fled on her own to the United States, it seemed, and had lost touch with her family. Meanwhile, the eighteen year old, traumatized by the rape, made a suicide attempt. Ms. Therese, increasingly terrified for her life and for the lives of her children, decided that she too must leave. Thus, leaving the eighteen year old with a friend in the far off countryside (to keep her safe from further rape and mental breakdown), Therese fled, taking along her son. They travelled together, led by a coyote,[42] mostly on top of a train.

Mid-trip, the train they were on was besieged by other gang members who attacked the coyote, and demanded all his money. When he resisted, they simply shot him, took his money out of his socks, and pushed him off the train! The coyote's blood spattered all over Therese, all over her son, and over others in their group as well. The Mara demanded their money too. Finally, they departed. Therese and her group were relieved.

The shame Ms. Therese felt, first about her rape, and then about her inability to protect her daughters, was so extreme, that in telling her tale, she threw herself onto her knees in front of me, grabbed my legs, and put her head in my lap, crying all the time. Eventually, with some encouragement, she was able to sit in her own chair again. We (my very good translator and I)[43] listened with concern as she continued her tale. She felt terrible guilt for having left behind her eighteen year old, she said. She had had no contact with this daughter since she had fled.

Beyond the need to speak to her daughter, her biggest internal question remained: WHY? Why had this happened to her? Where was God? Why had He abandoned her? What had she done to deserve this? Because the narrative sense she had had of her life—as having been poor, but good, having been blessed by God—had disappeared, nothing really made sense to her anymore. This she repeated, wringing her hands, two or three times.

At first I did not know how to reply to this question. I just felt stunned. Then I said something to reassure her that her question was normal, that anyone who had been through what she had been through would wonder why. I said that what had happened to her was not her fault, that she had done nothing wrong, that maybe the new reality at home, now completely out of her control because of the gangs, was different from the one she had known before. None of these words seemed to help. Finally, I added that perhaps, since all of this criminality was so new, that maybe God did not know what to do about it either. On hearing this, she was silent for a moment. Then she said, "God did save our lives," as if that, at least, was one way in which she could still believe He was there for her.

We then thought with her about how she could contact her daughter, the child she had left behind. We supported the plan that she herself came up with, which involved a visiting priest with a cell phone. The next day, when we saw Ms. Therese again, she had spoken to her daughter and felt reassured: her daughter was safe and was being well cared for, she told us. She was extraordinarily relieved and seemed a different person entirely, bowed down, almost meek, perhaps embarrassed, we did not know. The intense light in her eyes was gone. She did not want to stay with us very long.

It was clear to me, when we parted from Therese, that her "why" question about God still remained, that it was not a question she was going to be able to answer anytime soon. In all likelihood, it will take her years and many repetitions of her story, to fully address the trauma that she experienced and to recreate a sense of herself and a belief system that will support this. But, in telling her story to us, she had begun.

It is certainly true that pressing individuals to expose feelings of panic, shame, injury and despair, quickly, as we do during asylum interviews, is strongly advised against because of the potential of retraumatization. However, in contradiction to this is the evidence that empathically "witnessing" an account of survival can be a step, for the storyteller, towards reconnecting with others and making a new life. Perhaps I am biased in my belief in the positive nature of this experience.

Vicarious traumatization

Vicarious traumatization occurs in those who work with traumatized individuals of every kind. Trauma has a "contagious quality," as Ghislaine Boulanger (2016) has remarked. John Wilson, who has studied the transmission of trauma extensively[44] lists five "clusters" of PTSD symptoms that he believes are "omnipresent" during interviews with survivors. Many of these, he believes, inevitably get transmitted to the empathic listener. In an asylum interview, this process may be exaggerated because a quick lowering of defenses may take place under the pressure of fathoming an unfamiliar story in a short period of time. Often, during a telling, the feelings seem to "*live*" and encourage the "communicability of affect" as Agosta puts it (2015, *Preface*). It may also be that this feeling of openness includes an exaggerated willingness to over-identify with the asylee (Waugarman, 2009).

Speaking for myself, I am less vulnerable, more defended against the invasion of the other's experience now than I was fifteen years ago when I began interviewing asylum seekers. At the beginning, I was so affected by the stories I heard that sometimes I experienced myself as the torturer, a feeling that was unsettling, to say the least, but also helpful in understanding the asylee's experience. Once, inside a taxi, just after having completed an interview, I was so identified with the story I had just heard, in which my client had been witness to the killing of a child by gunfire outside the door of her house, that I found myself ducking to avoid the oncoming shots I heard. These, I quickly realized, were not shots at all, but no more than the backfire noises of a passing truck![45] More frequently I have had nightmares in which the army was after me or it was I who was receiving the beatings or trying helplessly to protect the person I had just interviewed. More recently, often after an asylum interview, I experience immense, very palpable sadness.

Vicarious traumatization among those who work specifically with survivors of political trauma is common. Its effects have been discussed from different perspectives, some more positive than others. Holmqvist and Andersen (2003), for example, compared the feelings of six therapists at work with survivors of political torture to a larger group of therapists who worked with a variety of other populations. The six experienced an unusually high level of responsibility for their clients, but this covered more devastating, unhappy feelings, which emerged over time. At the beginning of their contact with these clients, however, despite some ambivalence and feelings of judgment, they were enthusiastic and interested in the stories they heard.

Yael Danieli, in a series of studies of Holocaust survivors and their therapists (referenced in Danieli, 1984), first studied the effects on patients of the long- term neglect and avoidance of the pain caused during that period. Then, once survivor pain was acknowledged, therapist reactions to it, including guilt, rage, dread, horror, disgust, loathing, shame, enormous sorrow, and grief.

The experience of vicarious trauma when working with individuals who have been traumatized by victims of sex abuse, rape, and natural disaster, has been well documented by, for example, Shatan, 1973; McFarlane, 1994; Figley, 1995; Kleespies, 1998. Suggestions for self care include: a workbook on the subject (Saakvitne & Pearlman, 1996), the formation of ongoing support groups (McCann & Pearlman, 1990), and the careful balancing of trauma work with other less invading, more immediately satisfying experiences. The presence of a positive support system seems a necessity (Charney & Pearlman, 1998). I cannot agree more with the latter. If one is to engage in an ongoing manner with political asylum seekers, it is also a good thing to enjoy diversions of all sorts.

Along with its negative effects, vicarious traumatization can have positive effects as well. Boulanger (2016), for example, indicates that, not only is vicarious traumatization complex and variable from situation to situation, but in some long-term treatment situations, it can be very useful in accessing and then formulating dissociated material in both patient and therapist. She lists a number of other therapists (p. 4) who have had similar experiences.

3. How do we know the client is telling the truth?

It is not unusual to wonder if every asylum seeker tells the truth. Some stories are hard to believe, they are so detailed and horrible. And frequently, in telling their stories, clients seem to muddle details, especially in regard to the order in which sequences are reported. As a consequence, when I first began evaluating, I found myself distrusting my own willingness to be convinced.

A review of literature on the subject confirmed my intuitive response: I am correct to distrust my ability to make judgements in this area, for mental health professionals, in general, according to Paul Ekman (Ekman & Sullivan, 1991) and other researchers (for example, Di Salvo, 2011; Geiselman et al., 2013), are no better at this than the average person. Moreover, recent attempts to fix this (Evans et al., 2013; Whitbourne, 2014) seem too imprecise to be useful.

There are, however, a number of ways in which to confirm a client's account. First, it is possible to look online at conditions in the applicant's home country to investigate her claims in regard to threats to people like herself, people of similar race, religion, group membership, political affiliation, etc. It is also possible to find descriptions of the schools that the client reports having attended, as well as churches, medical facilities, etc. After such a search it has generally seemed reasonable to me to conclude that, if others like her are/were threatened at home, why would she not be threatened as well?

As for details of the trauma experienced, it is well known that a common symptom of trauma is difficulty in recalling the details of the actual event itself. Indeed, in the retelling of the story, details inevitably change (Herlihy & Turner, 2006; Stern, 2012), which is a difficult issue for trauma survivors themselves. This is especially the case when the victim has been unable to find anyone willing to listen to her story before the advent of the asylum process itself (Brewin, Andrews, & Valentine, 2000; Peskin, 2012). Even when she might previously have had an audience, details of a life-changing, traumatic experience can be "like unwieldy clay, stubbornly resisting efforts to mold or shape them into a form that an audience not used to such dense matter might recognize and accept" (Langer, 2003, p. 157). In the end, without the acknowledgment of another, the victim herself may have difficulty believing that the events that happened to her did actually take place.

Then there are differences in the ways in which people from different cultures conceptualize events. Individuals from Western European cultures, for example, tend to think sequentially, in contrast to the more holistic thinking common to cultures from other parts of the world. In interviewing a person from a culture of the latter kind, details may well emerge randomly. For example, one of the women I interviewed while working in the South Texas Family Residential Center (prison) in Dilley, Texas, a young widow, very attractive, from the mountainous region of a Central American country, spoke only Quiché, an ancient language with time boundaries (past, present, future) that are less detailed than in either English or Spanish. Moreover, it was difficult to read her facial expressions, for, when she interacted with us, she kept her eyes averted, which is customary in the culture from which she comes. In order to communicate with her, we engaged a translator by telephone. He spoke to her in Quiché and then to us in Spanish. Once we had him on the line, and she was conversing with him, her entire demeanor changed. She became animated, spoke easily, freely, rapidly, even using her hands.

She and her four-year-old son had been (illegally!) placed in this prison by the United States government, she reported. Two previous attempts to come to the United States had failed. She had been sent back home. Her immigration problems, she thought, had stemmed from the fact that she could not read the documents she had inadvertently signed, which were in fact deportation documents. She was the youngest child and only daughter in a family from a region of her country which had no electricity. She had been a weaver by trade, a tradition she inherited from her mother. At home, she had done well financially, but because she is female and descended from an artisanal tradition (she described her work with considerable pride), she was never sent to school. Thus she could not read or write. Nor did she learn Spanish. As a result, the details of the story she told were not always added in sequential order. They seemed to be spoken as she reimagined the picture of what had happened to her at the hands of the strangers who had entered her house, held her at knifepoint, and attempted to rape her and steal her money.

In communicating with us, the first thing she did was to show us the scar left by the knife wound she endured in struggling with them. Gradually other details emerged, one by one, in disorder. The men dropped their flashlight, could not see, they fell down, she ran out of her house into the street, made noise, bargained with them about money, etc. In the end it was clear that her intelligence, ingenuity, and courage had, in fact, saved her life and the lives of her children as well. With the help of Hugo, the translator on the phone, she understood which papers to sign. She had brought them with her to the interview. He was familiar with them and helped her. He also helped us get the details of her story in order.

Given all of the above, I came to the conclusion that, unless the story I am told is totally outrageous, doubting an asylum seeker is a waste of time. Perhaps it is prejudice on my part, but I almost always accept the stories I am told as sufficiently true to justify the client's asylum need.

Issues in regard to confidentiality

Because all the material the attorney will collect in support of the applicant's case will be submitted to federal court, it is by definition in the public domain. As a consequence, it is not confidential. This piece of information is generally unclear to asylum seekers. It is thus incumbent upon the psychologist to inform them of this, although the attorney might also have done so. In addition, it is appropriate to disguise personal information when and if data from asylum interviews is used elsewhere.

Working with attorneys

As described above, the attorney is in charge of presenting an asylee's material, including all relevant supporting documents, to the federal official (officer or judge) assigned to the case.

My experience has been with attorneys employed as follows: attorneys who work for non-profits (AFSC, Human Rights First, Kids in Need of Defense (KIND), and others); attorneys who work for large law firms who have been assigned an asylum case because the firm has volunteered a number of hours of pro bono work; student attorneys, under the supervision of their professors in law school; attorneys in their own private practices. These individuals vary enormously in both their knowledge of asylum law and their willingness to spend sufficient time to adequately represent their client.

The most consistently dedicated and collaborative of these attorneys, in my experience, have been those who work for non-profits. They have chosen to work for such organizations, are paid a standard salary, and want to do the work well. They know the law and are wholeheartedly involved in practicing it.

Next have been law students under supervision at their respective law schools. These students also have chosen to do asylum work as part of their legal training. They often regard it not only as important in the world, but important to them as a real clinical service they can accomplish, in contrast to the dryness of other law courses in which they are only reading law. Supervisors at law school asylum clinics are dedicated as well.

Lawyers completing pro bono assignments in large law firms, again in my experience, have been less consistently reliable. Many large law firms volunteer a certain amount of pro bono legal work in their respective communities because they believe they should. This is a good thing. But often the attorneys they assign to these cases are young and inexperienced. In addition, although they receive a salary from the firm while they are completing these cases, they are paid no bonuses. Nor do they necessarily get as much recognition as they might were they working under the supervision of an interested partner with prominent, more lucrative clients. Thus it has often seemed to me these individuals would rather do their other work, which may seem more time sensitive or important. At times, their interviews have been so poor that I have had to return them and ask for more information. More information has then graciously been supplied.

In contrast, however, at other times I have found some pro-bono attorneys from large law firms to be extraordinarily intelligent and conscientious. I have learned from them considerably.

Finally, there are attorneys in their own private immigration practices. I have had some positive experiences with these individuals and some rather negative ones. The good experiences have been with intelligent, compassionate professionals who, despite overwork, have done their best to represent their clients. But too often these individuals have seemed to care more about their fees than about the well-being of their client. Or, good as their intentions may have been, they have seemed so overwhelmed that they have failed to provide sufficient information to the court to document and/or validate the client's claim about politics in her country, about sexual practices, or at times, about the roots of sexual orientation.[46] When appropriate, I ask the attorney about the kinds of background information (s)he will make available to the court. When the answer seems wanting to me, I add it to my own affidavit in a footnote. Recently, for example, I interviewed a gay woman from an African country in which homosexuality is outlawed. My impression was that the attorney was not going to mention this in his own report to the court. Accordingly, I added a footnote on the subject to my own.

In working with attorneys it is wise to keep in mind that they too are subject to vicarious trauma just as the rest of the staff who work with asylum seekers are (Levin et al., 2011). Often they have fewer resources to contend with it than psychologists do.

Working with interpreters[47]

Increasingly, in the last two decades, both because of increased numbers of immigrants and refugees and greater sophistication about the nature of human interaction, questions are being asked about the complexity of interpreter contributions to legal, medical, and psychotherapeutic exchanges (Angelelli, 2004). In regard to psychotherapy, issues in regard to boundary crossing and role confusion (Darling, 2004; Baker, Izzo, & Trento, 2015), intrusion of the interpreter's personal issues (Darling, 2004), and the emotional effects on the interpreter of client material, (Doherty, MacIntyre, & Wyne, 2010) have been recognized as occasionally problematic. At the same time, real appreciation has grown because of the multi-faceted nature of the contributions interpreters can make in situations involving refugees. The need for the training of mental health professionals in regard to how best to work with interpreters has grown (Angelilli, 2004; Angelilli & Baer, 2016). Collaboration between all parties involved in this work is the goal (Costa, 2017). For interpreters themselves, there are a few training programs presently available.[48] These underscore the role of the interpreter, not only as a person who is translating words, but as an interpreter of one culture to another. All of this seems important indeed.

In my experience, however, interpreters who have been trained as such are rare. In fact, I have never worked with one. Usually, the interpreters who accompany my clients have been trained only by their on-the-job experience in the offices of attorneys. Sometimes they have been doing such work for years. At other times, they have had barely any experience at all. Most, however, seem very collaborative.

In general, I try to make a connection with the translators before we begin. I ask (and write down) their names, ask about their knowledge of the client, how the attorney found them, etc. I explain that I am seating them behind the client because I want the client to be relating to me. I have never worked with an interpreter who did not understand this.

In my experience, the effect of the presence of interpreters on an asylum interview varies considerably, depending on the following: their fluency in the client's language; their familiarity with the culture of the asylee's home country; their familiarity with the asylum seeker and the case.

Again, in my experience, interpreter and client have generally met before they arrive at my office, as the attorney (who is responsible for providing this service) previously has worked with both. Thus the interpreter is usually sympathetic to the client and the client feels positively towards her in return. When the interpreter is a native speaker of the asylee's language they share nuances of feeling, reflected in the language, which I do not share, even though I may understand some of the words they speak. Thus, inevitably, the interpreter plays an important dialogic role in describing the client's experience and is a definite presence in the room (Bot & Wadensjö, 2004).

However, as described in the first part of this chapter, I try to minimize the presence of the interpreter by placing him or her behind the asylee and connecting by eye contact with the asylee myself.[49] I also try to look at the interpreter as little as possible. In this way I try to establish myself as the main other in the room. Perhaps because of my own intensity, I have found this easy to do. Although, at times, I have experienced the interpreter as irritated by this, usually the opposite has seemed true: interpreters want to cooperate as much as they can. At times, it has seemed to me that the interpreter is relieved not to be confronted directly with the client's pain. At other times, it has seemed to me that (s)he is as interested as I in understanding the more elusive details of the client's story.

Often during the minutes in which the interpreter is at work, I am either writing rapidly or making facial contact with the asylee. I try to use my face to reflect back feelings appropriate to the words the interpreter is saying and/or to say encouraging words to the asylee myself. Asylees often understand these quite well, in English.

In general, I have found interpreters to be extremely helpful, sometimes even extraordinary. Once, for example, I had a client (my very first one) who was learning-disabled. It was quickly clear to me that she had difficulty finding the words she needed (in her own language) to describe things.[50] So we ended up drawing the prison cell into which she had been put and made stick figures to locate the policemen who had tortured her. The interpreter, a highly intelligent woman, already acquainted with the client, understood immediately and explained to the client what to do, helping her locate exactly where the policemen were in the room, etc. It was a remarkable experience for both myself and the interpreter.

Interpreters also have their own countertransference issues (Mellman, 1995). In addition, they too can suffer vicarious trauma. Once an interpreter was so affected by the client's story that she burst into tears. Once, working in a prison, an interpreter soliloquized at considerable length on the evils of men in her own home culture (one she shared with the client). In situations such as these, a little sympathy goes a long way. Interpreters know perfectly well that the interview they are assisting at is not directed at them.

Final comment

This chapter has covered factors implicit in the completion of psychosocial evaluations of asylum seekers. An outline of a prospective psychologist's affidavit appears at the end of Appendix I. The chapters that follow are focused on asylum seekers themselves.

Notes

1 Excellent descriptions of this process, forensically based, have been authored by: Meffert et al. (2010), Physicians for Human Rights Handbook (2012), and Vaisman (2003; 2014).
2 Every country has its own asylum laws, hence this book is limited to asylum seekers in the United States.
3 The United States is a cosigner of the 1951 Convention Relating to the Status of Refugees and its 1967 Protocol. These laws are known as the Geneva Conventions. They define "well-founded fear of persecution" as the grounds upon which asylum is to be granted. These international laws are not binding. Signators have only agreed, in front of one another, to abide by them. See more at:

- https://en.wikipedia.org/wiki/Asylum_in_the_United_States
- http://www.unhcr.org/4d93528a9.pdf
- https://www.uscis.gov/sites/default/files/.

Vaisman-Tzachor (2003; 2012) describes the manner in which the legal definition of persecution (the cause of "well-founded fear") has changed over time in the United States. At present, there must be "demonstrable physical or emotional harm to the asylum seeker" or potential for it in order to qualify. The clearest discussion I have found of the evolution of asylum law and its various present-day caveats has been written by PHR (2012). According to them, "even for an experienced immigration attorney, understanding the numerous sources of and interaction between immigration laws can be difficult and frustrating," (PHR, 2012, p. 3). Further changes have and still are being made by the Trump administration.
4 This principle, part of the Geneva Convention, is fully described at: http://www.unhcr.org/en-us/excom/scip/3ae68ccd10/note-non-refoulement-submitted-high-commissioner.html.
5 These words are from a Supreme Court decision, referenced in PHR (2012, p. 9). In fact the entire vague, discretionary nature implicit in asylum-related decision-making is based on Supreme Court rulings. These are referenced in PHR (2012).

6 For more on this, including numbers who have finally achieved permanent residency in the United States, see: http://www.migrationpolicy.org/article/refugees-and-asylees-united-states. Refugees in contrast, are asylum seekers who apply for asylum from a place outside of the country, usually an embassy belonging to the country to which they hope to go.

7 This training program covers "topics such as international refugee law and the U.S. Asylum Program's role in world-wide refugee protection, U.S. asylum law and its interpretation by the Board of Immigration Appeals and federal appellate courts, interviewing techniques, researching country of origin information, and decision-making/writing. Separate training sessions address interviewing survivors of torture, identifying possible cases of victims of trafficking, handling cases of children, and handling claims that may be specific to women" and more. It is described at: https://www.uscis.gov/humanitarian/refugees-asylum/asylum/asylum-division-training-programs. For a fine depiction of who these people are and the kinds of burdens they face, see an excellent documentary, *Well-Founded Fear*, available on line, through Apple and other places.

8 For a description of the utterly confusing nature of the asylum process, especially in regard to the question of the availability of the expert witness, whose statement presumably supports the credibility of the client's claim, internationally as well as nationally, see Lawrence & Ruffer, 2015.

9 The services of mental health professionals are being sought for immigrants who face other proceedings as well, including: cancellation of removal, hardship, rehabilitation, U visa. See Appendix I for more on these.

10 Asylum seekers without representation are "almost five times less likely to win their cases than those with representation." (Ardalan, 2015, cited in Harvard Law School, 2017).

11 In New York City there are a host of organizations that can access legal services for no charge. Among these are: Human Rights First, Catholic Charities; KIND. Such services are available in other parts of the country as well, although a guide to them does not exist. In addition, there are attorneys who specialize in immigration for a fee. Some are much more competent than others. See below for more on this.

12 The reasoning behind acceptance of PTSD and other psychological diagnoses as scientifically valid is legally stated in two "rules of evidence," The Frye Rule of Evidence (1923) and the Daubert Standard (1993). These rules evolve. In addition, some states accept one, some both. For more on this see: https://inns.innsofcourt.org/media/148127/daubert-frye_presentation_011917_final_011917.pdf and https://www.theexpertinstitute.com/daubert-v-frye-a-state-by-state-comparison/.

13 Although my services are offered pro bono, there are many honorable forensic health professionals who are paid for their services by the asylee herself or by a sponsoring organization.

14 I have been assigned asylum cases by seven different organizations: PHR, Doctors of the World, AFSC, KIND, Cardozo Law School, HRF, Dilley Prison Group. Indeed, there are many organizations nationally that provide legal and other services to asylum seekers. Unfortunately, I know of no guide to these services. Altogether, as a volunteer, I have evaluated more than one hundred and fifty people seeking asylum, from twenty-four different countries.

15 There are many of these, some of which are listed below. I have worked for: HealthRight International, AFSC, Cardozo Law School, KIND, PHR, HRF, and more. There are, however, health professionals who are recompensed for their work, either by the asylee herself or an agency.

16 PHR (http://physiciansforhumanrights.org/?referrer=https://www.google.com/) has offices in other cities which also receive requests for this service.

17 Laws protecting individuals threatened by gang violence do not clearly fit the U.N requirements for asylum, based on the five "protected" grounds which are accepted as bases for persecution. Thus UNHCR issues a note addressing gang based asylum claims, available at: http://www.refworld.org/pdfid/4bb21fa02.pdf. To quote from the last paragraph of the Conclusion of this note: "UNHCR's perspective is that the interpretation of the 1951 Convention grounds needs to be inclusive and flexible enough to encompass emerging groups and respond to new risks of persecution. Young people . . . who live in communities with a pervasive and powerful gang presence but who seek to resist gangs may constitute a particular social group for the purposes of the 1951 Convention." In such cases, of course, the burden of proof lies with the asylee.

18 These are available at: http://www.loc.gov/law/foreign-news/article/united-nations-new-international-guidelines-on-detention-of-asylum-seekers/.

19 See section "Working with Interpreters," for a more detailed discussion of this subject.

20 In my experience, clients whose children are living with them, if encouraged, often take home a bunch of cookies wrapped in a napkin. Often, because the asylee cannot work and money is scarce, little is available for food.

21 When I first began doing asylum evaluations, I often felt like a torturer myself. Later I read that Bergmann and Jacovy believed that "the therapist must be experienced by the survivor as a Nazi . . . if the unconscious identification with the . . .perpetrators is not to remain forever lodged in the unconscious of the survivor." (1982 p. xi, quoted in Ornstein, 2003, p. 93). If this is true it may perhaps be true in asylum evaluations as well.

22 In my experience, asylees often believe that their symptoms, intrusive feelings, flashbacks, despair, imply that they have become crazy. These are notoriously normal responses to severe trauma, as evident in the accounts of Holocaust survivors especially. See, for instance, Langer, 2003.

23 APA ethical standards (at: http://www.apa.org/ethics/code/) require informed consent to evaluations (paragraph 3:10), unless the testing is mandated by law (paragraph 9:03). Assessment of asylees is not exactly mandated by law.

24 The United Nations developed a protocol for mental health and other evaluations in 1999, titled The Istanbul Protocol. It is available at: http://www.ohchr.org/Documents/Publications/training8Rev1en.pdf.
25 A strong social network is often implicit in the client's description of how they raised the money necessary for them to leave home. I interpret this as a sign of emotional well-being.
26 An updated list of tests and questionnaires currently in use for this purpose can be found at: https://www.psychologicalevaluationsforimmigrationcourt.net/sample-page/. An outline of a prospective evaluations is available in Appendix III.

 I do not use tests because, along with Leanh Nguyen (2011), I think they restrict my ability to know about the client's life. As she puts it: "When we administer a test, we do something both *with* and *to* another. We limit and distort what can be experienced, known, and shared, of the other person's reality" (p. 36). The DSM criteria are often met in the story the asylee tells me and questions about their experience, when necessary, are less intrusive than test questions.
27 According to some, PTSD, as described by the DSM, poorly represents the entirety of a torture survivor's symptoms. For more on this see Kleber, Figley, & Berthold, 1995.
28 Fran Geteles Shapiro, Ph.D., who has done nearly two hundred evaluations, tells me (in a personal communication) that she just describes her clients' symptoms and broadly refers to PTSD. Her cases are generally successful at achieving asylum.
29 I understand that in some cases health professionals write nothing. Instead they appear in court. In my experience, a written affidavit has always been required. Although, lately, I have been asked to be "available to the court" on the day of the hearing, in most cases this has meant on the other end of a telephone. I have, however, never actually been asked to testify, perhaps because, as one judge told me: "It's all there. I don't need more." I believe this is the conclusion judges arrive at if the DSM is used in a report. They respect it.
30 According to one source (Randall & Lutz, 1991) "it is often the best adjusted who can leave their countries" in order to seek political asylum (p. 7).
31 Morning Edition, National Public Radio, 9/23/17.
32 More about this is at: http://www.pewresearch.org/fact-tank/2017/01/30/key-facts-about-refugees-to-the-u-s/.
33 Telling the story is helpful to most people who have lived through any kind of ordeal, according to Cave and Sloan (2016).
34 In fact, frequently, at the beginning of meetings with asylum seekers, when we are discussing the reason for an interview with me, the client has said that, since her attorney has sent her to me, she can trust me.
35 Gerson (2009, p. 1342), summarizing the work of others, describes three different fields of thirdness, which he calls the developmental, the relational, and the cultural (and, perhaps, the law). The relational is concerned with the ongoing

connection between two people, the cultural with the non-personal aspects of society, including the language in which individuals co-exist. See his article for more on this.

36 Astonishment and disbelief at the failure of empathy on the part of the torturer and the powerlessness of the victim to change this is common among survivors of genocide and trauma of other sorts at the hands of the enemy. See Auerhahn, Laub, & Peskin (1993) for more on this.
37 One can put oneself at risk in many ways, by being physically or psychologically endangered, by risking one's life in a crossfire, by risking one's personal or professional reputation, etc.
38 Ullman attributes the origin of this idea to Berman (2002).
39 This is apparently the only study of its kind to date.
40 The formal APA criteria for a diagnosis of PTSD includes three sets of reactions: the first describes intrusion experiences—flashbacks, nightmares etc.—of the traumatic event. The second describes avoidance and numbing responses, such as feelings of detachment, restriction of affect, etc. The third describes forms of hyperarousal such as sleep disturbances, irritability, outbursts of anger, etc. Particulars are available at: https://www.ptsd.va.gov/professional/pages/dsm5_criteria_ptsd.asp.
41 In my experience there is a surprising amount of information about different cultures available online as long as there is time to search.
42 Coyote is the word used in Central America to describe the leader of a group fleeing home. Coyotes are paid for their services and must proceed in secret.
43 I have a moderately good understanding of spoken Spanish; my ability to speak correctly, however, is far less proficient.
44 A paper summarizing this work is available in Wilson (2004).
45 Excellent and almost shocking experiences of vicarious trauma are described by McCann & Pearlman (1990).
46 Once in New Jersey, before knowledge about homosexuality was much extant, I went to court with a client, a gay man who had suffered brutal treatment in a country in which homosexuality is outlawed. The client lost his case, essentially because the judge was convinced he had chosen his sexual orientation and could have chosen another path. This was a surprise to the attorney as well as to me. She had not considered that this might be an issue for her client.
47 An excellent discussion of this subject from a linguistic perspective can be found in Bot & Wadensjö (2004).
48 See Costa (2017) for more on this.
49 Eye contact, in some cultures, is inappropriate, especially between men and women. Although I have interviewed a number of individuals from such cultures, with the exception of one woman from a mountainous region of Central America, mentioned above, I never found this to impede the willingness of asylees to look at me.
50 My first job as a psychologist was in a speech and hearing clinic in which we saw many language disordered individuals.

References

Agosta, L. (2015). *A Rumor of Empathy: Rewriting Empathy in the Context of Philosophy*. [Kindle Version]. Retrieved from www.amazon.com

Ainslee, R. C., Harlem, A., Tummala-Narra, P., Barbarnel, L., & Ruth, R. (2013). Contemporary psychoanalytic views on the immigrant experience. *Psychoanalytic Psychology*. 30: 663–679.

Angelilli, C. V. (2004). *Medical Interpreting and Cross-Cultural Communication*. New York, NY: Cambridge University Press.

Angelilli, C. V. & Baer, B. J. (2016). *Researching Translation and Interpretive Translation and Interpreting*. New York, NY: Routledge.

Auerhahn, N. C., Laub, D., & Peskin, H. (1993). Psychotherapy with holocaust survivors. *Psychotherapy, Theory, Research, Practice, Training*, 30: 434–442.

Baker, S. W., Izzo, P., & Trento, A. (2015). Psychodynamic considerations in psychotherapy using interpreters: Perspectives from psychiatry residents. *Psychodynamic Psychiatry*. 43: 117–128.

Bergmann, M. & Jacovy, M. (1982). *Generations of the Holocaust*. New York, NY: Basic Books.

Berman, E. (2002). Beyond analytic anonymity: Political involvement of analysts in Israel. In J. Bunzi & B. Beit-Hallahmi (Eds.), *Psychoanalysis, Identity, and Ideology* (pp. 177–200). Norwell, MA: Kluwer.

Blackwell, D. (2005). *Counseling and Psychotherapy with Refugees*. London, UK: Jessica Kingsley Publishers.

Bot, H. & Wadensjö, C. (2004). The presence of a third party: A dialectical view on interpreter-assisted treatment. In J. Wilson & B. Droždec (Eds.), *Broken Spirits: The Treatment of Traumatized Asylum Seekers, Refugees, War and Torture Victims* (pp. 355–378). New York, NY: Bruner-Mazed.

Boulanger, G. (2007). *Wounded by Reality*. Mahwah, NJ: Analytic Press.

Boulanger, G. (2012). Psychoanalytic witnessing: Professional obligation or moral imperative? *Psychoanalytic Dialogues*. 29: 318–324.

Boulanger, G. (2016). When is vicarious trauma a necessary tool? *Psychoanalytic Psychology*. Retrieved from: http://dx.doi.org/10 1037/pop0000089.

Brewin, C. R., Andrews, B., Valentine, J. D., (2000). Meta-analysis of risk factors for posttraumatic stress disorder in trauma-exposed adults. *Journal of Consulting and Clinical Psychology*. 68: 748–766.

Carens, J. H. (2015). *The Ethics of Immigration*. New York: Oxford University Press.

Caruth, C. (1995). An interview with Robert Jay Lifton. In C. Caruth (Ed.), *Trauma: Explorations in Memory* (pp. 128–147). Baltimore, MD: Johns Hopkins University Press.

Cave, M. & Sloan, S. (2016). *Listening on the Edge: Oral History in the Aftermath of Crisis*. New York, NY: Oxford University Press.

Charney, A. E. & Pearlman, L. A. (1998). The ecstasy and the agony: The impact of disaster and trauma work on the self of the clinician. In P. M. Kleespies (Ed.), *Emergencies in Mental Health Practice: Evaluation and Management* (pp. 418–436). New York, NY: Guilford Press.

Costa, B. (2017). Training therapists to work in a team. *International Journal for the Advancement of Counselling.* 39: 56–69.

Dailey, A. C. (2017). *Law and the Unconscious: A Psychoanalytic Perspective.* New Haven, CT: Yale University Press.

Danieli, Y. (1984). Psychotherapists' participation in the conspiracy of silence about The Holocaust. *Psychoanalytic Psychology.* 1: 23–42.

Darling, L. (2004). Psychodynamically informed work with interpreters. *Psychoanalytic Psychotherapy.* 18: 255–267.

Di Salvo, D. (2011). How do we know you're lying? *Psychology Today.* Retrieved from: https://www.psychologytoday.com/blog/neuronarrative/201106/how-we-know-youre-lying.

Doherty, S. M., MacIntyre, S. M., & Wyne, T. (2010). How does it feel for you? The emotional impact and specific challenges of mental health interpreting. *Mental Health Review Journal.* 15: 31–44.

Duckworth, M. P. & Follette, V. M. (2012). *Retraumatization: Assessment, Treatment and Prevention.* New York, NY: Routledge

Eisenman, D. P., Bergner, S. & Cohen, I. (2000) An ideal victim: Idealizing trauma victims causes traumatic stress in human rights workers. *Human Rights Review.* 106–114.

Ekman, P. & O'Sullivan, M. (1991). Who can catch a liar? *American Psychologist.* 46: 913–920.

Engstrom, D., Hernandez, P., & Gangsei, D. (2008). Vicarious resilience: A qualitative investigation into its description. *Traumatology.* 14: 13–21.

Evans, J. P., Michael, S.W., Meissner, C.A., & Brandon, S. I. (2013). Validating a new assessment method for deception detection: Introducing a psychologically based credibility assessment tool. *Journal of Applied Research in Memory and Cognition.* 2: 33–41.

Felman, S. & Laub, D. (1992). *Testimony, Crises of Witnessing in Literature, Psycho-Analysis and History.* New York, NY: Routledge.

Figley, C. R. (1995). *Compassion Fatigue: Coping with Secondary Traumatic Stress Disorder in Those who Treat the Traumatized.* New York, NY: Bruner/Mazel.

Freud, S. (1895/1950). Project for a scientific psychology. In J. Strachey (Ed.), *Standard Edition of the Complete Psychological Works of Sigmund Freud.* (Vol. 1, pp. 281–387. New York, NY: W. W. Norton.

Geiselman, R. E., Musarra, E., Berezovskaya, N., Lustic, C., & Elmgren, S. (2013). Training novices to detect deception in oral narratives and exchanges, Part II. *American Journal of Forensic Psychology.* 31: 1–15.

Gerson, S. (2009). When the third is dead: Memory, mourning and witnessing in the aftermath of the Holocaust. *International Journal of Psychoanalysis.* 90: 1341–1357.

Harvard Law School. (2017). The impact of President Trump's executive orders on asylum seekers. Retrieved from: https://today.law.harvard.edu/wp-content/uploads/2017/02/Report-Impact-of-Trump-Executive-Orders-on-Asylum-Seekers.pdf.

Hedges, C. (2003). *War is the Force that Gives Us Meaning.* New York: Anchor.*

Herlihy, J. & Turner, S. (2006). Should discrepant accounts given by asylum seekers be taken as proof of deceit? *Torture.* 16: 81–92.

Herman, J. L. (2004). Complex PTSD: A syndrome in survivors of prolonged and repeated trauma. In D. Knafo (Ed.), *Living with Terror, Working with Trauma* (pp. 35–50). New York, NY: Aronson.

Holmqvist, R. & Andersen, K. (2003). Therapists reaction to the treatment of survivors of political trauma. *Professional Psychology: Research and Practice.* 3: 294–300.

Kleber, R. J., Figley, C. R., & Berthold, B. P. R. (Eds.). (1995). *Beyond Trauma:Cultural and Social Dynamics.* New York, NY: Plenum.

Kleespies, P. M. (Ed.). (1998). *Emergencies in Mental Health Practice: Evaluation and Management.* New York, NY: Guilford Press.

Kuchuck, S (2008). In the shadow of the towers: The role of retraumatization and political action in the evolution of a psychoanalyst. *Psychoanalytic Review.* 95: 417–436.

Lacan, J. (1982). Le symbolique, l'imaginaire et le réel. *Bulletin de l'Association Freudienne.* 1: 4–13.

Langer, L. L. (2003). The pursuit of death in holocaust narrative. In G. D. Fireman, T. E. McVay Jr., O. J. Flanagan (Eds.), *Narrative and Consciousness: Literature, Psychology and the Brain.* New York, NY: Oxford University Press.

Laub, D. (1992). Bearing witness to the vicissitudes of listening. In S. Felman & D. Laub (Eds.), *Testimony: Crises of Witnessing in Literature, Psychoanalysis, and History* (pp. 57–74). New York, NY: Routledge.

Laub, D. & Auerhahn, N. (1982). Failed empathy: A central theme in the survivor's holocaust experience. *Psychoanalytic Psychology.* 6: 377–400.

Lawrence, B. N. & Ruffer, G. (2015). Introduction: Witness to the persecution? Expertise, testimony, and consistency in asylum adjudication. In B. N. Lawrence & G. Ruffer (Eds.). *Adjudicating Refugee and Asylum Status: The Role of Witness, Expertise and Testimony* (Introduction). New York, NY: Cambridge University Press.

Levin, A. P., Albert, L., Besser, A., Smith, D., Zelenski, A., Rosenkranz, S. & Neria, Y. (2011). Secondary traumatic stress in attorneys and their administrative support staff working with trauma-exposed clients. *Journal of Nervous and Mental Disease.* 199: 946–971.

Lewin, K. (1936). *Principles of Topological Psychology.* York, PA: Maple Press.

McCann, I. L. & Pearlman, L. A. (1990). Vicarious traumatization: A framework for understanding the psychological effects of working with victims. *Journal of Traumatic Stress.* 3: 131–149.

McFarlane, A. C. (1994). Individual psychotherapy for post-traumatic stress disorder. *Psychiatric Clinics of North America.* 17: 393–408.

Mailloux, S. L. (2014). The ethical imperative: Considerations in the trauma counseling Process. *Traumatology: An International Journal.* 20: 50–56.

Margalit, A. (2002). *The Ethics of Memory.* Cambridge, MA: Harvard University Press.

Meffert, S. M., Musalo, M. McNiel, D., & Binder, R. (2010). The role of the mental health professional in political asylum processing. *Journal of the American Academy of Psychiatry and the Law Online.* 38: 479–489.

Mellman, L. A. (1995). Countertransference in court interpreters. *Bulletin of the Academy of Psychiatry And Law.* 23: 467–471.

Modell, A. (1994). Trauma, memory and psychic continuity. *Progress in Self Psychology.* 10: 131–146.

Nguyen, L. (2011). The ethics of trauma: Retraumatizing in society's approach to the traumatized subject. *International Journal of Group Psychotherapy.* 61: 27–47.

Nguyen, L. (2012). Psychoanalytic activism: Finding the human, staying human. *Psychoanalytic Psychology* 29: 308–317.

Ornstein, A. (2003) Survival and recovery: psychoanalytic reflections. *Progress in Self Psychology.* 19: 85–105. (2012).

Pepper, C. (2005). Gay men tortured on the basis of homosexuality: Psychodynamic and psychotherapeutic perspectives. *Contemporary Psychotherapy.* 41: 35–54.

Peskin, H. (2012). "Man is a wolf to man": Disorders of dehumanization in psychoanalysis. *Psychoanalytic Dialogues.* 22(2): 190–205.

PHR. (2012). *Examining Asylum Seekers.* Cambridge, MA: PHR.

Poland, W. S. (2016).Warren Poland on: "The analyst's witnessing and otherness": *PEP/UCL. Top Author's Project.* 1(1): 7.

Prilleltensky, I. (1997). Values, assumptions and practices: Assessing the moral implications of psychological discourse and action. *American Psychologist.* 52: 517–535.

Randall, G. R. & Lutz E. L.(1991) *Serving Survivors of Torture.* AAAS publication Number 91-42S.

Reading, R. & Rubin, L. (2011). Advocacy and empowerment: Group therapy for LGBT asylum seekers. *Traumatology*. 17: 86–98.

Reis, B. (2009). Performative and enactive features of psychoanalytic witnessing: The transference as the scene of address. *International Journal of Psychoanalysis*. 90: 1359–1372.

Saakvitne, K. W. & Pearlman, L. A. (1996). *Transforming the Pain: A Workbook on Vicarious Traumatization*. New York, NY: Norton.

Shatan, C. (1973). The grief of soldiers: Vietnam combat veterans' self-help movement. *American Journal of Orthopsychiatry*. 43: 640–653.

Schock, K., Rosner, R. & Knaevelsrud, C. (2013). Retraumatization: The vicious circle of intrusive memory. In: M. Linden & K. Rutkwski (Eds.), *Hurting Memories and Beneficial Forgetting: Posttraumatic Stress Disorders and Social Conflicts* (pp. 59–70). Amsterdam, Netherlands: Elsevier.

Schock, K., Rosner, R., & Knaevelsrud, C. (2015). Impact of asylum interviews on the mental health of traumatized asylum seekers. *European Journal of Traumatology*. Retrieved from: https://www.ncbi.nlm.nih.gov/pubmed/26333540.

Schoen, S. (2017). The culture of interrogation: Evaluating detainees at Guantanamo Bay. *International Journal of Applied Psychoanalytic Studies*. 14: 133–142.

Smith, H. E., Stuart L. L., & Gangsei, D. (2015). Incredible until proven credible: Mental health expert testimony and the systematic and cultural challenges facing asylum applicants. In B. N. Lawrence & G. Ruffer, (eds.): *Adjudicating Refugee and Asylum Status: The Role of Witness, Expertise and Testimony* (Chapter 9). New York, NY: Cambridge University Press.

Stepakoff, S., Reynolds, S. G., & Charters, S. (2015). Self-reported psychosocial consequences of testifying in a war crimes tribunal in Sierra Leone. *International Perspectives in Psychology: Research, Practice, Consultation*. 4: 161–181.

Stern, D. B. (2012). Witnessing across time: Accessing the present from the past and the past from the present. *Psychoanalytic Quarterly*. 81: 53–81.

Stern, D. B. (2013a). Field theory in psychoanalysis, part I: Harry Stack Sullivan and Madeleine and Willy Baranger. *Psychoanalytic Dialogues*. 23: 487–501.

Stern, D. B. (2013b) Field theory in psychoanalysis, part 2: Bionian field theory and contemporary interpersonal psychoanalysis. *Psychoanalytic Dialogues*. 23: 630–645.

Stolorow, R. D.; Orange, D. M. & Atwood, G. E. (2001). World Horizons: A post Cartesian alternative to the Freudian unconscious. *Contemporary Psychoanalysis*. 37: 43–61.

Symonds, M (1980/2010). The "second injury" to victims of violent acts. *The American Journal of Psychoanalysis*. 70: 903–921.

Ullman, C. (2011). Between denial and witnessing: Psychoanalytic and clinical practice in the Israeli context. *Psychoanalytic Perspectives*. 8: 179–200.

Vaisman-Tzachor, R. (2003). Psychological assessment: Protocol in federal immigration court. *The Federal Examiner*. 12: 34–40.

Vaisman-Tzachor, R. (2014). Psychological assessment protocol for asylum evaluations In federal immigration courts. American Psychotherapy Association. Retrieved from: http://www.annalsofpsychotherapy.com/articles/2014/PDF/Vaisman-Tzachor_Nov14.pdf.

Waugerman, R.M. (2009). Coasting in the countertransference. Conflicts of self-interest between analyst and patient. By Irwin Hirsch. Book Review. *Journal of the American Psychoanalytic Association*. 57: 507–511.

Whitbourne, S. K. (2014). 9 ways to tell who's lying to you. *Psychology Today*. Retrieved from: http://www.pewresearch.org/fact-tank/2017/01/30/key-facts-about-refugees-to-the-u-s/.

Wilson, J. (2004). Empathy, trauma, transmission and countertransference. In J. P. Wilson & B. Drožděk (Eds.), *Broken Spirits: The Treatment of Traumatized Asylum Seekers, Refugees, War and Torture Victims*. New York, NY: Brunner-Routledge.

Chapter 2

Heroic Asylum seekers from around the world[1]

Introduction

"It is hard to understand unless you have lived through it," she tells me, slowly, in French, which to my surprise, is completely clear to me. "Many things happened there about suffering," she continues. "I cried and cried. The danger! There was no bed, no place to pee, no place to wash, no light. Food came once a day. My husband didn't visit. My brother didn't visit. They violated me. They burned my leg with hot wax." Here she briefly lifts her skirt to show me the scar left by the wax, just above her ankle. "I don't know how to explain the feelings. I can't think of a parallel situation. There are people who died there and they can't explain. If they torture you in prison, no one can do anything . . . I told myself this, but at the same time I wanted to have a visitor . . ." Here her voice trails off. Being alone there was the hardest to bear and the most difficult to talk about.

This storyteller is a pretty, diminutive woman, university educated, who married late and thereby inherited a house full of children. In part because she cares for these children and is anxious about their future, she had routinely joined peaceful protests against the extraordinary limits placed on everyone by the repressive government in the African country from which she comes. Twice she had been picked up by the police at protests and twice endured the terrifying isolation of prison. The third and final time, however, her captors not only raped her, but threatened to kill her were they to pick her up again. Only then did she decide to leave. With family help, she flew to the United States, tourist visa in hand. She applied for asylum once it became time for her to go home, for going home, she believed, would have threatened her life, given her past prison record.

My task was to get her to describe in detail what happened to her and to transcribe it. I wanted to be able to describe the symptoms her ordeal has left behind. Then I had wanted to make as formal a diagnosis as I could, of

PTSD (and/or depression or dissociative disorder). How useful my report would turn out be would depend not only on the facts of the case and the clarity of my presentation, but on the cleverness of the attorney who was representing her and on the discretion of the judge before whom she would testify. If the outcome had been in her favor, she would have wanted to bring her children here to her new country, where a better future for them, she hoped, would be possible.

This woman belonged to a special group of asylum seekers who I have designated as heroes. These are people who, seemingly of their own accord, chose to oppose their repressive governments, peacefully, by distributing pamphlets, making speeches, protesting in the street, because they were outraged by the restrictions placed upon them as ordinary citizens with divergent political beliefs. Often, in my experience, (but not always) these are individuals who begin to protest in the relatively early stages of a repressive political situation, which later becomes more chaotic because repression has led to war.[2] My heroes, in contrast to other asylum seekers,[3] still had connections at home with family members who were living more or less together, although sometimes they had moved into the countryside, hoping to remain as anonymous as possible.

Upon first encountering such people, I found myself thinking of them as modern-day heroes because they seemed willing to die for the kind of freedom that might have been more easily available to them if they had gone elsewhere. Thus far, I have interviewed perhaps eleven people of this kind. Intrigued, and wanting to know more, I found, as I completed my interviews, that individuals such as these come from all over the world, from very different cultural backgrounds. In reviewing their stories, I was surprised to discover that, in spite of their vast cultural differences, with one exception (a woman from Ghana, whose child was killed inadvertently by relatives), they shared four important, life-affecting experiences: (1) Each, as a child or adolescent, had witnessed the trauma (wounds, bruises, depression, etc.) of an older, esteemed relative, who had been tortured by oppressors. (2) None had been offered the opportunity to discuss the feelings evoked by this witnessing. (3) Later, each had been chosen by his or her family to protest the trauma-causing oppressors. (4) Finally, each had then been able to sustain repeated instances of punishment and/or imprisonment at the hands of these oppressors, until death was threatened. Then, and only then, were they able to change course completely and take flight. In doing this, they had had help from their families. In this context, their flight seemed to represent a family-sanctioned event, designed not only to preserve a single life, but also to provide an opportunity for a new family beginning somewhere else.

In Table 1 I have presented some personal data about each of these people in a manner which will make comparison among them relatively easy. I have numbered my hero subjects (in future pages to be referred to only as "protestors" or "subjects") from 1 to 11 for the sake of further discussion.

Initiating the protestor role

Seven men and four women make up my protestor group. Among the men, who ranged in age from twenty-four to forty-four when I met them, all but one (Subject 1) are first-born sons or only children. Of these seven, five came from an African country (Togo, Guinea, or Cameroon), two from Tibet. All of the Africans were literate, in both French (their school language) and their own native tongue.[4] The Tibetan monk (Subject 5) was also highly literate, and spoke English as well as Tibetan and Mandarin. Subject 4, also from Tibet, had earned his living by farming, was illiterate, and spoke only his native language.

In Tibet and in the African countries from which my heroes had come, it is customary for the eldest son, if he has sufficient intelligence and will, to carry on the most important family traditions. In the families of each of the men I interviewed, pride had traditionally been invested in political resistance. Thus it was the eldest son who was supposed to carry on that tradition, following the line begun by his father or grandfather, or sometimes both. Subject 7, for example, university educated, from Cameroon, the eldest son in his family, told me that, when he turned thirteen his father had taken him to visit an uncle who had been brutalized by the despotic regime in their country. Depressed and in great pain, this uncle was recovering in a hospital. In spite of the fact that his uncle's protests had led to great pain, this boy's father expected that, eventually, his first-born son would also protest. Indeed, Subject 7 did just what was expected of him. When he was older, having convinced himself that protest was valuable, he took up his father's unspoken assignment and began to protest/ resist. His siblings, meanwhile, had not been burdened with this work. Not a single one of them had become a political protestor.

Similarly, Subject 4, from Tibet, was also expected to continue the family tradition of protest. His father had died in prison, he told me, and

Table 2.1 Heroic asylum seekers: Personal data

Order	Country of origin	Gender/age Religion	Education Birth	Family background	Personal/work history	Prison/abuse history	Funders of escape
1.	Yugoslavia	M+. Age: 30 Muslim	Secondary School. 3rd of 3	Educated parents, brothers. Parents political outcasts. Parents suffered extreme hardship. No funds for his higher education.	Volunteered for parent's political party. Loved the work. Married a Catholic. Unable to get paid work.	Beaten in street, 3 times; last time with wife. Her religion plus his political activities were his so-called crimes.	Parents
2.	Togo	M. Age: 24 Christian	Only child French education. 1 year of secondary school.	Educated parents. Resisters. Father arrested. Released after 4 years. "All his strength was gone." Mother unable to work, sold vegetables in street.	At 14 began political resistance after arrest of father. Helped mother.	Imprisoned, brutalized once. Released. Fled when police came for him a second time.	Parents
3.	Guinea	M. Age: 34 Muslim	Eldest son. 4 half brothers. Educated.	Father educated, well-off. Grt grandfather, grandfather & father resisted. Father imprisoned, tortured. When released had PTSD, plus physical injuries, observed by all.	Married, 4 children. Erratic work history due to imprisonments. Engineer.	Imprisoned 5 times in 15 years. Badly tortured.	Family
4.	Tibet	M. Age: 44 Buddhist	Eldest of 4	Illiterate peasants. Political resisters. 3 generations. Uncle ill; sent home from prison to die, witnessed by all. Father died in prison.	Married, 7 children. Farmed while raising children.	Imprisoned from age 10–18. Again at 42 for 8 months. Tortured badly.	Family/ community
5.	Tibet	M. Age: 37 Buddhist	Eldest of 5	Monastery educated. Family: guerilla fighters. Witnessed uncle & father stripped of wealth; become desperately poor. Little food. Watched depleted father die.	Became a monk during adolescence.	Fled Chinese army as it attacked monastery and took fellow monks away.	Friend of deceased father
6.	Guinea	M. Age: 39 Muslim	Eldest of 5	Six years of French primary school. Qur'anic studies also. Saw father a resister, after prison, hurt, humiliated. Father encouraged son's political activities.	Farmer. Entered politics/ resistance at 28.	Imprisoned 4 times.	Family

(continued)

Table 2.1 (continued)

Country of origin / Order	Gender/age / Religion	Education / Birth	Family background	Personal/work history	Prison/ abuse history	Funders of escape
7. Cameroon	M. Age: 24 Muslim	Eldest of 4	Prosperous, educated family. Had B.A. Family also resisters for generations. At 13 saw tortured uncle after release.	Student. Politics/resistance Imprisoned 3 times.	Tortured. Lost his mind for a period.	Mother
8. Cameroon	F. Age: 25 Muslim	4th of 6	Poor, illiterate family of peasants. Good in school. Adopted by uncle Raised with his children. College educated. Uncle politically involved, a resister, encouraged her political interest/activity. Uncle arrested. Then disappeared. Traumatic for her	Became secretary of local student political group.	Tortured. Raped.	Parents
9. Myanmar	F. Age: 25 Buddhist	2nd of 2	Educated family. Many family members participated in pro-democracy movement, most notably her older sister (4 years older) who was imprisoned and tortured and then sent home, with bruises and PTSD. Witnessed by all	Student. Became politically active after sister left for United States.	Imprisoned once. Tortured.	Family
10. Belarus	F. Age: 24 Christian	Eldest of 2	Parents uneducated. Excellent student. Completed 2 years of university. Parents divorced. Mother politically active. Encouraged daughter. Mother imprisoned, probably raped, tortured. Effects seen by children.	Student. Became politically active following mother.	3 imprisonments. Torture, rape.	Mother
11. Ghana	F. Age: 31 Christian	Youngest	Poor family, unable to afford school for their very bright girl, who got funded anyway for high school. Was raped at 12 by family driver. Child born of rape died due to primitive mistreatment. Promised herself to have her children in the West. Older sister in United States helped.	Married, 3 children, born in United States. Entered politics in high school.	Paid to proselytize there.	Family/church

+ Female and male are abbreviated with the letters F and M.

his uncle, released, after years of imprisonment, an ill and severely weakened man, had died soon thereafter, in front of his extended family. When Hero 4 returned, at the age of eighteen, from the eight years of imprisonment which he himself had endured, he was informed by family members and members of the wider community that he was the one with the intelligence and strength to continue the fight and he should do so. Having suffered a great deal already, however, he chose instead to marry and have children of his own.

Nevertheless, many years later, at the age of forty-four, after having fathered seven children of his own, his anger against the oppressive Chinese regime returned. This occurred, he said, because the Chinese government had not let him mourn the death of his father following strict Buddhist tradition. Because of this, he believed, his father's ghost was condemned to wander the world forever without rest. His faith in Buddhism and the Dalai Lama, the very mention of whom is forbidden in Tibet,[5] had also increased, he said, through his attachment to certain nuns whom he had come to know. Thus, once again, with community support, he took up the protestor role, continuing in the footsteps of his father, uncle, and grandfather.

Subject 1, in contrast, European (from former Yugoslavia), was not the first, but the third of three sons. However, he was also the only member of his family who had been unable to obtain the university education customary in his family, because his parents, political outcasts at that point, did not have the money to pay for it. They themselves were barely surviving, he said. Unable to get steady work, he chose instead to volunteer for his father's political party, delivering aid to people who needed it. He loved the work and managed to get by, along with his parents, until the work he was doing, as well as his choice of a Catholic partner (he was Muslim), made him a specific target of the opposition. After a few instances in which he was beaten in the street and she was beaten as well, he fled, with his Catholic wife, to begin a family safely, in the United States.

The women in my group have less in common than do the men, especially in regard to birth order. Only one, Subject 10, from Belarus, is first born. In contrast, Subject 8 is the fourth of six children, born to illiterate (but very caring)[6] peasants. However, because she was obviously intelligent and "loved school," she told me, her educated uncle adopted her and took her into his urban family to be educated with his (four) children. In this environment, she performed outstandingly. Thus she was the one he chose to follow him into political protest. His brutal arrest by the police at his home, which she witnessed, and then his disappearance, were traumatic for her. This trauma only seemed to add fuel to her desire to continue his fight. None of his own children followed him into political protest as she did.

Subject 11 is perhaps the most exceptional person, male or female, in my entire group. The youngest member of her family, she was raped at the age of twelve by her family's driver and threatened with death if she told anyone about it. As a result a child was born, in secret, away from the gaze of neighbors. Her family then gave this child, a son, to uneducated relatives in the far away countryside to raise as their own. However, because of the primitive rites they practiced on him (they poured hot water on his head in order to shape it into a desirable form, she said), he died. As a result, his mother, only thirteen at the time, promised herself that she would never give birth again to a child at home. In the future, her children would be born in the United States. This, she thought, would be possible because an older, well-loved sister was living in the United States at the time and would take her in.

Subject 11 then went on to private secondary school in Ghana, which she paid for herself. Her parents, shamed by the birth of her son, had claimed they were unable to do so, although they had paid for her older sisters, she said. So she daringly asked other relatives to help her. She also went to work for a political party to proselytize and gain other party members at her school, which, she told me, is common in her country. After secondary school, she completed university and married the clergyman who had sponsored her political work. He came regularly to the United States for training and conferences. Then, just as she had promised herself, when she was about to bear each of her three children, she came to the United States herself. The most extraordinary aspect of her extraordinary story, however, is that, after each birth, she returned to Africa (where her minister husband worked, but was not much politically involved) to continue to protest, as she had been doing since adolescence. There she endured four imprisonments, including two rapes,[7] before she finally sought asylum in the United States. Her children, meanwhile, were already American citizens! Unlike my other subjects, her plan to start her family outside of Ghana was created alone, at an early age, and miraculously, with the help of an esteemed sister and the support of her husband, she succeeded in carrying it out! At this point, all of her children, along with her husband, reside here. I learn from the internet that, after she was granted asylum, she completed training in nursing, which she had told me she wanted to do, and opened her own nursing practice in women's health. The marriage to her husband continues.

How the protestor/resister role unfolds

Having briefly described the manner in which my group of hero subjects were chosen as protestors and took up the role, I want now to describe two cases (Subjects 3 and 10) to illustrate the course of events to which the choice can lead, including the final decision to flee and seek asylum elsewhere.

Mr. I (Muslim, from an African country, Subject 3): Mr. I, aged thirty-nine when I met him, was married and the father of three children. A tall, handsome man who seemed to radiate energy, he was the eldest of five and came from a family of farmers who, for three generations, had opposed their repressive government. His grandfather, the hero of the family, had spent five years in prison, where he had apparently been tortured repeatedly. When finally released, the grandfather returned home, a listless and crippled man, only to die. Mr. I, aged ten at the time, witnessed his grandfather's deteriorated physical state and then his death. No one, however, told Mr. I anything about the nature of the punishment his grandfather had endured while in prison. After the death, however, the family fled to a neighboring country to avoid further punishment. There they remained until Mr. I (a very bright child) reached high school age. At that point, they returned home, for the sake of the free, superior education, unavailable outside their own country.

Mr. I received a French primary and high school education and attended university. Eventually, in spite of political harassment, he trained as an engineer in both Africa and the West (Canada). Early in his student years, unlike his siblings, he became politically active. "I do it for the future," he told me, "as my grandfather did before me." Active for twenty years, he sustained four imprisonments. The first, after he had married and had children, lasted five months. He and his father, arrested together, were thrown, half-naked, into a crowded cell, where they were regularly kicked and beaten. There was little food and no bathroom facility beyond an overflowing bucket in the corner. Most painful of all, Mr. I experienced profound humiliation because he was unable to shield his father from harm or from witnessing the harm he himself endured. Bribery (collected from relatives) finally brought about their release. A month of recovery went by, after which Mr. I returned again to political opposition.

Mr. I's second imprisonment, a few months later, this time without his father, included similarly brutal treatment and lasted three months. Again, after his release, he quickly returned to political activity.

His third arrest took place in front of his family, which was a very humiliating ordeal for him. Again, he was taken to prison, where again, he was regularly beaten, this time while hung upside down. He remained in that prison for five months. Again, upon release, he returned to political work.

During his fourth and final imprisonment, Mr. I was kept for weeks in solitary confinement until, finally, his mother-in-law put up the funds to buy his release. In the process, he was forced to appear before her almost naked, which was another deeply humiliating experience for him. Upon his release, he was told that if he did not leave the country, he would be killed. This threat led him, finally, to flee and to seek asylum in the United States. He paid for the trip with funds his family raised. When I interviewed him, a few months after his arrival, he was hugely worried about the fate of his family, whom he hoped to bring here as soon as possible.

Ms. B (Christian, from Eastern Europe, Subject 10): Ms. B, tall, blue-eyed, very pretty, was twenty-four when I interviewed her. The eldest of two children (a brother is two years younger), her parents divorced when she was seven. A very good student, Ms. B graduated first in her high school class and completed two years of university before coming to the United States. She speaks and reads three languages, including English. Growing up, her family was deprived of all but the most basic subsistence because of her mother's political activities. Unlike her brother, Ms. B herself became involved in politics in high school, following her mother's example.

At the age of nineteen, during her first university year, she and her mother were attending a rally when the police attacked. Ms. B was beaten so severely that she lost consciousness. When she came to, she was lying in the street, alone, covered in blood. Upon returning home, her uncle told her that her mother had been taken by the militia to an unknown place. "People just disappear in my country," she said. Her mother, however, did return some days later, badly bruised and very depressed. Her mother never described the torture she had endured, "Because she did not want to worry me," Ms. B told me. Ms. B suspected rape.

Ms. B continued to participate in anti-government events. At the next big rally, she was beaten again. This time she was taken to prison, where she was thrown into a damp, cold cell. No food was provided and no toilet, other than a hole in the floor. Interrogated and beaten, she was released the next day, bruised and in pain. Nevertheless, she continued to believe that things could change. "I was so sure! You believe you can change the world," she added. Her mother encouraged this. Again, she participated in a demonstration and again she was taken to prison. This time prisoners were interrogated one by one. Once in the interrogation room with three policemen, she continued to deny knowledge of anything political. Enormously angered, the men began to torture her, first with electric shocks, then with punches. Finally they tore off her clothes, held her down and took turns raping her. She had been a virgin. She lost consciousness.

She came to, much later, alone, in a dark, cold cell. She wept copiously. On the following day, when she was released, they told her that if she were detained again, she would be imprisoned permanently. Nevertheless, despite the torture she had sustained, she continued to protest.

Ms. B's third and final arrest took place at yet another political demonstration. Again, the militia arrived and began to beat the demonstrators, several of whom they took to prison. This time in prison, there was an investigator who was "crazy-looking," she said. He cut her palm with a knife, telling her that the scar would be a "souvenir" of what had happened to her. She was released the next day, but given a summons to appear later for more interrogation. In order to escape, she left town. In her absence, officers arrived at her home to take her to prison, threatening to keep her there for eleven years. This was the turning point for her. Knowing she would not survive eleven such years, she began to take steps to come to the United States, which she finally achieved with the help of her family. Since she arrived, her mother has been pressuring her, on the telephone, to get married and have children.

Discussion

At the beginning of this chapter, I described my heroes as people whose lives included certain equivalent experiences. With one exception (Subject 11) each, I said, had: (1) witnessed the trauma of an older relative who had been tortured by oppressors; (2) never been given the opportunity to discuss the effect on them of what they had witnessed;

(3) later been chosen by his or her family of origin to protest those oppressors; and then (4) been able to sustain repeated instances of punishment at the hands of those same oppressors until, finally, death was threatened. Then, and only then, had each been able to change course entirely and take flight. This was accomplished with help from their families. In taking flight their mission had changed, from one in which they had been asked to protest, to one in which they were asked to survive, for the sake of both themselves and their families. The latter mission was a relatively hopeful one because, presumably, they had left behind the insurmountable reality they had faced at home. They were to begin elsewhere, in the United States, where they believed political freedom would be guaranteed.

In contrast to my heroes, research seems to indicate that other protestor/resisters,[8] for example those who chose the role in Europe during and following World War II, (Marton, 1974; Bar-Zohar, 2001; Oliner & Oliner, 1988; Klempner, 2006) and those who resisted in the famous Milgram laboratory experiments (Blass, 2000) were motivated differently from the people I have described above. A rebellious streak, rather than a family tradition, was common among them, plus values, sometimes bred at home or through religious belief, which allowed them to perceive individuals as unique, rather than as representatives of an objectified, hated *other* group. According to Oliner and Oliner (1988), World War II protestors seemed to possess sufficiently nurturing, internalized, early relationships to allow them to sustain a robust sense of their own values, which at the time were in opposition to popular thought.

Resisters in the era of World War II tended to begin resisting as soon as widespread oppression became obvious to them, as my heroes also did. However, in contrast to my heroes, they generally continued until captured or killed or, in more fortunate cases, until they were captured and released. They may also have felt the urge to resist because of the heightened sense of aliveness it afforded them. Such feelings are common among some individuals during wartime (Hedges, 2003).[9] The thrill of the fight often makes it difficult to abandon it, once it has passed on or they themselves have moved away from it. Indeed, for a host of reasons, resisters during World War II seemed to continue their fight until the very end, without much thought about either their own preservation or the future of their families.

In a different vein, individuals in a resister group, this time from Eastern Europe, have been described by Vamik Volkan (1998; 2006), as motivated by their own humiliation-based personal trauma, the result, he believes, of abuse at the hands of parents who possessed similarly "traumatized self-realizations" (1998, p. 4). The internal sense of self these resisters possessed had become fused (he believes) with centuries-old blood feuds between ethnic winners and losers. In this milieu, becoming a resistance leader had dual implications: it was a path by which to gain personal recognition on the one hand, and, on the other, to avenge personal and political wrongs.[10] In this way, what Volkan (1998) calls the "ethnic tent" (belief systems, animosities, humiliations, feelings of helplessness etc.) shared among people in this group became an acceptable part of identity and a rationale for aggression, a state of being which also may have been sustained by the thrill of the fight. Indeed, the rebels Volkan describes seem to have been rebels for life, until they either won their war or died in the process. Changing course, moving to a more nurturing landscape, one designed for family preservation, did not at all seem to be a part of their plan.

My heroic asylees do share a number of characteristics with each of the other two resister groups described above. Each of my heroes, for example, enjoyed being a rebel, at least at first; each also came from a family that had experienced humiliation and helpless rage at the hands of oppressors, while all the time sustaining its commitment to human rights. Each also wanted to be recognized by his or her family as a protestor. But, unlike those in the other groups described above, my heroes were quite ready to abandon the exciting aspects of their endeavor at the moment they became convinced that death would follow if they did not. Faced incontestably with their own death, they were able to switch gears and move on, into an unknown territory in which they hoped to survive.

Becoming a heroic protestor: Psychodynamic perspectives

Given the series of life events that my heroes shared, how, from a psychodynamic point of view, might their decision to take on the dangerous role of protestor/resister be explained? And how, then, did their willingness to abandon it, once death seemed imminent, evolve?

It would be difficult, I think, to arrive at one single factor that affected all of my heroes equally as a determinant of either of these two decisions. Rather, a number of factors seemed to have interacted, differently, within each person. For the sake of discussion, I will consider the choice of the role as an outcome of the combined effects of having, in childhood or youth, observed but not discussed the pain of an esteemed older protestor, on the one hand, and having been chosen for the task by their families, on the other. A third factor, the use of denial, seems to have allowed them to continue in the protestor role for a short time, despite its obvious dangers. Denial will be discussed as well.

To repeat, six of my heroes (all men) were first-born children who came from cultures in which first-born males were expected to carry on family traditions. Similarly, the only first-born woman, a European, was encouraged by her mother (her protestor/resister model) to join her in embodying the role. Despite being openly chosen by their elders for this role, however, each of these first-born heroes (and the five others on my list as well) had to make the decision to take it up him or herself. Moreover, as time went on and he or she experienced the pain brought on by protest, this decision had to become an extremely strong resolve. Without such resolve, each would have abandoned the task at the first threat from the opposition. My supposition, therefore, is that, in addition to having been chosen for the role by their elders, my heroes were themselves driven to take it on by the need to get closer to the unspoken, unprocessed, "unformulated" (Stern, 2003) pain of tortured elders (fathers, uncles, grandfathers, sisters) which they had observed as children or adolescents and which they were driven to understand. In this manner, the pain and possibly the guilt of members of non-protestor members of the older generation, was seemingly passed on to my youthful heroes without words.

In regard to the wordless transmission of trauma across generations, it is European Holocaust survivors and their children who have been most thoroughly studied, using psychoanalytic theory as a guide. In such families, it is believed that the psychic trauma experienced by the parents before their children were born tended to "annihilate the[ir] perceiving, experiencing sel[ves]" (Laub and Lee, 2003, p. 436). Thus, although it was "lived through," it was not "experienced as part of the self," according to these authors (Cohen, 1985, quoted by Laub & Lee, 2003, p. 438). In such cases, the capacity to reflect (an important aspect of self-experience) was absent, which implies that meaning-making either did not take place or, more likely, was "dissociated" (Bromberg, 1994, 2001, 2003; Stern, 2003; van der Kolk, McFarlane, & Weisaeth, 2006). As a result, the orderly, sequential structuring necessary for easy recall (Cohen, 1985; Yovell, 2000) did not exist, which left them without an easy way in which to discuss their experiences with their children.

In addition, as an outcome of their Holocaust experiences, these parents, according to Gubrich-Simitis (1981), often became engulfed in "ubiquitous depressive moods," which existed along with "grave guilt feelings, paranoid anxieties, and psychosomatic complaints" (p. 425). Although no single syndrome seems to be characteristic of all children of Holocaust survivors (Kestenberg, 1980; Jucovy, 1992) often their parents insisted on "a special conformity of behavior in the children." They depended on this because they believed that it would guarantee the family's survival. In such cases, according to Gubrich-Simitis (1981, p. 428), "[the] children had no opportunity to develop an individual identity" of their own.

In thinking about my heroes with this work in mind, it seemed probable that the well-being of the fathers of the first-born African men depended, to some degree, on having a son who would carry on the protestor tradition. No doubt, if the son had refused this role, his father, indeed, perhaps the whole family, might have been deeply humiliated.[11] Survivor guilt, another factor mentioned in regard to Holocaust survivors (see above), might also have been present in some of the fathers of my heroes. Subject 7, for example, told me that his father was very upset by the state in which they had found his uncle when they visited the uncle in the hospital. Moreover, after this visit, his own family (mother, father, other uncles/aunts) discussed ways in which they might help the uncle's wife and children. In a similar vein, Subject 3 told me that his father was deeply disturbed by how little they could do to improve his grandfather's health and state of mind after the latter was released from prison and sent home to die. To contend with the feelings this aroused, his father, he said, needed to continue the fight and needed him to be involved also. Altogether, it seems, the dedication of his eldest son to the cause of protest/resistance seems to have been motivated in part by the need to assuage the father's feelings of helplessness, guilt and humiliation.

In contrast to the Africans, Subjects 4 and 5, both Tibetan first-born sons, had fathers who had died by the time their own protesting began.[12] As the eldest son, however, Subject 4 was responsible for his father's ghost in the afterlife. Without the appropriate burial rites, this ghost would be unable to rest, he told me. Had he continued to live without protesting the Chinese regulations, he added, he would have accepted his father's unrest and, with it, the disapproval of his entire community. This would have led to a state of humiliation for himself and for his family, which, finally, he could not bear. Thus, in this case, it is clear that the expectations of his dead father shaped his behavior just as much as the expectations of the living fathers of the African men had shaped theirs.

Returning again briefly to the children of Holocaust survivors, both Bergmann (1982) and Kogan (2002) describe situations in which these children, as adults, seemed to be trying to concretize or enact aspects of their parents' past lives without any awareness of what they were doing. According to Kogan, behavior of this kind was most likely to occur when there had been no discussion by the parents of their experiences at the hands of the Nazis. It became especially prevalent in situations (such as the Gulf War) in which danger was potentially threatening. At such times, she tells us, survivors' children tended to "endanger themselves in reality by always being ready to rescue . . . others" (1993, p. 804).

It seems highly likely that unconscious motivation of this kind was present in the psyches of some, if not all, of my heroes, who did indeed seem to be trying to re-live trauma-related aspects of the lives of older relatives. This was the case not only for the men (each of whom had been encouraged along this path), but also for three of the four women. Among these, Subject 10 seemed to be reliving events she imagined her mother had lived through, of prison and probably rape. Subject 8 seemed to be trying to join her uncle along the path that she fantasized he had taken, to prison and torture, before his disappearance. Subject 9 seemed to be reliving the ordeal experienced by her older sister, the effects of which she herself had observed a few years earlier. Indeed, all of my heroes, except perhaps Subject 11, seemed to be reenacting events that they believed an esteemed older relative had experienced. Perhaps they were driven by the need to better understand both the experience of that relative and their own affect (what has been called "secondary traumatization" by Agger & Jensen, 1994), to which they in all likelihood surrendered unwittingly when, as younger people, they stood by helplessly observing their relatives' pain. (Krystal, 1988; Boulanger, 2007).

Moving on now to denial, Ilene Kogan (2002), in her work on children of Holocaust survivors, tells us that, in their actions, they tended to deny potential danger as they unconsciously attempted to enact aspects of their parents' past lives. Those I have designated as heroes also seemed to deny the danger they faced, sometimes for months, sometimes for years, as they struggled to protest their respective governments. Subject 9, for example, who did not begin protesting until after her older sister had left for America, had observed this sister, wounded and depressed, after her release from prison. When Subject 9 took up the protestor role herself, however, she told me that she "didn't realize how dangerous it was!" Thus, when it was her turn to be imprisoned, the torture she endured there was unexpected and altogether shocking to her.

In a slightly different vein, Subject 10 told me that she believed her protest would end in success. To repeat, she told me that she was "so sure! You believe you can change the world!" She was able to sustain this belief only by denying the implications of the fact that everyone else who had protested before her had entirely failed to change their political world. Indeed, denial of a number of the more painful aspects of the political struggle they undertook was common to all of my heroes.

Abandoning the heroic protestor role

Given the brevity of the interviews I conducted with each of my heroes, my hypotheses concerning the reasons they chose to abandon the protestor/resister role and leave home are just that, hypotheses. However, a number of factors must have interacted to determine their decision, six of which seem most likely to me. They are listed below:

1 **An experience of success at having taken up the protestor/resister role:** It seems reasonable to assume that because they were able to take up this role and endure the suffering it entailed, they experienced some sense of success. They had done the job their father, uncle, mother, or sister had required of them. Accordingly, any humiliation the family might have experienced had they refused the role was avoided. In addition, their success must have left them feeling much less encumbered by obligation in this regard than earlier they might have.
2 **A (probably unconscious) experience of success in joining the pained, beleaguered older relative, whose pain they had observed earlier in their lives and never discussed:** Without words, my heroes must have come to understand something of what those loved and respected ones had endured.
3 **A (probably unconscious) experience of success in reconnecting with the earlier feelings[13] they had experienced as they observed the pain of elders:** I am assuming that they had surrendered to these feelings earlier in their lives without reflection, as often happens in such family situations according to Krystal (1988).
4 **The weakening of the ability to deny:** Having accomplished 1 and 2 above, my heroes' ability to deny pain, fear, and powerlessness seems to have weakened considerably. Subject 7, for example, openly acknowledged that during his final imprisonment, he had been in such pain and so terrified that he had lost his "sense of reality," whereas earlier he had had no such problem. Having lost this sense, he did not know what he had said to his torturers, nor

did he much care. All he thought about was the possibility of release, which had not been true for him during earlier imprisonments.

In a somewhat different vein, Subject 9, imprisoned only once before she decided to leave home and follow her sister to America, said that, although originally she denied the danger of protest, the treatment she received in prison made it all too real to her and she did not want any more of it. Others, especially the African men who were imprisoned three and four times, seemed to express feelings of relief when, finally, they were threatened with death. Only then could they acknowledge the pain and difficulty of their lives as victims of the opposition and begin the journey away from home.

5   **The availability of alternative ways of perceiving themselves beyond the role of protestor:** All but two of my heroes were highly educated, at least in respect to the communities they came from. Thus they could experience themselves in important work roles completely unrelated to protest. Of the two without formal education, Subject 1, from former Yugoslavia, came from a highly educated family. Only circumstances had prevented his education, which, he told me, he hoped to get in America. Clearly he wanted more from life than just to be a protestor. And Subject 4, from Tibet, despite his lack of education, had had important leadership responsibilities in his community. The sense of self of all of my heroes, in other words, was not entirely bound up with protesting, seemingly in contrast to, for example, the protestors Volkan (1998, 2006) describes.

6   **The increased availability of escape routes:** Escape routes out of beleaguered countries have become more available recently than ever before because of easier access to more frequently scheduled air travel. At this time in history, for example, men from all over Africa commute to the United States, and presumably also to Europe, simply to work for short periods of time, on constructions crews or to sell goods in the street, etc. Once they have made sufficient money, they return home. As for Tibet, although there is great risk in getting out of the country,[14] there are recently established places to go (Dharamsala for example) where help is available, once escape has taken place. Thus, once sufficient funds have been raised to pay for flights, it is much less difficult to leave other parts of the world than was the case two or more generations ago.

These then, in combination, are some of the reasons my heroes, unlike other protestors at other times, were able to move their lives to the United States. Once they had arrived here, however, they were forced to contend with the dream of a new beginning. How did that unfold?

Pursuing the dream of family in America: Mr. I and Ms. B

The immigrant experience is notoriously difficult for all who leave home.[15] Not only must an immigrant begin life all over again in a land with a different language and culture, but the context in which his or her familiar self existed is no longer present. This familiar sense of self, therefore, often becomes minimized, even when it had previously been very well established, because there is no one to reflect it back.

Regardless of how chosen they may have felt at home, good adjustment in their new country for all immigrants, including heroic asylum seekers, will depend on a number of factors, including their early cultural and relationship history (the security of their early attachments), their earlier trauma history, and their ability to find various support networks to meet their needs. These needs include the need for work, for housing, for health care, and for companionship (Meaders, 1997; Mongomery & Patel, 2011).

In contrast to ordinary immigrants, the negative aspects of the immigration experience are often exaggerated for asylum seekers because, in addition to the exigencies all immigrants face, asylum seekers arrive here with no money and with no one ready to take them in. At the same time, they are often contending with the aftermath of torture.

At present, there is no definitive method for treating the symptoms of torture. According to recent reviews (Williams & Merwe, 2013; Peckel, 2017) the symptoms of torture vary widely, as do their implications for the individuals who experience them. They are, therefore, difficult to categorize. In addition, torture is often overlooked as the cause of a client's symptoms (which may well be presented as pain) because survivors often do not disclose their experiences. When torture has been identified, however, the number of studies comparing different treatment approaches is small and their outcomes not reliable (Jaranson & Quiroga, 2011; Montgomery & Patel, 2011). Jaranson and Quiroga tell us that the benefits of services for torture survivors have simply been assumed, based on the reports of both the survivors themselves and of their helpers. Reliability for this group is difficult to establish, in part because the creation of randomized control groups is deemed unethical. In addition, among the two hundred plus programs that exist worldwide, most are run by human rights organizations, which offer a wide array of services and a multi-modal approach to meet the vast array of client needs. Psychological interventions make up only a portion of these and are difficult to isolate for study. Trauma focused eye movement desensitization and reprocessing (EMDR) and cognitive behavioral therapy (CBT), however, seem to be useful, as is narrative therapy (Robjant & Fazel, 2010). In regard to referral for these services, there is no guarantee that this will occur since attorneys who work with asylum seekers are not required to make them.

I have been able to do ongoing therapy with only two asylum seekers myself. In addition, I was able to interview two of my heroes at length,[16] a few years after they had received asylum. I was also able to question the attorney of a third. My attempts to inquire about the lives of four others, through their attorneys, failed because the attorneys had moved on. Two others, however, did respond to my inquiries, once I found them. Both tried to contact their asylee-client. Neither of their clients was interested in speaking to me, however. Therefore, for the sake of discussion here, I have combined information gathered from all of these sources with the goal of comparing and contrasting two very different patterns of acclimation and adjustment among heroic asylum seekers. These are outlined below. In each case the mandate to plant the family elsewhere was evident in the telephone contact these individuals had had with family members at home, which were reported to me. These have multiplied since access to the cell phone has become routine.[17] In keeping with the previous cases, I have called the subjects in the following accounts Mr. I and Ms. B.

Mr. I – Follow-up: Mr. I, an educated, experienced, middle-aged man, had been exposed to the West briefly as a young man, when he was sent to Canada, briefly, to study engineering. As described above, he had well-developed abilities and an established family of his own by the time he came to the United States. The only experience of personal trauma he had as a child (as far as I know) occurred when, at age ten, without preparation, he observed the effects of torture on his grandfather.

Once he was granted asylum, Mr. I, a proud, very driven man, worked assiduously to master English. He also became an electrician. Although this was an occupation lower in status than the one he had had at home, he was able to accept it without feelings of humiliation because he found, in New York, a small community of fellow countrymen who encouraged and supported his choice. As has been the case with many male immigrants from Africa, he has done well at work, perhaps in part as an outcome of this community support.[18] In time, he may try to get the credentials he needs in order to work in America at a level more similar to the one he occupied at home.

For some months following his arrival, Mr. I attended the Program for Survivors of Torture at Bellevue Hospital, where he received individual and group therapy, in French, to help him contend with the symptoms (nightmares and flashbacks especially) of PTSD, which persisted. Although he resisted participating at Bellevue at the beginning (he comes from a culture in which, as he puts it, most people do not "take" psychotherapy), he was persuaded to try it by other men from his background who had found it useful. His participation at Bellevue was surprisingly successful and was concluded in under a year. Although he still has some symptoms of PTSD (which is now understood as a chronic ailment, according to Montgomery & Patel, 2011), these occur much less frequently than they did earlier. Generally, they tend to occur only when he is reminded of his imprisonment. In order to protect himself, he tries to avoid these reminders.

Since 2006 (when he was granted asylum), Mr. I has managed to bring his wife and his two oldest children to America. His youngest child will follow when he is a bit older, he hopes. Gradually they are adjusting to life here. He hopes the lives of his children will be less threatened than was his own, when he was their age.

Mr. I does not know how or what he will tell his children about his experiences in prison. Consequently, it is difficult to predict whether or not, in the future, his children will be affected by his trauma. It is certainly possible that portions of his experience will remain unprocessed and that its effects might be passed along, in, for example, unexplained inattention to their endangerment (see Stern 2010 for more about this), or by placing excessive demands on them, or in being grossly insensitive to their specific needs. As was described above, trauma experienced by a parent can have devastating effects on the next generation, if not sufficiently integrated into the present day life of the survivor (Gubrich-Simitis, 1981; Danieli, 1998; Laub & Lee, 2003; Davoine & Gaudilliere, 2004; Kaplan, 2006).

In considering his adjustment, it seems clear that, when he arrived, Mr. I's psychological make-up included a robust sense of himself, which, although affected by severe adult onset trauma (Boulanger, 2007), was not destroyed. As an outcome, even without on-the-spot family support, he has been able to sustain the motivation to do the task his family hoped he would do in the United States. He was the first to arrive here safely, to be followed by his wife and children. At present, because he has his family close by, and is sufficiently well employed and can care for them and, in addition, has the support of a like-minded community, Mr. I is doing well in his new country.

Ms. B – Follow-up: Ms. B's story is very different. Very attractive and already fluent in English when she arrived, Ms. B came to America on a student visa, in order to finish her education. In Russia, where she embarked for America, she purchased a student visa (with money provided by her family) to accomplish this goal. When she arrived here, however, she discovered that the school she was slated to attend did not exist! The visa apparently had been the invention of swindlers. Thus, she literally had no place to go.

Unlike Mr. I (who was middle-aged and had left a full life behind), when Ms. B arrived in the United States, she was barely 23. Although very pretty, with a superb academic record behind her, she had hardly established herself as an accomplished adult. Moreover, as a child, her family relationships had been problematic. In fact, after a relatively benign early childhood, her parents had separated. At that point (she was six or seven at the time), her mother had rejected her because of the striking physical resemblance she bore to her hated father, whose favorite she had been. In leaving his wife, this father had also abandoned his children. Thus, in early latency, Ms. B was rejected by both parents, a traumatic experience for her. Having only her mother to turn to, Ms. B had worked hard to distance herself from her father in her mother's mind, and did finally succeed in regaining her mother's respect. Her mother's acceptance, however, has always seemed tentative to her. Indeed, it was always her less intelligent brother whom her mother seemed to adore.

Ms. B's second traumatic experience occurred at age eight, when she was operated on for a hernia. During the operation, the anesthesia wore off. She felt such pain that she was sure she would die. Worst of all, her mother was absent and thus there was no one to comfort her.

Years later, in prison, Ms. B was raped. She suffered excruciatingly as a result, in part because she had been a virgin, in part because she could not make sense of the motives of the "terrible" men who violated her. To add to her despair, during her time in prison, her faith in God seemed to have abandoned her.[19]

Once in America, Ms. B suffered from severe depression and PTSD. She was especially plagued by a sense of a foreshortened future (one of the symptoms of PTSD), which can be particularly devastating for young people. In her own mind, she referred to her former self as "that poor girl." In the present, she told me, she felt "like a forty-year-old person whose life is over."

Although it is unclear how trauma experienced in childhood combines with adult onset trauma (Krystal, 1988), evidence seems to indicate that three separate experiences of trauma make recovery unusually difficult (Alexander, 2011). Ms. B had already had two by the time she became an adolescent, before she had to contend with the rape in prison. With three severely traumatic experiences in her past, Ms. B's trust in the world was severely damaged. People simply terrified her. Thus, she withdrew. She seemed to prefer to stay home unless she had to work or felt safe with the prospect of an upcoming social interaction.

Immediately after gaining asylum, Ms. B found work waiting on tables. She has consistently allowed her bosses to take advantage of her, however. Although she had the opportunity to go to school tuition free, through a scholarship she inadvertently discovered, she turned this down, afraid that she would do poorly. She was also worried that she would not have the time to support herself. She also turned down psychotherapy offered both privately and also at Bellevue's Program for Survivors of Torture. Many people had suggested this to her.

Unlike Mr. I, Ms. B is among a very small group of immigrants from her country.[20] Thus finding compatriots here has been difficult for her, a situation that has been compounded by the fact that she also has not looked very hard to find them. As a substitute, because she speaks Russian, she has tried to befriend Russian immigrants, but these are mostly students who remain in America only for short periods of time. Thus, when I last spoke to her (four years after the date upon which she was granted asylum), Ms. B had made only one lasting friend, a Russian immigrant who is also Catholic. The two women had shared a room, but saw very little of each other because of their respective work schedules.

Ms. B speaks to her mother quite frequently on the telephone. For more than a year after she gained asylum, her mother plagued her, during these calls, to find a man, get married, and have a child. However, for Ms. B, trusting men is difficult and having sex with them is beyond the pale. For the time being, therefore, having children is out of the question.

Briefly, probably in part because of the pressure from her mother, Ms. B had a few encounters with a man from her part of the world. He appealed to her. In the course of their few interactions, this man confided in Ms. B his wish to build his own business, for which he was saving his money. Convincing herself that he meant to marry her, Ms. B promised to help him. Encouraged by him, she began to send him money. When his visits stopped and his telephone attention decreased, as it did when he found her unwilling to have sex with him, Ms. B continued to send him money anyway, calling him occasionally to see how he was doing. Many months passed in this fashion, until one day, after she had sent him most of her savings, her telephone call was answered by a woman. When confronted, he confessed to having found someone else and promised to return her money. Needless to say, this has not happened. Nor has he been in contact with her since. Meanwhile, Ms. B has become more and more fearful of going anywhere alone other than work.

In summary, then, it is clear, from a comparison of the lives of Mr. I and Ms. B in the United States, that settling well in a new country is difficult indeed, regardless of the family mandate one has come with. Ms. B, in contrast to Mr. I, was unable to move beyond her anxiety sufficiently to embrace the opportunities open to her for help and for community. Hers so far has been a sad end to a story that earlier seemed full of possibility.

Conclusion

In this chapter I have described a group I have called heroic asylum seekers because, first, they chose to protest political repression at home, when they very well might not have done so, and then because they chose to abandon protesting, once they were threatened with imminent death. Rather than martyrdom, my heroes, with the blessings and help of their families, chose to seek asylum in the United States and thus to relocate their family here.

Six interacting factors, shared by them all, (and described in detail above) seemed to determine these choices. Instead of reiterating these factors here, I want to underscore the fact that the individuals I have called heroes came from seven different countries and three different hemispheres – Europe, Asia, and Africa – from backgrounds that were rarely the same. Nevertheless, the unfolding of their lives as protestors/resisters seemed to have been determined by surprisingly similar experiences, beginning early in their lives. Indeed, this demonstrates once again that, as Harry Stack Sullivan once said, "we are all much more human than otherwise" (2013, p. 18), alike in so many ways.

In spite of the promise my talented heroes seemed to show, in spite of the risks they took, and the luck that was on their side, it is clear that, once in America, their good adjustment was based on a host of still other interacting factors. These included the degree to which their sense of themselves, by virtue of early attachments and lifelong experience, was robust (Meaders, 1997) and their confidence as doers in the world had been well established. In addition, as the two examples presented above seem to indicate, a relatively brief trauma history (Alexander, 2011) makes adjustment easier, as does the availability of group support. The willingness to accept help from organizations with wide-ranging programs designed to meet their various needs also can have a positive impact, once referral to such an organization occurs. Indeed, once they arrived here, my heroic asylum seekers were subjected to the same roller coaster of seemingly happenstance events as all immigrants are, especially those who arrive without money and with no place to go. The United States has much work to do to improve the services it offers in this area, needless to say.

Notes

1 An earlier version of this paper was published in the *International Journal of Applied Psychoanalytic Studies.* 13: 279–304. Reprinted by permission of John Wiley and Sons, Inc.
2 Many political situations are of this kind. Syria and Somalia presently come to mind. According to Randall and Lutz, 1991 (referenced as well in footnote 23, Introduction) those who are among the first to protest in a political situation tend to be intelligent and relatively well educated. Later, as safety and survival become more and more difficult, everyone wants to leave and send family emissaries to lead the way who are much less carefully chosen. Sometimes this has devastating consequences. See footnote 25 in the Introduction for more on this.
3 Novelist Jenny Erpenbeck in *Go, Went, Gone* (2017) describes individuals from African countries who have fled to Europe and who live briefly in one European country after another, after they have lived briefly in one African country after another, who, in the desperation of their war-torn homes, do not know where any relatives are, if indeed any are still alive. They cling to their cell phones as their only remaining potential for connection to anyone at home.
4 Educated people from African countries (including those who are Muslim and have an education beyond the Qur'anic schools, which are commonly attended by Muslim boys) are usually multilingual. They speak French or sometimes English (presently the languages of the formal schools established all over Africa during colonialism), their own tribal language, and often one or two other tribal languages. This is because, in most African countries, there are people from many different tribes, each of which has its own language. There is much interaction among them. It should also be noted that, although different countries in Africa do not, by any means, have the same culture, often country boundaries (which were originally established by European invaders) are not always the same as tribal boundaries. Thus people with the same tribal inheritance actually live in different countries.

64 Heroic Asylum seekers from around the world

5 One can be put in prison simply for discussing the Dalai Lama in Tibet or exhibiting his picture. This law reaches outrageous proportions. On a recent trip to Tibet (2013), for example, my group was taken to see both the Potala Palace in Lhasa, for centuries the home of successive Dalai Lamas, and the Summer Palace, built by the present Dalai Lama, in part for his mother, but our guide to both these places, a Tibetan Buddhist, who held the Dalai Lama sacred, was forbidden to utter his name! Moreover, to our surprise, when we returned to mainland China, our guide there, who had organized the Tibetan portion of our trip, questioned us closely to find out whether our Tibetan guide had spoken of the present Dalai Lama by name. He had not. What punishments might have befallen the Tibetan guide, had he mentioned the Dalai Lama and we had reported this, I do not know.
6 Her mother came to her city abode to nurse her, after her most damaging imprisonment, and then raised the money for her to come to America.
7 Needless to say, perhaps, the rapes she sustained caused great strain in her marriage.
8 Resisting in this context seems equivalent to me to protesting, as my heroes did.
9 Here, I am presuming excessive attachment to the thrill of the fight from various readings on war, including those referenced above, as well as Lagouranis (2008), and Soli (2010).
10 See, for example, the case of Abdullah, Chapter 11, in Volkan, 1998.
11 Here, I am assuming, based on experiences with individuals from African countries (including Mr. I in this chapter and Ms. A in the previous chapter) that avoidance of humiliation in the eyes of others is a primary mode of socialization in many African cultures. This seems to require the ongoing maintenance of family roles. A well-researched discussion of the ways in which the experience of humiliation creates political differences has been written by Lindner (2000). This author has a number of publications on the subject, which are available online at: http://www.humiliationstudies.org/whoweare/evelin.php.
12 Unfortunately, I know least about the second Tibetan man I interviewed, other than that he was quite educated.
13 This is designated secondary traumatization by Agger and Jensen (1994).
14 Escape from Tibet often requires days of walking over treacherous mountain paths.
15 See, for example, Elovitz & Kahn, 1997 and Akhtar, 1999 for more on this.
16 I had an ongoing relationship with Hero 10 for sometime before we finally lost contact. I was also able to interview Hero 8 on the telephone. She now lives in Alaska. She became a nurse and lives and works in a community of people who share her background. She has never married, but is happy, she said. She is gradually bringing her nieces and nephews to the United States. She believes she owes this to her family. She will help them adjust once they arrive, she told me.
17 Hero 8 told me that access to the cell phone had changed the lives of survivors such as herself, since it made contact with people at home, even those in hiding, relatively easy.
18 According to Pew National Trust (at: http://www.pewresearch.org/fact-tank/2017/02/14/african-immigrant-population-in-u-s-steadily-climbs/), in 2015,

African immigrants made up 4.1% of all immigrants to the United States. Of these, 41% are estimated to have bachelor degrees or higher (http://www.universityworldnews.com/article.php?story=2014101521150498). One in three speaks limited proficient English. Perhaps because of their skills, men from these countries are more likely to be employed than are men from other immigrant groups.

19 Various authors seem to indicate that those who best contend with torture either have to begin with, or later develop, some sort of belief system or rationale by which to understand what is happening to them, either while it is happening or later (Frankl, 1946/2006; Alexander, 2011). Alternately, the capacity to reflect in the situation itself seems to help in preserving a sense of oneself that is separate from the status of victim (Kaplan, 2006).

20 It is unclear how many immigrants there are annually from her country. The numbers are so small that they do not register in any account that I have been able to find.

References

Agger, I. & Jensen S. B. (1994). Determinant factors for countertransference reactions under state terrorism. In J. P. Wilson & J. D. Lindy (Eds.), *Countertransference in the Treatment of PTSD* (pp.263–287). New York. NY: Guilford.

Akhtar, S. (1999). *Immigration and Identity: Turmoil, Treatment, and Transformation.* New York, NY: Jason Aronson.

Alexander, A. (2011). Introduction. *Torture*. Retrieved from: http://www.irct.org/media-and Resources new/library/torture-journal/archive/volume-21,-no.-1,-2011.aspx.

Bar-Zohar, M. (2001). *Beyond Hitler's Grasp: The Heroic Rescue of Bulgaria's Jews*. New York, NY: Adams Media Corp.

Bergmann, M. V. (1982). Thoughts on superego pathology of survivors and their children. In M. S. Bergmann & M. D. Jucovy (Eds.), *Generations of the Holocaust* (pp.287–309). New York, NY: Columbia University Press.

Blass, T. (Ed.). (2000). *Obedience to Authority: Current Perspectives on the Milgram Paradigm*. Florence, KY: Taylor & Francis.

Boulanger, G. (2007). *Wounded by Reality: Understanding and Treating Adult Onset Trauma*. New York, NY: Routledge.

Bromberg, P. M. (1994). "Speak that I may see you!": Some reflections on dissociation, reality and psychoanalytic listening. *Psychoanalytic Dialogues*. 4: 517–547.

Bromberg, P. M. (2001). The gorilla did it: Some thoughts on dissociation, the real, and the really real. *Psychoanalytic Dialogues*. 11: 385–404.

Bromberg, P. M. (2003). Something wicked this way comes: Trauma, dissociation, and conflict: The space where psychoanalysis, cognitive science, and neuroscience overlap. *Psychoanalytic Psychology*. 20: 558–574.

Cohen, J. (1985). Trauma and repression. *Psychoanalytic Inquiry*. 5: 163–189.

Danieli, Y. (Ed.). (1998). *International Handbook of Multigenerational Legacies of Trauma*. New York, NY: Plenum Press.

Davoine, F. & Gaudilliere, J.-M. (2004). *History Beyond Trauma*. New York: Other Press.

Elovitz, P. H. & Kahn, C. (Eds) (1997). *Immigrant Experiences: Personal Narrative and Psychological Analysis*. Cranbury, NJ: Associated University Press.

Erpenbeck, J. (2017). *Go, Went, Gone*. [Kindle version]. Retrieved from www.amazon.com

Frankl, V. E. (2006). *Man's Search for Meaning*. Boston, MA: Beacon. (Original work published 1946).

Grubrich-Simitis, I. (1981). Extreme traumatization as cumulative trauma: Psychoanalytic investigations of the effects of concentration camp experiences on survivors and their children. *Psychoanalytic Study of the Child*. 36: 415–450.

Hedges, C. (2003). *War is the Force that Gives us Meaning*. New York, NY: Anchor.

Jaranson, J. & Quiroga, J. (2011). Evaluating the services of torture rehabilitation programs: History and recommendations. *Torture*. 21. Retrieved from: http://www.irct.org/Files/Filer/TortureJournal/21_02_2011/Evaluating_the_services2-2011.pdf.

Jucovy, M.E. (1992). Psychoanalytic contributions to Holocaust Studies. *International Journal of Psychoanalysis*. 73: 267–282.

Kaplan, S. (2006). Children in genocide: Extreme Traumatization and the "Affect Propeller." *International Journal of Psychoanalysis*. 87: 725–746.

Kestenberg, J. S. (1980). Psychoanalysis of children of survivors from the holocaust: Case presentations and assessment. *JPAP*. 28: 775–804.

Klempner, M (2006). *The Heart Has Reasons: Holocaust Rescuers and Their Stories*. New York, NY: Pilgrim Press.

Kogan, I. (2002). Enactment in the lives and treatment of Holocaust survivors' offspring. *Psychoanalytic Quarterly*.71: 251–272.

Krystal, H. (1988). *Integration and Self Healing: Affect, Trauma, Alexithymia*. Hillsdale, NJ: The Analytic Press.

Lagouranis, T. (2008). *Fear Up Harsh*. New York, NY: NAL Trade.

Laub, D. & Lee, S. (2003). Thanatos and massive psychic trauma: The impact of the death instinct on knowing, remembering and forgetting. *Journal of the American Psychoanalytic Association*. 51: 433–463.

Lindner, E.G. (2000). How humiliation creates cultural differences and political divisions: The psychology of intercultural communication – Germany, Somalia, Rwanda/Burundi, and the international community as cases. Retrieved from: http://www.humiliationstudies.org/documents/evelin/HumiliationCulturalDifferences.pdf.

Marton, S. (1974).*Wallenberg: Missing Hero*. New York, NY: Arcade.

Meaders, N.Y. (1997) The transcultural self. In Elovitz & Khan (Eds.), *Immigrant experiences: Personal narrative and psychological analysis*. Cranbury, NJ: Associated University Press.

Montgomery, E. & Patel, N. (2011). Torture rehabilitation: Reflections on treatment outcome studies. *Torture*: 21. Retrieved from: http://www.irct.org/Files/Filer/TortureJournal/21_02_2011/Torture_rehabilitation2-2011.pdf.

Oliner, S.P. & Oliner P. (1988). *The Altruistic Personality: Rescuers of Jews in Nazi Germany*. New York, NY: Free Press.

Randall, G. R. & Lutz, E. L. (1991). *Serving Survivors of Torture*. Washington, DC: American Association for the Advancement of Science.

Peckel, L. (2017). Treatment of torture survivors in a global environment of refugees seeking asylum. *Psychiatry Advisor*. Retrieved from: http://www.psychiatryadvisor.com/ptsd-trauma-and-stressor-related/refugees-torture-rehabilitation-ptsd-physical-mental-and-sexual-trauma/article/719726/.

Robjant, K. & Fazel, M. (2010). The emerging evidence for narrative exposure therapy: A review. *Clinical Psychology Review*, 30: 1030–1039.

Soli, T. (2010). *The Lotus Eaters: A Novel*. New York, NY: St. Martins Press.

Stern, D.B. (2003). *Unformulated Experience: From Dissociation to Imagination in Psychoanalysis*. New York, NY: Routledge.

Stern, J. (2010). *Denial: A Memoir of Terror*. New York, NY: Routledge.

Sullivan, H. S. (2013). *The Interpersonal Theory of Psychiatry*. New York, NY: Routledge.

Van der Kolk, B., McFarlane, A. C., & Weisaeth, L. (2006). *Traumatic Stress: The Effects of Overwhelming Experience on Mind and Body*. New York, NY: Guilford.

Volkan, V. E. E. (1998). *Blood Lines: From Ethnic Pride to Ethnic Terrorism*. New York, NY: Basic Books.

Volkan, V. E. E. (2006). *Killing in the Name of Identity: A Study of Blood Conflicts*. Charlottesville, VA: Pitchstone.

Williams, A. C. de C. & van der Merwe, J. (2013). The psychological impact of torture. *British Journal of Pain*. Retrieved from: http://journals.sagepub.com/doi/full/10.1177/2049463713483596.

Yovell, S. (2000). From hysteria to post-traumatic stress disorder: Psychoanalysis and the neurobiology of traumatic memories. *Neuropsychoanalysis*.2:171–181.

Chapter 3

Female genital mutilation and the wish for "life"

Cultural considerations in the development of personal agency[1]

Introduction

Eight of the asylum evaluations I have completed have been of women who were either threatened with or subjected to FGM. According to UNICEF, 200 million girls and women have endured this cutting,[2] in thirty countries, including the United States (Akinsulure-Smith & Sicalides, 2016).[3] The procedure is usually performed before the girl is old enough to choose it herself.[4] Although a recent article in the New York Times (Dugger, 2013) indicates that the incidence of FGM is decreasing,[5] this is difficult to investigate because often the procedure is performed against the law, in secret, and the police are bribed to keep quiet (Berg & Denison, 2012). Urban residency and education, however, do seem to decrease its occurrence[6] (Diop & Askew, 2009; Dalal, Lawoko, & Jansson, 2010; Cloward, 2016).

Since 2008 the effects of FGM have been ruled, beyond a reasonable doubt, the cause of ongoing pain and therefore "well-founded" grounds for the granting of asylum in the United States.[7] Despite this, however, there are still instances in which a judge will doubt the asylec's credibility and therefore deny her asylum.[8] As a result, frequently both a medical and a psychological evaluation are requested as validation of the asylee's claim.

FGM varies in its degree of severity,[9] based on the degree to which the girl's body is invaded. Regardless of its severity, however, proponents of the procedure believe it ensures cleanliness, lessens the woman's sexual desire, increases male sexual pleasure, insures virginity before marriage and fidelity after, and altogether makes the woman more appealing as a marriage partner (Akinsulure-Smith & Sicalides, 2016). FGM is an initiation rite of sorts; it seems to imply submission to paternalistic traditions, which continue, despite the infection, hemorrhaging, difficulties with child bearing, and death that can result. The pressure to have undergo the procedure is sometimes so great that, among schoolgirls, those who have avoided it can be cruelly ostracized by those who have not (Ali, 2007). Indeed, girls and women seem to play a large part in the continuation of the practice. In fact, the person who actually does the cutting is usually a woman, a paid traditional practitioner whose livelihood depends on the work. Usually she has had no medical training and uses no antiseptic or anesthetic.

The origins of FGM are unknown; it is not connected to any one religion. Whatever its origin, however, it is obviously a huge invasion of a girl's body and growing sense of self, a human rights violation of the first degree! Although we know a considerable amount about its physical effects, we know far less about the impact FGM can have on the way women perceive themselves, especially in regard to their feelings of power and personal agency. Nor do we know if this sense of power and personal agency can change, once they come to the West, and if so, how? What, in fact, is required to engender changes in these feelings? In the following pages, I would like to address these questions using psychoanalytic theory as a guide.

My clients

My FGM clients have almost all been middle-aged women with children who came from four different countries. Some had borne their children in the United States. Because of the nature of my contact with them, which, in most cases, consisted of one or two in-depth interviews, necessary to the process of completing an asylum evaluation,[10] my knowledge of their lives before they came to America is not extensive. In addition, in most cases, my interviews were conducted soon after their arrival and, therefore, I was unable to learn a great deal about their adjustment to life here. A more detailed description of these women appears in Table 3.1.

Ms. A and Ms. G, however, were exceptions to this pattern. Ms. A had been living in the United States for nine, and Ms. G for seven years when I met them. Both claimed to be illiterate, but because they spoke English, I was able to have longer and more in-depth interviews with them than was true with the other six women. Consequently, I was able to learn, in some detail, about their lives before they arrived in the United States and also a bit about how each had adjusted to life in New York City. I learned that both of these women had not only learned to

Table 3.1 FGM asylee: Background characteristics

Asylee name	Ms. A	Ms. B	Ms. C	Ms. D	Ms. E	Ms. F	Ms. G	Ms. H
Country of origin	Guinea	Gambia	D. K	Guinea	Senegal	Congo, DAR	Gambia	Senegal
Ethnic/religious group	Fulani/Muslim	Fulani/Muslim	Yacouba/Evangelical Christian	Peuhl/Muslim	Mandingo/Jola: Christian mother, Muslim father	Don't know: Muslim	Serahule/Muslim	Fulani/Muslim
Age at time of evaluation	34	36	46	56	33	31	22	27
Education	Thru grade 3, French school: illiterate	Thru French secondary	University	Professional school: computer	Thru French secondary	Thru English secondary	No schooling: illiterate	Thru French elementary
Number of languages spoken	5	3	3	5	3	7	3	3
Profession	Tailor	Accountant	Unsure: Political observer?	Gov't telecommunications	Hair salon	Not working: Health care interests	Paid housekeeper	Homemaker
Immigration type, originally[1]	Tourist (to join husband)	Alien (asylum)	Alien (asylum)	Alien (asylum)	Alien (asylum)	Alien (asylum)	Tourist (to join husband)	Tourist (to join husband)
Time already in United States	9 years	7 months	Don't know	15 months	7 years	3 years	6 years	6 years
Age at FGM	7 or 8	10	4 or 5	8 or 9	Escaped it	2 months	2–3 weeks	8
Type of FGM	Most severe	Most severe	Most severe	Most severe (botched)	None	Most severe	Most severe	Most severe
Marital status/history	Married at 14, a man of 30. Divorced	Married at 18; arranged; husband also 18	Married; no details.	Marriage arranged "late" (27)	Unmarried	Married, age unknown; arranged; husband loving	Married at 15; arranged; husband 29	Married, age unknown; love match
Number of children, gender	4 male	1 male; 3 female	6, gender unknown	2: adult, gender unknown	2, gender unknown	3, gender unknown	2 female; 2 male	2 female

1 For some, immigration status changed during their time in the United States.

speak English fluently, but had become the sole economic supporters of their children. Moreover, earlier in life, at home, each had contended with considerable abuse from a much older husband, but nevertheless had not offended her family of origin by flouting convention and abandoning him. Then, once she had arrived here, each had succeeded in ending her marriage and living on her own.

From a psychodynamic point of view, how can we explain the ongoing nature of the strength and resilience these women demonstrated in striking out on their own, once they perceived they had the opportunity to do so? From which aspects of their early experience did their capacity for independence come? Hoping to learn more about this, using psychoanalytic theory as my guide, I will present the case of one woman – Ms. A – as an example of others who come from a culture very different from my own, in which female submission and the hardships it entails can nevertheless be employed to develop a robust sense of personal agency with the outcome of independence.

Ms. A: Ms. A, a pretty, lively woman, was thirty-four when I met her. Her mother was Fulani and her father Malinke.[11] She was born in Sierra Leone, their third daughter. Although presumably breastfed for a year or more in the traditional Fulani manner,[12] her two older sisters (one five, one seven) helped with her care once she could walk.[13] These sisters were not always around to guide her, however. Perhaps as a consequence, she learned early that the best way to understand a new situation was to throw herself into it and then to figure it out. As her story unfolded, it appeared that she had done this often.

When Ms. A was approximately a year old, her father died. Soon after, her mother moved back to Guinea, to the small town from which the family had come. Without a husband, a woman like her mother, with no education and unable to read, "has no life," and, for all intents and purposes, is rendered powerless, Ms. A told me.[14] Thus, once returned to Guinea, her mother married a second time. She and her daughters then moved into an apartment adjoining the apartment of her husband's second wife, whose children were much older than Ms. A. All members of this extended family were (are) strict observers of the Muslim faith.[15]

Once married, Ms. A's mother was bound to do the will of her new husband, even in regard to the management of her daughters. Hence the three sisters were sent by their stepfather to the local French primary school, where French was the language in use. Learning this language was very difficult for her, Ms. A said, but she threw herself into the project and mastered it well.[16] When the stepfather's money ran out, however, schooling came to an end. This occurred just as Ms. A was completing third grade. Once she left school, she left reading behind. The skill was not valued by the women in her immediate family, in which girls were supposed to learn to sew and cook. Nevertheless, over the course of her life, Ms. A learned to speak five languages fluently:[17] Fula, Malinke, Sesotho, French and, most recently, English.

At the age of seven, Ms. A was subjected to the most extreme form of female genital mutilation, a full excision of her clitoris and labia minora. The procedure was forced upon her by her mother, grandmother, and other women in the community who believed that, without it, prospective suitors would think her unclean. The operation was performed without anesthesia, in the "usual way," by a woman qualified only because she "owned a switchblade," Ms. A told me. No information or preparation had been given to the little girl (who had no memory of her older sisters' experiences in this regard) and no calming words were offered at any point. "It is not our custom to discuss such matters," she told me.[18] Only later, in the United States could Ms. A acknowledge that the entire event, which included infibulation (the sewing up of the open, bleeding vagina) was extremely painful; it also scared and shocked her to such a degree that she shook uncontrollably for days.

Less than a week after the procedure, an aunt,[19] who was a nurse, happened to stop by. Upon seeing Ms. A's fevered state, the aunt became furious. Proper medical precautions had not been observed,[20] she screamed. She insisted that Ms. A be taken to a hospital and given antibiotics right away. The family complied. Ms. A believes that this intervention saved her life.

A lively child, with a mind of her own, Ms. A got along well with the other wives and enjoyed the freedom this gave her to roam their living quarters as she pleased. As a consequence, her mother began to rely on her to make good relationships with all of them, not always an easy task, given the jealous competition frequent among the three women and their children. In fact, as far back as she can remember Ms. A said she had always been the child who had helped her mother get along. Because of this, the two developed a loving, respectful relationship, which still endures.

When Ms. A was approximately twelve, a thirty-year-old stepbrother tried "to take advantage of me," she said. He sent her to the store to buy him cigarettes. When she returned, he grabbed her breasts from behind and brutally began to massage them. This both hurt and terrified her and she cried out in fear. Her mother, nearby, rushed in and told him to stop, explaining that this was his sister and that such behavior with a sister was not allowed. For permission to touch her this way, her mother explained, the brother would have to marry Ms. A and this would be impossible for a few more years.

Two years went by during which Ms. A did her best to stay out of the way of the obstreperous stepbrother. Once she turned fourteen, however, the two were formally betrothed by their parents.[21] Upon being told this news, Ms. A was horrified: she screamed and yelled in protest. A cycle of attempts to run away then began. Finally, to stop this, the family locked her up for two days, with no food or water, during which time the stepbrother (Mr. W) came to the window and said, "Tell your mother you love me! If you don't, they're going to kill you in this room." He alternated this threat with one to kill himself. Eventually, under this pressure, she gave in, believing that one of them would die if she did not.

As soon as they freed her, the family covered her in bridal garments. Wanting to wait a bit, she threw them off. In the end, however, the decision to marry was made by the stepfather and the marriage took place.

On the wedding night, the infibulation made during the FGM procedure when she was a child, was cut open by the same old crone. The pain this caused was exacerbated by sex, for her husband (unlike other kinder husbands I have heard about) showed no sympathy and brutally forced her to have sex with him immediately, and frequently, despite her cries. This made the first months of her marriage utterly miserable. Attempts to leave him, again by running away, inevitably failed. Each time, her stepfather beat her and forced her to return. Finally, having no alternative, Ms. A learned to cope, perhaps by not being "there" during sex. In fact, in describing these episodes to me, she simply reported the facts, in an emotionless monotone.

Two boys were born to the couple, in 1991 and 1994 respectively. Ms. A, who enjoyed being a mother, cared for them lovingly. Soon after the arrival of the second, however, Mr. W announced that he was leaving. He was going to join his brother in America, he said, where it was possible to earn good money. He then departed. Once there, he sent no money home. Desperate, Ms. A moved into her mother-in law's compound, now in another location, and worked locally as a tailor (a skill she had previously mastered) to support her family.

With her husband gone, Ms. A felt totally unprotected. At her mother-in-law's she was treated so wretchedly that, after two months, she moved back to her own mother's house. However, without a husband, she repeated, "a woman like me has no life." Any social life is potentially scandalous, because it can include exposure to other men. Given this, Ms. A decided she had no choice but to go to America to join her husband. Her mother (always her closest ally) encouraged this. Accordingly she saved her earnings (something she could do because her children were being cared for by her mother)[22] and eventually obtained a tourist visa and a ticket.

While she waited for her visa, her decision to go to America was reinforced, she said, by a dream, in which her much idealized, deceased biological father came to her and said he was sorry that she had been forced into such a terrible marriage. In the dream he promised the marriage would end, once she had established herself in America. In addition, and crucially important, she also has an abiding faith in Allah. He often comes to her at night and talks to her, she told me. He tells her that if she works hard to help herself, he too will help her. To propitiate his good will and to give thanks, she fasts often. Fasting this way for Allah also has helped to put a positive spin on days when there has been little in her house to eat. Indeed, there have been times since her arrival in America when the family has had very little money for food.

Upon arriving in the United States (2001) she moved in with her husband. She had barely unpacked when he insisted that she go to work. He "gave me nothing," she said. As a result, a few days later, she got a job braiding hair. Her husband did not even accompany her, a complete stranger to New York, with no ability to speak or read English, on the long subway trip from one borough in New York City to another, to meet her prospective employer. She was forced to go alone.

In keeping with his extraordinary self-centeredness, her husband (who is literate) gave her no information about what she needed to do to address her immigration situation. In fact, he had done nothing to address his own. All he was interested in was "having babies," she told me. If she did not produce another baby for him immediately, he said, he would send her back home. Once again, he repeatedly forced her sexual submission. She became pregnant in two months. Eventually, two more sons were born to the couple in the United States.

Gradually, Ms. A learned, from her contacts in the African community in New York City, that she needed to address her immigration situation if she wanted to remain. Her husband had introduced her to a Mr. Bah, to whom she paid a fee, because (she was told) Mr. Bah would help her do what was necessary to get asylum. "I didn't know nothing," she said. "I did what they told me." Mr. Bah, who asked her no questions, filled out her I-589 form,[23] with the wrong information, and she signed it. Then he took her to her first immigration hearing and translated for her. Not surprisingly, her first request for asylum was denied. Two other attempts to gain asylum, each of which cost money, were denied for similar reasons.

Meanwhile, in their home, her husband became even more abusive. This culminated in 2010, when he called her mother in Africa and said he did not want to be married anymore. Much in need of money himself, despite his employment as a taxi driver, he requested the dowry gold he had given her family upon their marriage. This he succeeded in getting.[24]

Then, however, instead of moving out, for the next six months, ignoring his children, her husband isolated himself in a bedroom, relying entirely on her to pay the rent, despite the fact that their apartment was in his name.

Twice, the police were called. The first time, in 2010, a visiting niece made the call because Mr. W had punched Ms. A in the face. The injury was severe enough for the police to take her to a local hospital for treatment. They also jailed Mr. W, briefly, as an abuser. Ms. A, fluent in English by this time, was referred to a helping agency. With support from this agency, she considered filing charges against him in order to secure an order of protection.

However, her mother in Africa, with whom she is always in contact, objected and begged her not to press charges. The reputation of the family at home was at stake, her mother said. In addition, the family worried that such an order would threaten Mr. W's United States immigration status. Willing to go along with their wishes yet again, Ms. A agreed to drop charges. Nevertheless, the couple finally separated: Ms. A moved with her children to a different rent-controlled apartment, in a public housing complex, and signed the lease herself. She had received help in finding this apartment from the organization to which she was earlier referred. This organization also provided some short-term counseling, which, she said, helped her to understand her "rights," in light of her husband's brutality. In addition, they referred her to a competent immigration attorney.

The second incident with the police was created entirely by her husband. For reasons unknown to Ms. A, he took it upon himself to go to her new apartment, where he immediately began verbally abusing her. Then he called the police!

When the police arrived, he told them that Ms. A had been harassing him and was throwing his clothes out of the window. But there were no clothes in the street, the police observed. They also read the lease, which was in her name. With help from the children, the police quickly understood the situation and forthwith they encouraged Ms. A to go again to Family Court to get a temporary restraining order against her husband. This time she agreed to do this.

However, again, she reported everything to her mother who again urged her to drop the case. The family at home was so worried about being shamed, should the brutality of this son become widely known to others in their community, that her brother-in-law (also in the United States) promised to take her to a local Imam to get a Muslim divorce if she, in turn, would promise to drop the request for a restraining order. With alacrity, she agreed to this. Thus the visit to the Imam then took place and he (the Imam) granted the divorce. Since then, Ms. A has been living peacefully with her two American-born sons in their own apartment. Her now ex-husband, meanwhile, has apparently not yet discovered a successful route to citizenship himself. Proudly describing her present situation, Ms. A said, "My mother would never understand how I live. In our country, the idea of an independent life is unheard of for women like me."

In addition to her mother at home, Ms. A is in regular contact with her two older sons. I discovered this because, while she was in my office, she received three telephone calls. Two were from her eldest American-born son, one to tell his mother that he and his brother had gotten on the school bus and were going home, one to tell her that they had arrived. This seemed to amuse and please her. The third was from one of her sons in Africa, to report on how things were going for the family there. To speak to him, Ms. A stood up and turned away from me, perhaps to focus better on her conversation with him. Indeed, Ms. A seems to be very important to all of her children and vice versa. Family, fundamental in Fulani culture, is more important to her than anything, she told me, except perhaps her faith in Allah. Her opinion of men, however, has soured completely. "I don't need one," she told me. "These days I can take care of myself." Although still quite anxious, most of the symptoms of PTSD, which had plagued her at home and when she first arrived here, are in remission. For the time being, things are going well.

In summary then, Ms. A has been able to move to America, to learn English, and to adjust quite well to a culture completely different from her own. She has found work and is managing, alone, to care for her children financially and emotionally. She is doing this with considerable pride and satisfaction; she has also secured relatively safe, affordable housing for them all. Presently Ms. A's life includes a number of contacts with people, visitors from home and those she meets here. These contacts, sometimes with men, would have been forbidden to her at home, as a woman living alone. Her present life also includes the right to keep all of the money she earns for her own needs, whereas previously, as custom decreed, she had been forced to give her earnings to her husband.

As for a love relationship, in America, she can choose whether to have a partner or not. It is this part of her life which seems to have been most affected by her past experiences, first as a victim of genital mutilation and then as a victim of marriage to a much older, extremely abusive husband. Based on the manner in which she described her sexual relations with her husband (e.g., that sex was forced upon her), my guess is that she learned to dissociate when this took place.[25] Her interest in being in a relationship with a man, at this point, seems to be nil.

In interviewing Ms. A, I was surprised at her seeming openness to my questions. She worked hard to answer them in as much detail as possible. When I used the word rape, to describe the way in which her husband had treated her sexually, she paused and seemed to think about the word before she used it herself in responding to me. In fact, this word had not appeared in any of the documents I had received from her attorney before interviewing her. In contrast, in revised documents, which I received later, the word rape did appear. It seemed as if she had not, herself, processed her husband's brutality in just this way before we met. Indeed, for the entirety of our interview, I had the experience that Ms. A was vigilantly observing me, working hard to connect, to make sure I was on her side, certainly, but also, it seemed, in order to learn. Labeling behavior as Americans do, in more generalized, more encompassing, terms, use of such words as rape, to describe a series of individual events, particularly ones that might have been painful to her,[26] had not been her custom before. My guess is that she has learned to do this, partially as an outcome of the counseling she received, both from her attorney, during the lengthy asylum-seeking process, and from her counselor at the helping organization to which she had been referred by family court. She has used this ability, this sensitivity, to change and reorient herself to America. Indeed, she seems to have experienced what Salman Akhtar (1995) might call a "third individuation process." In her case, she has become a different person, in many ways, from the person she was at home, certainly a person she would describe as "having a life."

Discussion

My clients in light of others who have experienced FGM

To date, I have been unable to find any psychodynamically oriented study of women, such as Ms. A, who have grown up in cultures that practice FGM and who have then immigrated to the West.

In wider reference groups (e.g., MEDLINE and the American Psychological Association's PsycINFO), among the two hundred odd studies I found, the one most focused on the affect in women who have suffered FGM, took place in the Netherlands and was completed in 2012 by psychologist E. Vioeberghs. He describes four different reaction patterns, from very depressed and alienated, at one extreme, to well adjusted and connected, at the other.[27] Individual case studies, however, were not presented.

Of my eight clients, none seemed either depressed or alienated. Perhaps I was blind to their more depressed affect. Depression is present in many, I have read.[28] Among the women I interviewed, Ms. H seemed to have suffered the most. She reported that she had, as an elementary school student, become so ill, as a result of the FGM procedure, that she had missed months of school and had been left back. A committed student at the time, she had never forgotten this humiliation. It had apparently de-railed her academic pursuits completely. Eventually, however, she grew up and married an adoring man, whose sister had died from the consequences of FGM. As a result, rather than take any chances bearing children at home, the couple had decided that their children would be born in the United States. Thus they were the parents of two American-born girls. The father supported his family by commuting to businesses abroad, while the mother, my client, lived here. As a couple (both came to her interview with me) they were altogether pleased to have managed their lives in this way. For both of them it was the outcome of terrible experiences at home.

Personal agency: Its development in Ms. A

In order to better understand the capabilities exhibited by Ms. A, and by others like her, I have turned to the concept of personal agency because it provides a strikingly flexible way to grasp the multifaceted nature of ongoing development and motivation in human beings. Lately the concept has become increasingly popular among psychoanalysts, as it has also among philosophers (Juarrero, 2000) sociologists/social psychologists (Bandura, 2006), neurologists (Jeannerod, 2001; Freeman, 2001), and computer simulators (Franklin & Graesser, 1996). I like best the definition of agency provided by the last of these authors. They define an autonomous agent as "a system situated within and a part of an environment that senses that environment and acts on it, over time, in pursuit of its own agenda and so as to affect what it senses in the future" (1996, p. 4). Within human beings, according to neurobiologist Walter Freeman (2001), such a system seems to become more robust as life tasks are successfully negotiated.

According to psychoanalysts, agency emerges early in life (Rustin, 1997), as an outcome of mutual recognition in the caretaker–infant pair. From the infant's point of view, agency implies that the infant begins to know her or himself as (s)he discovers that another is there for her or him (Winnicott, 1971) to whom (s)he matters (Slavin, 2014). It is mattering in this way that seems to register as a distinct feeling-set, one that emerges gradually from carefully sorted bodily sensations (Frie, 2008; Modell, 2008, 2009; Slavin, 2014) in ways that are congruent with the specifications of a given culture. Agency, as described by Modell, is:

> the feeling that we can make things happen and that we are masters of our own domain. When this is true, we feel good about ourselves . . . We know that our sense of self is deeply and fundamentally embedded in our bodies. Correspondingly, our sense of agency remains wedded to feelings derived from our bodies, but attributed to the self . . . Only a fraction of what we feel is attributed to the self as a causal agent. *We constantly receive sensations from our bodies that are not necessarily*

> *attributed to the self as agent. Pain is one clear example; pain is something we do not cause and therefore is outside the agency of the self.*
>
> (2008, p. 358, italics mine)

The suggestion here is that body-based agency helps to direct ongoing activity, much of which is out of conscious awareness, from the very beginning (Pollock & Slavin, 1998). Because agency is concretely based in the body, it is in the body that memory is stored. Bodily sensations provide the feeling that " [one's] story makes sense" (Slavin, 2014, p. 26). Freeman (2001) describes the direction of this agentic force as already determined before we ourselves become aware of where it will lead. Presumably, it includes certain self-protective qualities, including the capacity to behave appropriately in social situations and to observe and reverse personal actions and revise one's approach, if original plans do not work out (Caston, 2011). Life, as seen by the person living it, according to this point of view, suggests that conscious intent is preceded by unconscious neural activity (Jeannerod, 2000; Freeman 2001; Modell, 2008), which mentally prepares the individual for what is to come. Such activity may be especially helpful when the person moves from one culture to another and must adjust to different customs.

Resistance and rebellion, common among developing adolescents, before self-direction is clear, can also be helpful. It can provide a private space in which the nascent, emerging self can grow (Pollock & Slavin, 1998; Gentile, 2008).

This broad, very inclusive concept is useful in explaining the unfolding of Ms. A's feelings about herself, apparent to her long before she arrived in America and apparent to me when she described her wish to "have a life." A closer look at Ms. A's childhood may provide more specific information about how these feelings developed in her.

Based on Fulani child-rearing tradition, in which mothers are expected to be attentive (see DeLoach and Gottlieb, 2000), it is probable that Ms. A was nursed by her mother alone.[29] If standard Fulani procedure had been followed in other ways, Ms. A was also fed a kind of gruel, which her mother prepared. This feeding requires sustained attention between mother and child, as the child is generally not sitting in a high chair.[30] Probably because of this care, Ms. A made a good attachment to her mother. How "secure" this attachment actually was, when measured by modern research standards, is difficult to say, but certainly the bond between mother and child became strong and continues to be strong to this day.

Once Ms. A could walk tolerably well, much of her care was turned over to her two older sisters, as is also traditional among Fulani (Riesman, 1992). This care was probably a bit haphazard, which meant that she learned to rely on herself.

When her mother remarried, Ms. A developed better and better social skills, so good in fact that her mother came to rely on her to ensure that good connections were made with the new husband's other wives and children.

When sent to a French elementary school, she adjusted there as well and learned to speak French, despite its difficulty for her. When forced to leave the school, however, she quickly abandoned reading and writing because these skills were unimportant for women in the culture of her family and she herself had no interest in them. Instead she learned to sew (evident later in life when she tailored in order to support herself) and (presumably) to cook.

The genital mutilation, which was forced upon her around the age of eight, did not seem to create resentment. Ms. A did not blame the cutting she endured for future ills in her life. In fact, she accepted it as the custom in the community from which she came. In keeping with the values of Fulani culture, in which pain should be overcome (Riesman & Fuller, 1998), she did not complain about this or about any of the other hardships she was forced to endure.

In regard to her brutal stepbrother, however, her reactions were not so forgiving. He frightened her profoundly and was, therefore, never a person she liked. These feelings were clear to her at the age of twelve, when he first tried to molest her, and lasted through the years of marriage they shared. Her desire to be free of him thus seemed to have been present always. When, later, she was forced to marry him, she rebelled first, although she did eventually comply, for she believed her very life might be sacrificed if she did not. After the marriage, however, she ran away from him often. This rebellion, this running away is, according to Riesman (1992), common among Fulani brides, perhaps because so many of them are married as children to older, abusive men, chosen for them by their parents. The short vacations afforded by these home visits from the responsibilities of marriage, including the pain and violence of sex, must be welcome reprieves for such women and may be welcomed by their mothers as well.

Altogether then, the sequence of events described above indicates a pattern of ongoing submission to the rules of her culture, but with periods of personal exploration, self-assertion, and even rebellion, especially as a child. Later, the short vacations she took from spousal abuse, when she ran home to her mother, must have helped to bolster her sense of having some freedom to make decisions of her own.

Submission as the route to personal agency and power

It seems clear from Ms. A's account of her life that she seemed to understand, from an early age, that, in the end, her only choice was to submit to all the requirements of her culture. Certainly, in the eyes of her family she occupied a subordinate position, which she maintained. She did what the stepfather and the husband told her to do. She eventually married the person they chose for her and made the marriage work. She gave birth to four boys. She journeyed to America because that was where her husband was and it was supposedly correct for her to follow him. Her mother encouraged this. Her mother, who she mentioned many times during our interviews, may be the most important relationship in Ms. A's life, beyond her own children.[31] It is her mother, however, who has represented the stepfather's will. Even after she arrived in America, Ms. A subordinated herself to this will. She did what her husband told her to do, at least at the beginning, before she learned to speak English, before she was referred, by the police, to family court. When he beat her, it was not she who called the police, but a visiting niece. When her mother urged her to drop charges against him, she did. When a Muslim divorce was suggested as a bargaining chip, it was not she who suggested it, but her husband's brother, who then took her to an Imam to procure it. Remarkably, throughout all of this, she never actively judged her husband as a limited man, even when she witnessed him lie to the American police or try to use misplaced ruses that might well have succeeded in her home country, where the police, I have been told, side with the man, because he has the money and they expect to be bribed.[32] In addition, she never seems to have concluded that not only is she more courageous than her husband, but she is probably more intelligent, as demonstrated, among other things, by the fact that, through trial and error, she has come to understand some important aspects of American law, school policy, and health care, which he has not. She has used her understanding to find a relatively safe, affordable living space, to earn a living, and to win asylum. Indeed, despite all this, she seemed unwilling to label her husband negatively or to make any higher order judgment about him unless someone seemingly with greater knowledge did so first, as I did when I called him a rapist. Above all, perhaps, she did not see herself as a victim. To feel pity for herself or to make judgments about her husband might well have jeopardized not only her mother's love (it is humiliating in Fulani culture to acknowledge pain), but also the ability to subordinate herself sufficiently to succeed in getting to have the "life" she wanted.

But how exactly did submission lead her gradually to the feeling that she had power and thus to the further development of her own sense of personal agency? How did it lead her to a position in which she could finally embrace the relative freedom that coming to America offered her?

Here Jessica Benjamin is helpful in pointing the way. In two papers (1995, 2004), she has summarized recent psychoanalytic contributions in regard to the dynamics of gender role separation. "Feminine" and "masculine," as she sees them, are constructed, in part, by the requirements of separation,[33] which in turn are determined differently in different cultures. In the act of defining the boundaries between the two, the girl (and later the woman) functions as the container, into which the boy projects those aspects of himself that his culture asks him to repudiate as he moves into a world which will require more active thrusting than was ever required of him before. Indeed, earlier in his life, the warm, engulfing comfort of his mother's embrace required only his passive surrender. But he must relinquish this pleasure if he is to be accepted by other men as a man, as a person who is aggressive in the world outside.

Meanwhile, for girls and women, in cultures in which their submission is required, three choices are open to them as they mature, according to Benjamin (1995): they can actively fight the requirements to which they must submit; they can surrender willingly and master these, one by one; or they can effect some kind of compromise between the two.

Of the three choices Benjamin lists, the third seems to provide the greatest opportunity for satisfaction. In compromising, the girl may, if she is clever and imaginative, have the opportunity to gain a greater sense of power, the power of the "father," as Benjamin calls it, and then be able to use it to further her own ends. Indeed in some cases, the girl may succeed at this so well that she begins to feel as capable as he, in "having a life" on her own terms.

In a unique, creative manner, this is the route that Ms. A seems to have taken. In hearing her story, it was clear to me that, even as a child, she had been able to make her way uniquely, guided by her own resources. Please recall that, as a child, unlike her sisters, she had known all of the people in her extended family and felt free to interact with them herself. Indeed, she got along so well with them that her mother came to depend on her for help in establishing positive connections among them all. When she was forced to marry an abuser, she rebelled. She gave in only when death was threatened if she did not. Later, as an adult, "having a life" seemed to mean having the freedom to continue to socialize freely, just as she had as a child, with others, outside of her family, without fear of humiliating herself or any of them. The wish to keep the money she earned accompanied this: she needed money to do the things she wanted to do. Men, in contrast to women, have both money and the freedom to socialize as they please in the culture from which she comes.

But who exactly was the most powerful figure, the "father," in Benjamin's terms, from whom she garnered her greatest power? To whom did she turn for support in pursuing a "life," when her husband, stepfather, and mother let her down?

The greatest support Ms. A has had, as an adult, has been her faith in Allah. According to her, she hears his voice in their almost nightly conversations. He tells her that things will turn out well for her if she obeys him. In talking with him this way she is, once again, sustaining the correct subservient female role, in service to the "father," this time to the ultimate religious authority in her land. Allah is the all-powerful substitute for the father she never had.

The implications of hearing voices for Ms. A

Is Allah's voice in her head a symptom of psychosis in Ms. A? The answer here is no. Hearing voices, which, in the past, was often labeled as symptomatic of schizophrenia, seems to occur frequently in people who are not schizophrenic at all. To date, an eloquent voice-hearer, speaking from a personal point of view, is psychologist Eleanor Longdon, whose extraordinary account can be watched online (TED Talk, 2013).[34]

In a more scholarly review, Hill and Linden (2013) document the fact that there are voice-hearers who are neither distressed by the voices they hear nor in need of psychiatric care. An appraisal by the voice-hearer him or herself may be the determining factor in regard to whether the voices become distressful. Presently there are groups of voice-hearers who have come together to support one another and to assist in learning to use their voices productively (Hornstein, 2009).

Ms. A, as a voice-hearer, is clearly a member of the non-clinical group. Her voice supports and encourages courageous acts. Moreover, in the culture from which she comes, conversing with Allah is perfectly acceptable. Indeed, it gives her power, the ultimate power of the "father" (Benjamin, 2004), which, in turn, has allowed her to live a life of increasing personal agency. Unlike the angry or depressed victims of FGM described in the Dutch study referenced above (Vioeberghs, 2012), Ms. A seems relatively at peace. Her ability to subordinate herself, first to the expectations of the culture from which she came, and now to ours, seems to have saved her from the ill effects of helpless rage and to have helped her solve very large problems rather well.

Summary and conclusion

In this chapter, I have presented a group of women I came to know as they were in the process of applying for political asylum in the United States. Nearly all were subjected to the FGM procedure as children. Many, although not all, were also forced to marry older men who treated them quite brutally.

Focusing on one of these women, Ms. A, I have described the manner in which she developed a strong sense of personal agency (Modell, 2008; Slavin, 2014). I have suggested that this emerged early in a life which included, first, a solid primary attachment to her mother and then, as she moved into toddlerhood, haphazard care by two older sisters, which forced her, in turn, to rely on herself to master new situations. This sequence of events, in conjunction with innate intelligence, liveliness, and curiosity, gave her a platform from which to explore the world. She did so by using a concrete, largely body-based trial and error mode of exploration, well within the norms of her culture. Later, still exploring in this way, she developed excellent social skills within the boundaries of family. She came to relish the freedom this allowed.

However, once married off to an older man who treated her with incredible cruelty, the requisite submission to the female role became so difficult that she required the help of an outside aid in order to sustain her own sense of agency. The creation of this aid, the voice of Allah in her head, gave her a sense of power, perhaps the sort of power "fathers" in her culture might have assumed (Benjamin, 1995, 2004). With "Allah's help," she followed her husband to America. Here, still pursuing a course of trial and error, she finally succeeded in "having a life," having the social and economic freedom she had wished for. In addition, she has learned that not only can she be independent in America, but she can take a step back and reflect on events, label her husband a rapist, label other events in her life, without negative consequences. In accomplishing this, she has moved into a world her "mother would never understand . . . In our country the idea of an independent life is unheard of for a woman like me," she said. This pleases her. She is glad as well that she has accomplished this without offending her mother, whose support she needs and to whom she still speaks lovingly many times a week.

Knowing Ms. A, and a few others like her, has taught me that women can flourish in circumstances that I, from my Western perspective, consider almost unimaginable. It has been my privilege to know her. May she do well here and continue to "have a life," as she has wished so steadfastly, for so many years.

Notes

1 An earlier version of this paper appeared in *The International Journal of Applied Psychoanalytic Studies*. 2016, 13: 279–304. Reprinted here by permission of John Wiley & Sons, Inc., lic # 4201980052508.
2 Online at: https://data.unicef.org/topic/child-protection/female-genital-mutilation-and-cutting/ describes 200 million women and girls already cut. http://www.unicef.org/protection/57929_58002.html.
3 FGM has been performed on an estimated 500,000 women in the United States according to a recent report at: http://www.cnn.com/2017/05/11/health/female-genital-mutilation-fgm-explainer-trnd/index.html.
4 According to the World Health Organization (at: http://www.who.int/mediacentre/factsheets/fs241/en/) the procedure is usually performed on girls between infancy and the age of fifteen.
5 An example of how this is happening appeared in another recent New York Times article (Benanav, 2013) which describes a Maasi chief who had "persuaded the family [of an uninitiated girl] to join his campaign to end female genital mutilation." Thus, instead of the usual procedure, "inside the hut the girl would receive a ritual nick on her thigh, while screaming loudly enough for people outside to hear. 'The screaming is the important part.'" The chief said. "'We are not changing our culture, we are ending a harmful practice'" (p. 6).
6 In regard to FGM, a wonderful movie, *Moolaadé*, directed by Senegalese film director, Ousmane Sembène (2004) is an example of this. It is available at Amazon.com.

7 More about this is available at: https://repository.law.umich.edu/cgi/viewcontent.cgi?article=1182&context=mjgl
8 For more on this see: https://immigrationidaho.com/asylum-granted-fgm-domestic-violence/.
9 For a description of FGM degrees of severity, see Appendix IV.
10 This process is described in Chapter One.
11 The Fulani (called alternately Fula, Peul, and Fulbe), one of the largest ethnic groups in West Africa, numbers perhaps ten million (DeLoach & Gottlieb, 2000). They are scattered in different countries in a wide swath of Africa from West to East, along the southern edge of the Sahara. Islam was adopted by most of these people a long time ago (perhaps 5th century AD), although it has always been combined with other folk religious traditions. For a map and further description, see Anter (2011).
12 Offering love and good nutrition, are highly valued female qualities in Fulani culture, according to DeLoach and Gottlieb, 2000.
13 This, according to sociologist P. Riesman (1992), is customary among Fulani.
14 Among Fulani, it is the status of the man that matters. This tends to render solo women quite powerless. This is the case in much of Africa. In *Infidel*, for example, Aryan Hirsi Ali (2007), who later became a member of the Dutch parliament and is now living in the United States, quotes her grandmother as follows: "a woman alone is like a piece of sheep fat in the sun. Everything will come and feed on that fat. Before you know it, the ants and insects are crawling all over it, until there is nothing left but a smear of fat." In another book, *The Orchard of Lost Souls* (Mohamed, 2014), a novel set in Somalia, the separate fate of three different women, each alone, is described in harrowing terms.
15 Muslim men are permitted four wives.
16 In many African countries the best available schooling takes place in the language of the country's European invaders, that is French, English, or German. Sending one's children to such a school is a sign of well-being because the tuition is high. Alternative or even conjunctive schooling is sometimes provided, usually for boys, in madrasas, in which the object is to memorize the Qur'an.
17 Most Africans, educated and not, learn a number of languages by virtue of the fact that different linguistic groups live in close proximity to one another. Daily interaction requires considerable linguistic flexibility.
18 To acknowledge discomfort and pain of any kind is humiliating to most Fulani (Riesman, 1986; DeLoache & Gottlieb, 2000).
19 I have observed that friends, as well as relatives, are referred to as aunts in the culture from which Ms. A comes.
20 The aunt informed her mother (who did not know because such matters were never discussed!) that it would have been possible to have the procedure done in the hospital, with anesthesia and antibiotics, with much less loss of genitalia and much less pain.

21 Marriages among close relatives are traditional among Fulani (Riesman, 1992), most traditionally among first cousins.
22 I have been told by asylees that the collaborative nature of childcare, in which the mother, or mother-in-law, and the husband's various wives and children help each other, is very much missed in America by women who come here. Once I interviewed a woman who was actually afraid to have children in the United States because she did not know if she could raise them on her own! The expression "it takes a village," is a reality in many parts of the world.
23 This is the Application for Asylum and Withholding of Removal Form, referenced in Chapter One, necessary for asylum applicants to submit, within one year of their arrival here.
24 Again, according to Riesman (1992), such a request is not unusual among Fulani, although it generally occurs earlier in the marital relationship than it did for Ms. A.
25 In a study of women victims of FGM, recently completed in Holland (Vioeberghs et al, 2012, described in more detail in Appendix I), it was found that all of the subjects dissociated during sex. Sometime ago, I myself had, in my practice, a woman who had been severely sexually abused repeatedly as a child and adolescent. At approximately the age of eight, she learned to dissociate. This continued into adulthood, so that dissociating during sex was almost automatic. One of the effects of the work we did in therapy was that she gradually lost this ability, in spite of her ambivalence about doing so (Eisold, 2005).
26 According to Riesman (1998), Fulani culture emphasizes the virtue of overcoming pain.
27 To repeat, this study is described in more detail in Appendix V.
28 Political activist Aryan Hirsi Ali (2007) ascribes the suicide of her sister to a series of humiliating events, beginning with FGM. This sister had to undergo the FGM procedure twice, as a child, because her grandmother deemed the first time insufficiently complete.
29 Among the Fulani, according to DeLoach and Gottlieb (2000) sometimes other nursing mothers, within a single family compound, are enlisted to help in nursing a baby. This was unlikely for Ms. A because her mother was her biological father's only wife.
30 Pictures of this feeding process are available in DeLoach and Gottlieb.
31 This kind of close tie to the mother, as representative, among other things, of the rules of the family, was true of other women in my cohort as well.
32 According to other women I have interviewed, the police in some African countries are often bribed to keep quiet, not only about the performance of FGM, but about sexual and physical abuse. One twenty-seven-year-old woman I interviewed, for example, had been repeatedly raped by her stepfather who informed her that it was hopeless for her to go to the police because they would not listen to her. He had bribed them all to keep quiet. Because she believed him and also because she was ashamed, she kept quiet about the situation until she arrived here.

33 See also Nancy Chodorow (1992).
34 A video of her recent TED talk can be seen at: http://www.ted.com/talks/eleanor_longden_the_voices_in_my_head.html.

References

Akhtar, S. (1995). A third individuation: Immigration, identity, and the psychoanalytic process. *Journal of the American Psychoanalytic Association.*43: 1051–1084.

Akinsulure-Smith, A. M. & Sicalides, E. L. (2016). Female genital cutting in the United States: Implications for mental health professionals. *Professional Psychology: Research and Practice.* 47: 356–362.

Ali, A. H. (2007). *Infidel.* New York, NY: Atria.

Anter, T. (2011). Who are the Fulani people? Retrieved from: http://tariganter.wordpress.com/2011/09/17/who-are-the-fulani-people-their-origins/.

Bandura, A. (2006). Toward a psychology of human agency. *Perspectives on Psychological Science.* I: 164–180.

Benanav, M. (2013). Through the eyes of the Maasi. *New York Times, Travel.* August 11.

Benjamin, J. (2004). Deconstructing femininity: Understanding "passivity" and the daughter position. *Annual of Psychoanalysis.* 32: 45–57.

Benjamin, J. (1995). Sameness and difference: Toward an "overinclusive" model of gender development. *Psychoanalytic Inquiry.*15: 125–142.

Berg, R. C. & Denison, E. (2012). Effectiveness of interventions designed to prevent female genital mutilation/cutting. A systematic review. *Studies in Family Planning.* 43:135–146.

Caston, J. (2011). Agency as a psychoanalytic idea. *Journal of the American Psychoanalytic Association.*99: 907–938.

Chodorow, N. (1992). Heterosexuality as a compromise formation: Reflections on the psychoanalytic theory of sexual development. *Psychoanalysis and Contemporary Thought.* 15: 267–304.

Dalal, K., Lawoko, S., & Jansson, B. (2010). Women's attitude toward discontinuation of female genital mutilation in Egypt. *Journal of Injury and Violence Research.* 2: 41–47.

Cloward, K. (2016). *When Norms Collide: Local Responses to Activism against Female Genital Mutilation and Early Marriage.* New York, NY: Oxford University Press.

Deloach, J. S. & Gottlieb, A. (Eds.). (2000). *A world of Babies: Imagined Child Care Guides for Seven Societies.* New York, NY: Cambridge University Press.

Diop, N. J. & Askew, I. (2009) The effectiveness of a community based education program on abandoning female genital mutilation cutting in Senegal. *Studies In Family Planning.* 40: 307–318.

Dugger, C. W. (2013). Genital cutting found in decline in many nations. *New York Times*. July 23, p.1.

Eisold, B. (2005). Notes on life-long resilience: Perceptual and personality factors implicit in the creation of a particular adaptive style. *Psychoanalytic Psychology*. 22: pp. 411–425.

Franklin, S. & Graesser, A. (1996). Is it an agent or just a program? A taxonomy of autonomous agents.Third International Workshop on Agent, Theories, Architecture, and Language. Springer-Verlag. Retrieved from: http://www.msci.memphis.edu/~franklin/AgentProg.html.

Freeman, W. J. (2001). *How Brains Make up Their Minds*. New York, NY: Columbia University Press.

Frie, R. (2008). Fundamentally embodied: The experience of psychological agency. *Contemporary Psychoanalysis*. 44: 367–376.

Frie, R. (2011). Situated experience and psychological agency: Meaning and morality in worldly contexts. *International Journal of Psychoanalytic Self Psychology*. 6: 340–351.

Gentile, J. (2008). Between public and private: Towards a conception of the transitional subject. *International Journal of Psychoanalysis*.89: 959–976.

Hill, K. & Linden, D. E.-J. (2013). Hallucinatory experiences in non-clinical populations. In K. Jordi, A. Cachia, P. Thomas, & D. Pins (Eds.), *The Neuroscience of Hallucinations*. New York, NY: Springer.

Hornstein, G. (2009). *Agnes' Jacket: A Psychological Search for the Meanings in Madness*. Emmaus, PA: Rodale.

Jeannerod, M. (2001). Neural stimulation of action: A unifying mechanism for motor cognition. *NeuroImage*. 14: S103–S109.

Juarrero, A. (2000). Dynamics in action: Intentional behavior as a complex system. *Emergence*. 2: 24–57.

Modell, A. H. (2008). Horse and rider revisited: The dynamic unconscious and the self as agent.*Contemporary Psychoanalysis*. 44: 351–366. (2009). Metaphor: The bridge between feelings and knowledge. *Psychoanalytic Inquiry*. 29: 6–11.

Mohamed, N. (2014). *The Orchard of Lost Souls*. New York, NY: Farrar, Straus, & Giroux.

Pollock, L. & Slavin, J. H. (1998). The struggle for recognition: Disruption and reintegration in the experience of agency. *Psychoanalytic Dialogues*. 8: 857–873.

Riesman, P. (1986). The person and the life cycle in African social life and thought. *African Studies Review*. 29: 71–138.

Riesman, P. (1992). *First Find Your Child A Good Mother*. New Brunswik, NJ: Rutgers University Press.

Riesman, P. & M. Fuller. (1998). *Freedom in Fulani Social Life: An Introspective Ethnology*. Chicago, IL: Chicago University Press.

Rustin, J, (1997). Infancy, agency, and intersubjectivity: A view of therapeutic action. *Psychoanalytic Dialogues*.7: 43–62.

Slavin, J. H. (2014). "If someone is there:" On finding and having one's own mind. *Psychoanalytic Perspectives*. 11: 23–34.

Vloeberghs, E., van der Kwaak, A., Knipscheer, J., van der Muijsenbergh, M. (2012). Coping and chronic social consequences of female genital mutilation in the Netherlands. *Ethnicity and Health*. 17: 677–695.

Winnicott, D. W. (1971). *Playing and Reality*. London, UK: Tavistock Publications.

Chapter 4

Central American women on the run

Feminicide and its history[1]

Introduction

The past is never dead. It's not even past.
W. Faulkner: From: *Requiem of Nun*

The land is the body. They are equivalent.
Professor Nadera Shadera-Kevorkian,
personal communication, March 26, 2018, Jerusalem

Recently, I have interviewed fifteen asylum-seeking women from the Central American countries of the Northern Triangle.[2,3] I have seen these women in three different settings: in my office in New York City; in the South Texas Family Residential Center in Dilley, Texas,[4] and in the Delaney Hall Detention Facility in Newark, New Jersey. Of these, ten had suffered abuse at the hands of male partners, fathers, or brothers.[5] Five, all without partners, had been seriously threatened by gang violence. Life for women in the Northern Triangle is terrifying. Because of this, in spite of the erratic immigration policies of the United States, many from that part of the world continue to arrive.[6]

In listening to their stories, I have been surprised again and again at the degree of neglect and brutalization these women experienced at the hands of men, day-to-day, all of their lives, in spite of local and international laws which exist to protect them.[7] The accounts of Anna and Maria below exemplify this:

> Anna, a woman of thirty, had been raped by her elder brother three times between the ages of eight and eleven. When her mother threatened to kick him out of the house if he did not stop, he told her that she had no right to do this; only his father could make him leave.

Her mother then took Anna to a doctor, looking for help. He prescribed vitamins. Soon after, to escape her brother, Anna married. Soon after this, her husband left her and their newborn child and moved to the United States. She moved back in with her parents. The brother's abuse of his sister began again. Their father, upon hearing of this, told Anna she should fight back. Finally, Anna fled, taking her child with her, to seek asylum in the United States.

Maria, a married woman, successively beaten and sexually abused by her husband, had left him several times, but inevitably he found her. Finally, the last time this series of events took place, he locked her in a room, telling her that she was his, that he owned her. Then he tried to sell her to his friends in exchange for alcohol. Finally, when he threatened to hit their infant son, she managed to escape, her son in her arms. Knowing that he would find her anywhere she went in her home country, she and the child made their endangered way to the United States.

The commonness of abuse, the extent to which it occurs, the fact that it is more extensive in Central (and other parts of Latin) America than in other parts of the world,[8] may not be known by the women themselves. Certainly it is not fully acknowledged when they label it "machismo." Having grown up accepting patriarchy (a social system in which men are deemed the heads of families) they use the term machismo to describe a wide range of exaggerated, often demanding male behavior, which they have come to perceive as the normal performance of masculinity. The term itself, however, does not specify the violence to which this can lead.

Recently, the extreme violence with which men treat women in Central America (and in Latin America at large) has been labeled "feminicido" by professional researchers (Sagot, 2005, 2013; 2017; Ruhl, 2006; Ladutke, 2013), because so often it leads to death. Although it has existed for years,[9] in the past ten it has become so terrible and has led to an exodus so extraordinary that, in 2013, Antonio Guterres, then UNHCR, published a working paper entitled "Women on the Run,"[10] to alert the world at large about its details.

Feminicide, the *intentional* killing of women, because they are women, describes vast, culture-wide violence.[11] It seems to have emerged from the socialization of men, machos, as individuals whose behavior towards women is so privileged, so uncontained, that it can imply a kind of overarching ownership, which is protected from outside interference and can lead to murder. Such socialization, which must begin early and be accommodated by women, seems to represent what psychoanalyst Lynne Layton (2006) has called "normative unconscious processes." According to her, in spite of their negative effect and/or the ambivalence that some may feel about them, these processes "refer to that aspect of the unconscious that pulls to repeat affect/behavior/cognitive patterns that cause psychic distress to begin with" (p. 269). They represent "the psychological consequences of living in a culture in which many norms serve the dominant ideological purpose of maintaining the power status quo." They "tend ... to idealize certain subject positions and devalue others ... by splitting human capacities and giving them class, race or gender assignments" (p. 268). In this way wider "identity categories," in which, for example, classically male and female qualities/roles might be shared, are closed. Rosa's account of her struggle with her peers in regard to her treatment of her son exemplifies the nature of these "processes."[12]

Rosa and I met in the South Texas Detention Center where she and her nine year old son, asylum seekers from Honduras, were being held illegally by the United States, having completed a journey which she described as "hard: it was very cold; we had little to eat; we slept in caves." A pretty, articulate young woman, Rosa had completed three years of university and had also supported herself as a sales person in her home town. Originally she had come from the countryside, I learned. Her parents were dead. She was the only person in her family who had sought education beyond elementary school.

Her problem, the reason she asked to see someone, she said, concerned her relationship with her son. His father, an uneducated but moderately successful man, had beaten her, and the boy, week after week, while they were still at home. This had been humiliating to her, to say the least, and had also hurt her son. Finally, to escape this brutality, she, the boy, and his aunt (who had been living with them) had daringly moved to an apartment of their own. Soon after, however, the boy's father had broken in. He had thrown their new furniture into the street, claiming he owned it, claiming he owned her as well. Finally (the epitome of humiliation for her, she said) he had shown up at her job on his motorcycle and dragged her outside. There, he had beaten her publicly, leaving her lying wounded on the pavement as he rode off. Her co-workers, none of whom had dared intervene while the battle continued, took her to the hospital at its end. There recovery had been slow, but it had given her the time necessary to make the decision to leave. She knew (she said) that her partner was crazy and that nothing she could do could stop him.

Once she had decided to flee, she continued, her son seemed glad to be going. He would be safe, finally, from his brutal father. However, at the same time, perhaps to hold onto his father and thus to diminish their separation, she speculated, perhaps to overcome the humiliation he had sustained during his father's beatings, he began to play the role of humilator himself. He began using the age-old mechanisms of shame and humiliation to control and manipulate his mother, just as his father had done. When she refused to give him the things he wanted, her boy threatened to tell the other women in the prison about how often she had been the victim of his father's abuse. At age nine, he already knew just how much these stories would humiliate his mother, just how powerful humiliation could be when used by a male of any age to control a woman! Her problem, she said was how to handle this. So far, whenever her son had tried to manipulate her this way, she had not given in. Instead, she had told him that she was proud of what she had done. Coming to America had been a good thing, she had said. She had done it to save them both.

BUT, she wondered, was this the right thing to say? She wasn't sure. Would it be better for him, whom she had deprived of his father and his home, to be able to experience at least *some* "machismo" (the word she used), the power available to the men they knew? *This was the advice the other women in the prison had given her*, but should she, in fact, be giving in to him, or should she not?

At this point, there was a knock on the door and then it opened. Her son, having finished what passed for school in prison for the day, ran quickly into the room and stood directly in front of his mother and glared at us.[13] It looked to me as if he was stationing himself in front of his mother to protect her, in case we should try to hurt her.

In telling this story, Rosa was reporting a real dilemma. Already at the age of nine, her boy was enacting a mode of manipulative abuse by divulging her shame, the shame he knew she had experienced because, at home, he had learned, shame comes to the woman who is abused.[14] In addition, it seemed he had already learned that, as a male, his role was to protect his mother, which role he seemed prepared to play the moment he joined us. However, seemingly in exchange for this, he was demanding that he get from her what he desired, to which he was entitled as a male. Aware of all this, Rosa's fellow inmates, many of whom had also been abused, were apparently so unable to resist the pull of familiar "normative unconscious processes" (Layton, 2006) that they were encouraging her to give in to him and to support what they labeled his "cute" display of "machismo." Rosa, her education notwithstanding,[15] needed me, a credentialed outsider, to reassure her about her right to follow a courageous, alternative path, one which required that she pull herself out of passive submission to brutality in order to assume a larger, more articulated identity which included independent agency and self-protective skills.

The organization of this chapter: Two questions and three parts

In contending with Rosa's situation, I found myself with two large questions:

1 **Male/female relations today:** How did an array of "normative unconscious processes" (Layton, 2006), requiring complete submission on the woman's part, become so powerful that Rosa (and so many others like her) had, before her escape, been forced to occupy the passive position of abused, humiliated partner of an abusive man?
2 **Female compliance and compliance in regard to the raising of children:** What culturally based unconscious processes so constrained the women imprisoned with Rosa that they could come up with no alternative, in regard to raising her son, beyond encouraging her to nurture in him the same "normative unconscious processes" that had victimized them?

In the pages that follow I want to address these questions. First, however, in part one, as a demonstration of the extent of the devaluing attitudes of men towards women, the ways in which the power differential between male and female is maintained, I describe in greater detail just how widespread, hurtful and demeaning is the manner in which women from this part of the world are treated today. Then, in part two, I speculate briefly about history and what it seems to imply in regard to male-female relations today. In part three, against this background I address the two questions above.

Part one: The nature and extent of negative attitudes towards women in Central America

It is well known that although an unusual degree of violence exists in all of Latin America today, it is especially prevalent in Central America. According to one report, Honduras has the highest murder rate in the world and is followed closely by El Salvador and Guatemala (Martinez & Anderson, 2017).[16] Partner abuse and drug related gang violence contribute most to this.[17] There are 50,000–60,000 gang members in El Salvador (population six million) and half a million others who are economically dependent on them.[18] Although gangs target men and children as well as women, they prey disastrously on women. However, it is less gangs than men in their families who seem to do women the most harm (Sagot, 2005).

Indeed, according to sociologist M. Sagot (2005, p. 1293), "the violence executed by men and directed towards women" has been apparent for many years in a surprising number of society-wide interactions.[19] As a result, it has become a serious public health issue. It not only threatens the physical and mental well-being of women, but also the socio-economic development of the respective countries from which they come. In general, however, because this abuse is unacknowledged, it is vastly under-reported.

Sagot's evidence (2005) is based on interviews conducted with women (240–405 in all) over the ages of fifteen, in sixteen communities in ten different Latin American countries, including those Central American countries that are my focus here. In these interviews, not only was abuse documented, but the manner in which it is totally disregarded by society at large was well documented as well.[20] Sometimes, she reports, seemingly gratuitous abuse, had begun in childhood and was connected to what she calls the "authoritarian way" all children in those countries are raised. One woman, for example, told Sagot that her father had hanged her, then aged ten, from a tree because she had eaten a piece of cheese without his permission.

In other cases, abuse had begun with the beginning of sex. Sex seems to give the man a "sense of ownership," she reports. As his violence continued, the man not only injured his partner, but threatened her precious objects and/or to take away her children. Contraception of any sort was (is) often deplored. Even financial support is, at times, denied, a devastating situation because, in Central America, men control most of the land and other resources (Deere & León, 2001). Above all, the most difficult to bear, according to Sagot's interviewees, was the humiliation they experienced as victims, especially when the violence was sexual. Thus sexual violence was the most difficult for Sagot's subjects to report.

Humiliation was also part of the process when women tried to get help from the outside in order to address their injuries. When they revealed these to health-care providers, for example, but did not produce any causal evidence (witnesses, photos, etc.), often their stories were not believed. Indeed, in some places, violence was only recognized as a crime if injuries had taken ten or more days to heal. Often, as a result, the cause of the injury was blamed on the woman herself. In addition, frequently, there did not seem to be protocols in place by which to categorize differing forms of physical abuse, nor any means of following up. Sagot continues:

> This lack of [any treatment protocol] placed women who sought help at a disadvantage when attempting to get what they needed . . . and resulted in re-victimization through indifference, or mocking or at times additional abuse. The persistence of such practices on the part of many of the service providers and in the community at large has led to the generalized perception that family violence does not represent a real danger for women . . . Only a few service providers and community members expressed views outside of the patriarchal conceptions that cast this form of violence as natural . . . and justified or blamed the women . . . [Altogether, this manner of treatment puts] women at greater risk and promote[s] the aggressors' impunity.
> (Sagot, 2005, pps.1304 &1315)

Meanwhile, in countries in which there are laws specifically established to protect women (true, for example, in Guatemala), often the women themselves were/still are unaware that these exist and/or unaware of anyone to help them in tendering their applications. This is still often the case, "even for those with better economic resources and higher levels of education" (Sagot, 2005, p. 1303; Musalo & Bookey, 2013).

As for the police, when the women go to the police, sometimes in tears, "the police tell them not to be irresponsible and waste their time . . . They tell them, 'tonight your man is going to be between your legs again.' In other words, besides not helping them, [the police] disrespect them" (Sagot, 2005, p. 1307).

In those cases in which the law is known to the woman and she resorts to it, she may well find that her precise situation is not covered and/or that the law may be incorrectly applied. In addition, she may be forced to wade through endless paperwork, have little privacy once she meets with someone, or find no personnel available to deal with her problem. In El Salvador the police are associated with repression. In Guatemala, where, according to attorneys Musalo and Bookey (2013), feminicide rates are the highest in the world, no one cares to enforce the specific laws that address family violence.[21] Moreover, there is insufficient free legal counsel for women and little protected shelter in which to hide. For indigenous women (Maya), there are even fewer services because these people tend to live far from cities and often do not speak Spanish.

Above all, according to Sagot, women themselves are ambivalent about taking what she refers to as the "critical path" (presumably because such a path would be critical of present circumstances) away from a culture in which, despite their immense contributions at home, their safety and well-being are dismissed. Thus my client, Rosa, in turning to fellow inmates for their support as she struggled with her son, was fighting a widespread belief system with very deep roots, towards which she herself still felt pulled.

In demonstrating just how widespread is feminicide in Central America and how difficult it is to combat, I find Sagot's contribution especially compelling because she underscores how long it has existed, how little it is being addressed, and how little, as well, women perceive roles for themselves in which they might avoid abuse. However, she does not tell us how, historically speaking, this situation came about. In fact, Central American governments have presumably agreed to uphold international legal codes,[22] systems of law which psychoanalyst Jessica Benjamin might call the "Moral Third," which, according to her, should prescribe an expectancy in the minds of everyone of the idea of a lawful world in which wrongs (violations of rights) can be acknowledged, disruptions repaired, and relationships "put right" (2018, p.117). In Central America, however, despite the fact that such a legal system exists, it does not function as a presence in the minds of all. Thus no one expects it to "put right" violence against women. Why? How has the law that addresses such treatment come to be so overlooked?

These are large questions most of which are well beyond the scope of this book. Nevertheless, based on some exposure to the historical, anthropological, and sociological writings of others, I am going to take the liberty of "get[ting] the kind of facts [I] want," to quote historian E. H. Carr (as cited in Kuriloff, 2013, p. 22). Indeed, since "history means interpretation," as psychoanalyst Emily Kuriloff has pointed out (2013, p. 22), I will take the liberty of interpreting some historical facts to support my contention that, as others have implied (Tylim, 2016, for example), *men* in Central America have experienced shame/humiliation and the feeling of demasculinization again and again, in cultures in which codes of honor, built around the need to avoid feelings of shame and humiliation, have guided their behavior for years. At the same time, their horizons have been vastly limited. Meanwhile, their female partners, while they often shoulder the burden of keeping life going, also have little opportunity. To add to their burden, however, their deeply scarred men often turn upon them, denying them the right to agency of their own. Let me try here to trace this path in more detail.

Humiliation, based on the Latin root word "humus" (Burton, 2014), means dirt. Being treated like dirt implies the presence of a constant feeling of abasement. It implies loss of status, which, in a highly stratified society, as Latin American society is today (Caravallo, 2012) is a crucially demeaning experience. Loss of pride and dignity accompanies loss of status. As psychoanalyst Sam Gerson (2011) describes it, humiliation cuts deep and may be experienced as traumatic. It causes a person to feel excluded from the "benign recognition" of others. In order to save face, humiliated men, according to expert psychiatrists (Gilligan, 1997; Jabr & Berger, 2017, for example), often turn to violence and feel justified in doing so because of their own terrible experiences.

Here, I turn to history in order to better understand which sort of events have transpired in Central America to create, in men, such an all-encompassing experience of humiliation, so all-encompassing that, in order to overcome it, they turn on their women. I begin with the Maya.

Part two: History as background to the creation of "normative unconscious processes" which encompass feminismo

The Maya

Although many different peoples have occupied, indeed still do occupy, Central America, including the Garifuna, the Quiché, and the Mam (Kellogg, 2005), my focus here is on the Maya because, not only were Maya the largest indigenous group in the area when the Spanish arrived in the sixteenth century, but they still are[23] (Lebrun, 2008).[24] According to anthropologist June Nash (2002), gender-related age markers from ancient Maya times (for example, in regard to rites of passage from one stage to the next) are still extant among their descendants.

Very recent laser technology has indicated that, at its height, the Maya may have numbered ten million. They were spread across many miles, in separate communities, and spoke different dialects/languages.[25] In any single community, however, people lived in close proximity to one another in socially stratified fashion, with a king at the pinnacle of an elite group of supporters. The height of Maya civilization lasted from approximately 250–900 AD. Thereafter, the outward spread of communities, as families grew larger, seems to have diminished the power of any single king. Maya culture, which seems to have been family-centered, was strong nevertheless until the arrival of the Spanish.

The Maya had a highly developed, hieroglyphic/iconographic/phonemic written language (Hirst, 2006), which was engraved on steles and other monumental architecture, and written in codexes (books).[26] It was used to record history and myth, later also preserved by scribes, in the Spanish script they learned from clergymen, a tradition that has been passed down across generations and continues today (Lebrun, 2008).[27] It is from these writings and the artifacts preserved in ancient grave sites that a picture of gender roles has emerged (Plumer, 2011).

As a civilization, Maya was, with a few exceptions when no male heir was available, a patriarchal society.[28] Males were hierarchically organized into distinct classes and castes. Although commoners did most of the work and made up ninety percent of the population, description of their lives was apparently not recorded (Marcus, 2004), no doubt because no one believed that they were worth writing about. Community involvement on the part of the elite, in other words, seemed to extend only to those within their group and especially to family members.[29] Members of the elite were appointed and were subservient to their king (Jackson, 2013), who inherited his "right" from his father and was believed to be divine. This divine being was identified with the ruler-god of maize, who was believed to have given the gift of maize to the Maya people, thus making their civilization possible. Maya kings presumably were fierce warriors who, with the assistance of their courtiers, aimed to destroy the power of neighboring rivals, thus humiliating them (Foster, 2002). To demonstrate prowess, Maya kings have been pictured with the heads of those they vanquished hanging from their belts.

The greatest humiliation that could befall an enemy, once he had been conquered, was to be sacrificed to the gods. These always angry gods needed ongoing placation with ritual and sacrifice and the most valuable sacrifice was the blood of defeated male rivals (Sharer & Traxler, 2006). Kings were always trying to satisfy the gods and humiliate their rivals. Meanwhile, day to day, dead ancestors were presumed to be go-betweens, between the angry gods and mortals. In keeping with this, individual family dead were kept nearby; they were buried beneath the floors of peoples' homes, in a ritualistic ceremony befitting the status of the family. Altogether then, this was a culture concretely tied to its land from which came both physical and spiritual sustenance.

Meanwhile, women (elite women) participated in every realm of society, but were perceived by their men as a resource to be controlled (Plumer, 2011). They did not (could not) own property (Foster, 2002). In addition to bearing and rearing children, in largely monogamous relationships, they also wove. Weaving, in general (no single woman was identified as particularly gifted at this), was a highly prized skill because it produced cloth that had considerable trade value (Plummer, 2011). The skill was passed down, in any one family, across generations.[30] In addition, elite women cooked, often competitively, at feasts and rituals. While men harvested foodstuffs in the fields away from home, women remained at home, making the food edible. They also tended deer, an important source of protein, which women ate considerably less of than did their men, again, a sign of their lower status. In spite of all they did, however, as individuals, women seemed to have gained little recognition.

According to one account (Bell, 2002), no single woman is portrayed anywhere in the iconographic texts in Copan, a central Maya city.[31] Childbearing, a very important part of society, probably poorly understood, was nevertheless deemed so important that men seemed to want to absorb, control, and/or emulate it. Indeed some steles that represent men were created with female symbols placed on top of them, seemingly to indicate unity with female power or absorption of it. In addition, men bled their penises in apparent imitation of menstruation (Gustafson & Trevelyan, 2002) and/or to emulate/take in some part of female power, as much as it was understood. Generally, it seems, "individual [female] personality was obscured in favor of a formalized emphasis on their regenerative power," anthropologist Tracey Ardren reports (2002, p. 87).

Altogether then, the ancient Maya were a rather violent, patriarchal society, tied to the land not only through the life-giving maize and other staples they raised, but because the ancestors they worshipped were buried in it, in their homes. Honor was maintained through male aggressive prowess, which was elaborated in the creation of art, legend, and architectural sites. Honor achieved by virtue of male prowess, generalized as the "chosen glory" of the culture (Volkan, 1988), was exaggerated, as an outcome of the shaming and humiliation of defeated males. Indeed, the victor in any competition for honor "finds his reputation enhanced by the humiliation of the vanquished," according to social anthropologist Pitt-Rivers (1966, p. 24). Shame and humiliation were the generalized "chosen trauma" of the culture (Volkan, 1988), intimately tied to honor, because these are what individuals presumably experienced when honor was lost. Again, according to Pitt-Rivers, (1966), this duality (honor versus shame/humiliation) is typical of honor bound societies.

The gifts of women, meanwhile, despite their importance, were subordinated to, blended with, if not even usurped by men, their singularity denied. Clearly, as anthropologist June Nash (2002) reports, Maya ambivalence in regard to women was extensive. In regard to the continuity of culture between then and now, she observes, "The specificity of age-related ritual roles in contemporary Maya communities and in [the ancient] codices is one of the most impressive signs of continuation of culture over time" (p. xi).[32]

The Spanish

The Spanish, a diverse group of variously motivated male invaders, some poor, many illiterate, arrived in Central America in the sixteenth century, accompanied by slaves (Restall, 2003). Representatives of an exceptionally honor-bound European culture (Pitt-Rivers, 1966), the Spanish were looking for riches, the means to support, among other things, wars in Europe. They did their best to decimate the indigenous peoples, Maya and others – family based patriarchal agrarian communities – by forcing them into slavery, abusing, robbing, raping, and slaughtering many, especially their kings. They carried all this out in a manner designed, above all, to be deeply disrespectful and humiliating (Restall, 2003).

With the Spanish came not only a culture of invading violence (Munévar, 2012; Restall, 2003), but also disease, which, by itself, eliminated vast numbers of the original peoples. Equally destructive perhaps, not only were the Spanish convinced of their superiority because they had superior physical strength, but they believed the tenets of Catholicism were the only spiritual truth and they used this belief system to justify their categorization of indigenous groups as heathens, savages, and representatives of the devil, worthy only of immediate death. Those who survived this intent to kill were converted to Catholicism, while traces of their own religion (steles, books) were ruthlessly destroyed. In addition, because the Spanish arrived without partners, indigenous women, perceived as impure, were also forcibly taken, while their (humiliated) men stood helplessly by (Munévar, 2012). Indeed, at the same time as they were categorizing native women as pagans, impious, and seductive, the Spanish were also enjoying female "gifts," (e.g., making women their concubines), thus perhaps fulfilling two needs at once, the projection onto natives of their own presumably "impure" fantasies (Feldman, 2012; Tylim, 2016) and actual physical satisfaction.

Here greater examination of the concept of honor seems appropriate, since it was implicit in both Maya and Spanish cultures. According to Pitt-Rivers (1966), the first to study the subject at length in Andulasia, honor codes came into being there in the fifteenth and sixteenth centuries.[33] Honor was tied closely to personal behavior in medieval and early European societies, but then seemed to disappear when states became stronger, with more centralized codes of behavior determined by kings.

Recently, however, honor codes have reappeared in some communities (Pitt-Rivers, 1966; Stewart, 2013). Honor, these authors tell us, represents not only the value a person places on himself, but also his value to society. Accordingly, effort must be made to gain good repute. During the period in which the Spanish invaded the Americas, honor codes and the behavior they encouraged were well established, for honor is, in fact, fundamental to the idea of kingship and aristocracy. According to Pitt-Rivers:

> Honour pertains to social groups of any size, *from the nuclear family whose head is responsible for the honour of all its members to the nation*, whose members' honour is bound up with their fidelity to their sovereign. In both the family and the monarchy a single person symbolizes the group whose collective honour is vested in his person.
> (1966, p. 35–36, italics mine)

In regard to gender, honor has very specific, rather concrete implications, Pitt-Rivers continues:

> Masculinity means courage ... the concept is expressed as the physical quintessence of the male (cajones) ... Lacking the physiological basis, the weaker sex cannot obviously be expected to possess it. ... On the other hand, female honour is not entirely without a physical basis ... in that sexual purity relates to maidenhead. The male therefore both lacks the physical basis of sexual purity and risks the implication that his masculinity is in doubt if he maintains it; [should this occur] it [will] come ... to mean for him ... exclu[sion] from the popular concept of male honour. The natural qualities of sexual potency or purity and the moral qualities associated with them provide the conceptual framework on which the system is constructed ... It delegates the virtue expressed in sexual purity to the females and the duty of defending female virtue to the males. The honor of the man is involved therefore in the sexual purity of his mother, wife and daughters, and sisters, ... the woman remains with her own respect alleviated [because the man takes it on for her].
> (Pitt-Rivers, 1966, p. 45)

Finally, it is important here to note, still according to Pitt-Rivers, that honor codes have implications in regard to national codes of law. The latter, because they apply to all, are wider, less specifically personal in their application. In the more recent past, personal insults and shaming events were often settled outside of the established legal codes, in duels, even though increasingly these became illegal. Shame and humiliation were often so painful for individuals to bear, and their legal settlement so lengthy, that duels seemed the most immediate way to set things straight. The tradition in which a man takes the law into his own hands, empowering himself to do so, preferring this kind of rule rather than the more widely accepted rules of law, has been, and apparently still is, alive and well in some parts of Andulasia (Pitt-Rivers, 1966). Certainly it came with the Spanish to the new world.[34]

Thus, at least in so far as they were both clearly paternalistic and hierarchal, Spanish culture in the sixteenth to eighteenth centuries was much like the indigenous Maya culture of Central America. Both were also built around personal codes of honor in which male prowess was valued and shame befell the man who failed to attain it. Passivity and submission, meanwhile were split off, to reemerge, among the Spanish, as ideals for women who, as a result, were treated as second-class citizens. Although in the Spanish upper classes women were often idolized as objects of purity and beauty, in actual daily life, as with the Maya, they managed the household work, were subservient to men, and generally went unrecognized for their contributions. Education was available to Spanish women only if they were members of the upper classes, and then it was offered only at home. Education for men, meanwhile, was available in schools, but again only to descendants of the upper classes. These European prejudices were wholly transferred to the new world as women of the upper classes began to arrive and the Spanish truly settled in.[35]

In regard to public life, in accordance with the above, male descendants of the Spanish were considered more suitable as occupants of these roles than were women: "The few women who held public office were the exceptions who prove that strictures of class took precedence over norms of gender in colonial politics," anthropologist I. Silverblatt tells us (1987, p. xxx).

Meanwhile, all throughout Latin America, the progeny of Spanish/Indian relationships, mestizos, their mixed-blood descendants, were, according to psychoanalyst Montecinos (1991), initially despised by both groups. It was they, however, eventually the largest group, who became the worker/artisan class, the laborers who were paid for their services. The explicit nature of these layered social groups reaffirmed the layering that was present in both indigenous (Maya) and Spanish tradition and thus brought about what one researcher has designated as the most rigid class system in the world, equivalent only to that in India. A rigid class system, along with rigidly defined gender roles, further limits the potential for expanded identities. Although unacknowledged, this class system, according to him, has remained (Caravallo, 2012).

Then there were the relationships between Spanish men and their often multiple, frequently abandoned, indigenous female partners. This led to the development of the mother-child-orphan family,[36] for which, in religious symbolization, the Virgin Mary became the model. Meanwhile, the ongoing humiliation of indigenous men continued, for it was their land, their women, and their resources that the Spanish usurped.

In all of this, the Catholic Church was and continues to be central. For women, the figure of the mother abandoned, the virgin mother, Mary, the steadfast attachment figure for her son, was/has become more and more significant and is especially related to machismo (Munévar, 2012), which is explored in greater depth below.

The United States of America: Bananas/Coffee

In the late nineteenth/early twentieth century came still other colonizers, in particular, the United States, the country with the largest investment in agricultural production, especially the production of bananas. Large scale banana growth and exportation were made possible by the industrial revolution, particularly by the building of extensive railroad systems and the creation of better modes of refrigeration on better cargo ships. According to historian McCracken (1998), agricultural colonizers created huge plantations to produce first bananas and later coffee. The history of the upheaval this caused in many countries, including those in the Northern Triangle, is complex.[37] Suffice it to say that, along with bananas, came war, corruption, and enormous change in local communities. Above all, agricultural patterns were drastically altered. Land, on which sense of place and family identity had been based for centuries, was taken away from individual farmers and redistributed unequally. Many farmers were consequently forced to settle elsewhere, in places without great fertility (McCracken, 1998), far from the graves of their ancestors. Many chose to become employees of plantation lords on land which, previously, they had owned, where, every day, they were now exposed to poisonous pesticides. In addition, the workday was long, ten to twelve hours, with no relief, even on Sundays. Many became migrants, who moved from location to location. Since this mode of employment continues, often, today, men live far from home in barracks in which prostitution and alcoholism are common. Because these industries have become so important to the economy of the countries involved, their impact on politics, as well as on human communities, has been great. In addition, because they have taken up so much arable land, many food supplies must be imported. The outcome of all this has not only been a high degree of extreme poverty,[38] but rootlessness and still more humiliation for the men. Too little has been left that they can hold onto.

Machismo: The seeds of feminismo?

The word machismo was probably first used at the end of the nineteenth century (Paredes, 1967, referenced in Ramirez, 2008), around the time that large land masses were lost to farmers because of the arrival of bananas.[39] The word was used then to describe a theme character, a strong man in Mexican folklore, folklore that spread throughout other parts of the Latino world. More recently, machismo has been defined as representative of a "sense of masculine pride so embedded in culture that it is not only accepted, but often expected" (Mendoza, 2009). Sociologist Alfredo Mirandé (1997) believes that it may well have come into being out of a compensatory need, based on what he labels "deep feelings of inadequacy" (Mirandé, 1997, p. 67), which presumably resulted from the effects of successive invasions and the eradication of a more agriculturally based sense of self. More recently, according to writer Octavio Paz, "the macho," has become an individual who is isolated, "closed up in himself." (1961/1994, p. 29) He appears to be guided by a distorted sense of honor about things he imagines are being done to him. According to Paz:

> everything serves [the macho] as a defense: silence and words, politeness and disdain, irony and resignation . . . he is afraid even to glance at his neighbor because a mere glance can trigger . . . rage. . . . He builds a wall of remoteness between reality and himself. . . . Lying plays a decisive role in [his] daily [life].
>
> (Paz, 1961/1994, p. 29)

Use of the word itself first emerged in the countryside (Ramirez, 2008), because it was there that change most affected family-centered communities in which men were implicitly respected as "the guardians, the gatekeepers of their families and their land" (Callahan, 2005, p. 356). In these circumstances, honor, and its opposite, shame, guided male behavior. Callahan tells us:

> If a woman's good name is earned and maintained through her various duties . . . (and the avoidance of the appearance of infidelity), a man's reputation is dependent upon his ability to protect himself and his family from a host of largely financial threats (as well as the appearance of sexual indiscretions on the part of the women in his life).
> (Callahan, 2005, p. 356)

Anthropologist Elizabeth Brusco (1995), in a study of machismo and its effects, describes the macho as a transitional role for men, as they were forced to abandon land-based identities, described by Callahan above, and then to take up less concretely based, multiple identities in new communities. She portrays the machismo as an individual who plays out his "hypersexuality, cuatismo (male camaraderie), violence, risk taking, courage, . . . authoritarianism, and independence" (1995, p. 78) away from the home, in the company of other men, to gain male respect. Machismo is based on personal qualities, an honor code built upon honor codes of the past, but with far fewer concrete means to demonstrate one's prowess other than role play. Such play, appears to be an attempt to fix what psychoanalyst Virginia Goldner (2004) refers to as the "ruin" of the old ideals, ideals with roots reaching into the past, based on honor as the guardian/protector of land and family.

In women, meanwhile, a role complementing machismo emerged at about the same time, in the late nineteenth century. Designated as marianismo, it has had devastating results.

Marianismo, a set of characteristics modeled on idealized qualities presumed to have existed in Mary, the Virgin Mother, requires sacrifice of self to the needs of men, of fathers and brothers, and especially of husbands. Fidelity is implicit here, as indeed it was in older honor codes. Although Latina women may perceive themselves as morally superior to their men as they play this role (Mendoza, 2007), in actuality, they occupy the same drastically inferior social position they have occupied in Central America for ages, in which there is an absence of recognition for their labor, which is exploited, and they must suffer whatever abuse comes their way. They are expected to do all the chores and to bear and care for many children in order to prove their husband's machismo, which at home, is often the absolute law. Above all, the marianismo role is culturally the "normative" one for women (Layton, 2006). The Catholic Church has lent unquestioning support to this division of the sexes by telling women that maintaining the family is more important than their own well-being (Torres, 1987) and by discouraging contraception.

Sometime later, even more devastation unfolded in Central America.

The United States again: Devastating interventions and other events in twentieth-century Central America

Perhaps not surprisingly, in reaction to the devastation of their land, the control exerted on their lives by big industry and government, and the resultant upheavals described above, some peasant groups in Central America began to rebel. These rebellions, which took place in the early to middle years of the twentieth century, induced terrible fear in the United States of spreading Communist influence. Hence, the United States reacted with violence, providing funds to accommodating local governments to train their armies to fight these rebels on the ground and in the air.[40] The CIA, meanwhile, trained on-the-ground elite forces, torture teams in fact, whose only goal was the inspiration of terror.[41] All the while, however, those in the United States government either denied this evil or dissociated themselves from it, in part because it was believed to be necessary for protection of the United States from Communism. As historians Booth, Wade, and Walker describe, in their report:[42]

> U.S. policies [in Central America] . . . at a minimum intensified political conflicts that by the early 1990's had killed over 300,000 people (mainly civilians), nearly ruined the economies of the region and displaced millions, left countless others jobless, orphaned or physically or psychologically maimed. U.S. Policy was by no means the only cause of the Central American tragedy, but it contributed importantly to its onset and evolution. . . . [The] main goal of U.S. policy was to keep as much control as possible over events and policies in Central

America. . . . The presence of US backed rights abusing dictatorships helped spark insurgencies . . . from the 1960's through 1990's.
(Booth, Wade, & Walker, 2006, pp. 169–170)

Adding to the above and creating crises in the late twentieth and early twenty-first centuries in Central America, has been considerable population growth, exacerbated by increasing power disparities between a small upper class, partnered with an also small middle class, and the majority poor. The poor majority has very limited access to education[43] and thus little economic possibility because skills otherwise have been so difficult to come by. As a consequence, adding to the four million Central Americans who are already in the United States,[44] more are arriving every day. As a group, Central Americans are enormously hardworking and resilient, according to historians Booth, Wade, & Walker (2014), and are thus a positive addition to the population of the United States.

However, the ongoing experience of those who have remained at home, as depicted by journalist Oscar Martínez (2017), has included more land loss, loss of family members, and extreme poverty, which together have caused still more deeply humiliating wounds to the development of a positive sense of self, especially to male heads of families. Martínez describes, for example, a peasant who weeps because he feels helpless to have an impact on the desperate circumstances in which his family lives. There are families, he says, tens of thousands of them, who cannot always put food on the table. Partly as cause, partly as result, "today," he reports, "criminal violence has replaced the political violence with levels of bloodshed that come, at times, chillingly close to those of wartime"(2017, Kindle location 71).

Part three: Returning to my questions

Male-female relations today: Machismo to feminismo

I have reviewed history here in order to better understand the roots of abuse of women today as it leads to feminicide in the Northern Triangle of Central America. I have focused on these countries, despite the fact that feminicide is widespread in *all* of Latin America and the Caribbean,[45] because these are the countries from which many of my asylee clients have come.

In reviewing the history of this area, I have pointed to the fact that, in the past four to five hundred years, there have been a series of hugely destructive invasions, disruptive of land ownership, government, and family bonds, with the effect of repeated male humiliation. These occurred in what were originally and continue to be patriarchal, honor-bound societies with rigid class structures, societies in which men have had most of the power and have been, at best, to quote June Nash (2002) "ambivalent" about acknowledging female creativity, uniqueness, and contribution. As is often the case in such situations (Dutton, 2007), spousal abuse has often been accepted as "normal" behavior. I have described the emergence of a new behavioral stance, or identity, for men –the macho - which emerged in response to the industrial revolution/colonial restructuring of work and society as compensation for the more solidly grounded identity of the patriarch, the landholder/farmer/protector of old. I have described the ongoing, present-day absence of easily available basic education for the majority of the population, the poor (male and female) in these countries, as compared with modern countries elsewhere, which makes it difficult for individuals to take advantage of higher educational opportunity, even when it is available. This, along with a population, which, in many places, is increasing in size,[46] affords little choice for adults in regard to work opportunity.

Thus, for the man whose identity has been severely diminished, who feels deeply humiliated by circumstance, the easy power available to him is the power he has at home. Under these circumstances, it is hardly surprising that the more recent national and international legal codes designed to protect women from abuse are not respected or that bribery of the police and legal officials, in the infrequent instances of their involvement, is used to avoid them. Where is the motivation to confront the long-existing "normative unconscious processes" (Layton, 2006) which delineate the tightly determined roles each gender is supposed to play and which give the man total power at home? It is this compound of factors which has put the individual man in the position of determining, himself, how he will behave. Given the unbounded, uncontained nature in which aspects of self such as patriarch (male as head of family), macho (male as alone, defended in his stance of presumed potency), and feminicido (male as a killer of women) can exist in one person, side by side, it is individual personality factors in the man that seem to determine how much, in fact, he will slip from one of these positions to another.

When it comes to understanding such personality factors in men, Erich Fromm (2006) suggests that anger can create a feeling of great power in a person who previously has felt impotent. Given the enormous degree of dishonor/humiliation so many men in Central America must/do experience, as a result of all that has been taken from them, it is not difficult to imagine that, in familial relationships, enormous feelings of impotence can emerge if the man has any fantasy narrative of his own weakness and sees it played out in the behavior of his women. Such a fantasy, for example, might be that his woman (daughter, sister) is trying to control him, cheat on him, steal money from him, shame him in any way, especially by disregarding his will. "People often fail to recognize the deadly chain of events that leads to feminicide," a report by the UN informs us.[47] "An abusive relationship doesn't start with murder, but the abuse escalates and without timely intervention and support, the woman may end up murdered." Violence is even more likely to emerge if such behavior has been modeled for the man by members of previous generations (Dutton, 2007), which in Central America has been the normative case for years. Considering all this, I can understand how a man can commit murder, perhaps in spite of himself. And, on the part of the women in his life, it is easy to understand how they might feel forced to do as he says in order to avoid being killed.

Female compliance and compliance in regard to the raising of children

Women: what bonds, what fears not only keep them tied to the men who abuse them, but make it difficult for them to model other ways of raising their children beyond the male as abuser, the female passively abused?

As a recent report tells us (Nguyen & Martin, 2017) women who stay in abusive relationships do so for a host of practical reasons including: economic worries, family pressure, self doubt, concern for their children, and lack of community support. Added to these, however, are less conscious ties, connected to the potential for loss of deeply held ideals and shame and humiliation of their own, which is shared with the important men in their lives. Elena, an asylum seeker I interviewed, provided an example of the complex interconnectedness of these factors.

I met Elena in a tiny, windowless room in a prison in Newark, New Jersey. A shy, petite, pretty woman, from a northern country in Latin America, educated (BA; MA in business), she had married "late" (at thirty), because singleness was unacceptable to her father. She was the youngest of his five children and his favorite. Although he maintained a certain distance from his children, she felt great pleasure whenever he seemed to show pleasure in her. He thought she was smart, she said, and occasionally told her so. This never happened with her siblings.

In regard to a life outside the family, Elena had few female friends, but she was popular with men and had dated. Only one man, however, had ever wanted to marry her. At first she had disliked this man, but eventually she had convinced herself to love him in order to please her father. To her surprise, this man had met her father's standards because his father had "honored" their country by serving in the military, as Elena's father also had done.[48]

Elena thought her father's "machistic" attitudes (her word) towards his family were based on "pride." His personal honor meant everything to him, she said. Accordingly, his rank in the military had been high and, as a private citizen, he had been a successful (wealthy) business owner/businessman. Although good to her and encouraging of her business skills, he had beaten her oldest brother whenever he seemed to do wrong and had bossed his other children around, insisting that they do as he decreed. In addition, he had yelled regularly at their mother, insisting that, without him, she would never have had a life.

Elena's uneducated, very religious mother, meanwhile, had raised her two daughters to believe that the wife must serve her spouse, regardless of how horrible he was in return. In addition, regularly, every day until they had married, she and her sister were made to pray alongside their mother to the Virgin Mary at the family altar, a routine that Elena despised, but complied with nevertheless. Elena did as she was told because her mother's love seemed to depend on this. When it came to her father, any seeming rebellion made him rage. When this happened everyone suffered.

Despite her mother's apparent obedience, however, perhaps as a reflection of changing times, she had insisted that her daughters, as well as her sons, go to university. To pay for this she had secreted household funds and then begged money from her husband. Although he grumbled over this, the daughters' tuition got paid.

Elena's privileged education notwithstanding, she followed her mother's agenda when it came to marriage. Thus, as her mother advised, she had gone with her fiancé to the United States, where he had found work, and married him there. However, once married, "he turned into a different person," she said. Far less intelligent and less well educated than she, he had reduced her to working as a domestic and taken all of her earnings. He also had begun to beat and sexually misuse her on a regular basis. Although at first she tried, and tried again, to "do better," to please him in every way, she soon realized that nothing was good enough for him. Gradually, the marriage became a loveless, abusive one, in which the abuse caused her shame, so much in fact that she shrank from the thought of asking for help, even from the priest in her Long Island town, whom she had come to love.

A year later, when the couple returned to their home country, Elena was shocked to learn that her older sister had divorced. Her husband, it seemed, had also been an abuser. As a consequence, this sister was no longer welcomed by their father in the family home. Pitying her, Elena wondered how she could bear this state of affairs. In fact, her sister was having quite a hard time.

Meanwhile, Elena's husband continued his abuse. Ever humiliated by the bruises this caused, she hid them beneath her clothes, but her mother, she thought, noticed them nevertheless, without ever uttering a word! In addition, Elena's husband manipulated her in order to secure loans from her well-to-do father, much of which he spent on alcohol. With the rest, following his orders, she opened a business, a food market, in which she worked from dawn 'til dusk, while he boasted about the place and drank. This business, meanwhile, survived because of the ongoing financial help she procured from her father. Knowing how dependent on this they were, her husband never beat Elena on parts of her body that outsiders might see. The fact of her father's wealth, in other words, contained him.

By then the couple were parents of a little girl. As the abuse continued, Elena found herself extremely concerned about the amount of paternal violence and maternal humiliation this daughter was witnessing. The presence of her child seemed to plant in Elena, for the first time, the capacity to observe herself from a perspective different from her father's, one more consciously critical of her own passivity. But still she did not ask for help. To report her suffering to anyone would not only have been humiliating for her, she said, but would have humiliated her father, as well. For years, this man had presented himself to other men as a wealthy patriarch with a large obedient family. The thought that he might be perceived otherwise was inconceivable to him. Abandoning her, she knew, would have been easier for him than this. Her mother, she knew, would have followed his lead. The idea of relinquishing parental support and moving out on her own opened up an unknown chasm for Elena, a place in her imagination into which she was afraid she literally could fall. Its hollow bottomless, emptiness made her afraid, afraid of going crazy. In letting herself become consumed with this fear, she completely obliterated any thought about her own quite extensive personal resources. They ceased to be useful to her.

Then suddenly, unexpectedly, in a car accident, her father had died. Elena's response, a surprise to her, was a feeling of utter liberation. Once he was dead, she told me, she could no longer strive for his positive regard. Nor would she humiliate him or be abandoned by him if she divorced. This feeling was wonderful.

Immediately following her father's death, however, her husband's abuse accelerated. He knew, she thought, that she would try to free herself from him, but if she died, he would inherit her father's estate. Indeed, his abuse became so severe that she seriously began to think he would kill her. Thus, over the following months, she tried to hide from him in various other parts of the country, leaving her daughter behind with her mother, taking work with her, but he succeeded every time in uncovering her whereabouts and following her. Finally, upon finding her, he beat her so badly that, once he had left, neighbors took her to the hospital, where she remained for some time. Realizing then that he would not let her escape, Elena decided to leave the country. To her surprise, her mother supported this decision and provided the funds for the trip. Rapidly, therefore, Elena made her way to the United States. Once here, she applied for political asylum from the prison site in which she was placed. Once her case was granted, her mother brought her daughter to live with her.

In considering her future, Elena told me spontaneously that once settled in the United States, she hoped to find a partner with whom it would be possible to have a non-abusive relationship. But, she said, given her background she did not know if she could judge which man would and which man would not be an abuser. Her attorney, with whom she had discussed this dilemma at some length, had suggested psychotherapy as possibly helpful in figuring this out. Our interview ended with a discussion of psychotherapy, in regard to the ways it might or might not help Elena reach her goal.

In describing her father and the hold he had on her, Elena's use of the word "machismo" seemed to cover many intimate details of his behavior and its implications for her. It hid the hard work her father did to protect his honor, the apparent essence of his "machismo," which was based on the identity he had created for himself as the wealthy patriarch of a large, productive family. She herself seemed to honor him for this and to want to assist him in his desire to present himself to the world as a man of wealth, with an orderly family at home. As insurance against shame, should any "order" be lost, her father policed everyone rigidly. He also clung to the "order" represented by the military. This too contributed to his feelings of security about himself. Indeed, Elena's father seemed a perfect illustration of the typical "macho" described by Octavio Paz (1961/1994), as a person who clings to "form or . . . formalities [which] are very apt to become formulas . . . [in which] order . . . brings security and stability" (p. 32–33) regardless of the sacrifice this requires of everyone it affects.

Elena, meanwhile, despite her good education, seemed unable to strike out on her own until her father was no longer in the picture. Her behavior seemed determined by a number of factors, many "normative unconscious processes" (Layton, 2006), many infused with fear. These factors, which appear as the rules which govern behavior, are commonly held in her part of the world by many and make it very difficult for women to break free and learn to perceive themselves as in possession of a more personally organized sense of agency. I have listed some of these below as they seemed evident first in Elena and then in Rosa, the woman I described earlier in this paper. These two are two among many from their part of the world who display varying combinations of a group of "normative unconscious processes" (Layton, 2006) which are prevalent in the culture from which they come.

a) **Fear of the loss of the ideal of masculinity, the "split-off" notion of perfection** (Brady, 2017): In Elena's case, this ideal was embodied for Elena by her father. Indeed, in her culture men are perceived as all-powerful protectors in a brutal world with few ideals other than those implied by personal honor and, by extension, the purity and honorableness of their women. The opposite of such honor, personal shame and humiliation, were, in Elena's case, anathema to her father. Indeed, Elena seemed merged with her father in this regard. In her mind, her humiliation (were she to admit that she was being abused, for example) was equivalent to his and (presumably) vice versa. In other words, she seemed to have "lost" herself (Bragin, 2007) in her identification with her father's idealized power and his potential for deep humiliation. In preserving this merger, she minimized her own reaction to the physical pain she regularly experienced at the hands of her husband. This continued until her own daughter was old enough to observe the goings on between her parents. It was only then that Elena could begin to think about the future, the future beyond her father's lifetime. Only then could Elena begin to think of the need to model, for her daughter, a woman who stands up for herself.

In Rosa's case, the notion of male perfection, I presumed, existed in her partner's mind. I am presuming that he believed in the ideal of himself as the all-powerful male and that this belief encompassed Rosa, to whom he referred as his property. She was his and therefore could be used by him as he pleased. However, perhaps because of the education she had received, she had gradually come to think otherwise, to have and be able to keep her own mind. Thus, she wanted to refuse "machismo" and the humiliation it/he had thrust upon her and then to act on these feelings. This wish became especially strong when her partner became "crazy," as she put it, and his power to abuse took over. But even then she was not absolutely certain that she was doing the right thing in breaking the chain of "machismo" as she was raising her son. In taking up an alternate way to behave, which included belief in her own ideas/self-respect, she sought and found in me, the credentialed outside authority, the support she seemed to need to confirm her. Change, challenged by her son, was difficult for her indeed.

b) **Fear of the loss of the patriarch's recognition:** Elena's fear of the loss of her unique, very special place in her father's eyes, as a person of intelligence and capability, was the only real recognition she had ever known. She needed this recognition to feel positively about herself. As Jessica Benjamin (1988) describes it, the need for recognition by the "loved protector" is "elemental" (p. 117). Should he have abandoned her, Elena would have felt annihilated. All of her success in the world (at school, in business, as a wife and mother) had taken place to please him. Losing this would have meant leaping into the unknown, a space which she feared, perhaps because it felt bottomless, even insane. Until the birth of her daughter nothing had mattered more than her father's recognition.

Rosa's need for recognition from her partner seemed less pressing than Elena's in regard to her father, but here I hazard a guess that, once she began university studies, her needs in this regard, whatever they had been before, lessened. Certainly, once he tried to destroy the home she and her sister had created on their own and then dared to beat and humiliate her in public, it became clear to her that his recognition, if it was possible at all, was not for traits (submission the first among them) for which she herself any longer wished to be recognized. Rosa had moved on. For many other women, however, women with fewer opportunities than Rosa had, recognition from a partner may be the only manner of recognition they can imagine. In addition to this, without his protection they may feel vulnerable to the predations of other men or to gang violence.

c) **Fear of the loss of the patriarch's** more concrete, very real protection, evidenced first by virtue of **his financial help/support and** then by **the protection felt** as a member of his family from the criticism of others and possibly also f**rom the unwanted attention/potential violence of other men:**[49] Elena's fate, had she divorced, would have been an uncertain financial future and the potential for gang violence or rape or the possibly less threatening ongoing sexual attention of other men. As her father's married daughter, she did not have to worry about any of these. Her divorced sister apparently did.

Rosa was also protected from the incursions of other men during the time she was living with her partner.

d) **Fear of the loss of her mother's affection**/protection as well as her father's: for her mother, in turn, also seemed merged with him in her willingness to support his ideals/demands, even if it meant abandoning her children.

e) **Fear of having to make it on her own in the outside world, supporting herself:** In Elena's case, in spite of her good intelligence and good education, she did not seem to have much of an idea of how she would go about supporting herself. Work in the grocery store, which she had opened with her husband and which her father subsidized, would have been unavailable to her. She seemed to lack the confidence to strike out at all on her own economically.

In contrast, Rosa and her sister (also employed) were able, together, to support themselves, but her partner would not allow this. Presumably, he wanted their earnings for himself.

f) **Lack of any palpable awareness of the existence of an effective "Moral Third" (Benjamin, 2018), e.g., of an over-arching, universal code of laws, respected by all** which might help them address their respective situations and offer a means of repair: A code such as this exists beyond the scope of a personal honor code in that it is designed to apply to all citizens of a country, regardless of gender or status. In contrast, diminished identities/possibilities, such as those that exist in honor-bound societies, cut out awareness of broader possibilities for justice, even when they exist. Thus, as far as I know, it did not occur to either Elena or Rosa that laws might exist in regard to their need to protect themselves from their partners, because neither had ever witnessed the success of the law in a situation in which normative expectations were based on faith in the male's personal sense of honor. Thus the only reliable escape from this situation, they believed, was to leave.

g) **Lack of willingness to avail themselves of any on-the-ground psychosocial service that might have helped them contend with their husband/partner**: Apparently, for Elena to have sought such services would have meant an acknowledgement of her suffering, which would have been too humiliating to bear. Furthermore, if Sagot's research, described above, is correct, professional help for either Elena or Rosa would, in all likelihood, have offered little beyond dismissal or further humiliation. Thus any kind of search to find decent, respectful, confidential counseling services was apparently never considered by either woman.

Routes to a less threatened future for the sake of the children and for themselves

Long ago, psychoanalyst Therese Benedek (1959), described "parenthood as a developmental phase." In language heavy with Freudian theory, less popular now than it was then, she pointed out a fact that seems undeniable, regardless of time or the theory to which one subscribes. As a parent, one is forced to review one's own childhood, and the parenting one received then is the model of parenthood that lives within each of us, however much it gets revised in the reliving.

Both Rosa and Elena wished to change things for their children. Neither wished her child to grow up with a mother who sustained the ongoing pain and humiliation of abuse. Partially motivated by this desire, Elena eschewed the path her mother had taken in relation to her father as much as the one she herself had occupied with her husband.

Similarly, Rosa, raising a son, recoiled at his attempt to humiliate her. She did not want him to occupy the position his father had occupied in abusing and humiliating her. She did not want to be abused and humiliated herself. For both women the first step towards the lives they desired was secured by leaving home to seek an environment in which the law is respected as a means of protection of women against men and of men against their own uncontained urges to violate, when these exist. Their determination was typical of the women (and sometimes the men) I have interviewed who came from their part of the world. However, the struggle to overcome patriarchy and the grip of honor codes that are historically, culturally, individually determined is complex and often requires help from those other orientations. Let us hope they can find the help they may need.

Notes

1 I am grateful for the guidance of Philip Boxer, Ph.D., in the organization of this chapter.
2 A list of languages spoken in the countries of the Americas is available at: http://www.nationsonline.org/oneworld/american_languages.htm . According to this source, in Guatemala alone twenty-three Amerindian languages are spoken, including Quiché, Mam and Garifuna by people who speak nothing else (Booth, Wade, & Walker, 2014). Central America is apparently the most difficult linguistic area to parse, in terms of what is a language and what a dialect, according to linguist Campbell (1997). Guatemala is probably the incubator of the original Maya languages, which apparently have many dialects.
3 Central America, in all, is made up of seven countries, Belize, Costa Rica, El Salvador, Guatemala, Honduras, Nicaragua, and Panama.
4 I worked in this prison for a week in August 2015, and again briefly in August, 2018.
5 As this chapter is being written, the United States government is threatening to remove domestic violence from the list of justifiable grounds upon which to seek asylum. See: https://cis.org/Cadman/Asylum-Law-Not-Intended-Domestic-Violence for more about this.
6 Statistics on this subject can be found at: https://www.migrationpolicy.org/article/frequently-requested-statistics-immigrants-and-immigration-united-states#CurrentHistoricalNumbers.
7 Information on the subject of international law specifically addressed to the rights of women is at: http://www.ohchr.org/Documents/Events/WHRD/WomenRightsAreHR.pdf. This document reports that, although presumably women's rights have been guaranteed for some time by UN human rights conventions, it was not until 1994 that the Organization of American States adopted a set of laws specifically addressing the prevention, punishment, and eradication of violence against women in Central America.
8 More about this is available at: http://www.who.int/reproductivehealth/publications/violence/9789241564625/en/

9 Feminicide exists in other parts of Latin America as well, as described on NPR at: https://www.npr.org/sections/goatsandsoda/2016/03/19/469932998/what-did-you-expect-the-question-that-women-are-sick-of-hearing.
10 At: http://www.unhcr.org/publications/operations/5630f24c6/women-run.html.
11 Because feminicide is widespread in *all* of Latin America and the Caribbean. The UN, aware of this, has an initiative against it, including the creation of law, education, etc. about it. Sixteen countries have apparently signed up to it. Change, however, is slow. For more on this see: http://www.unwomen.org/en/news/stories/2017/2/take-five-adriana-quinones-femicide-in-latin-america.
12 An earlier version of this case was first presented on the website, Public Seminar, a publication of the New School of Social Research, as "Dilley in retrospect: Machismo and lasting emotional injury," Part II, Barbara Eisold – March 21, 2016. It is reprinted here with their permission.
13 There were two of us present besides Rosa, myself and my interpreter, Ms. Beatriz Tapiz. I am not sufficiently fluent in Spanish to get all its nuances.
14 Sagot's findings described below (2005) lucidly describes this.
15 According to a recent (2016) report from Vanderbilt University (at: https://www.vanderbilt.edu/lapop/insights/IO927en.pdf) education lessens acceptance of spousal violence in Latin America, but by no means eliminates it.
16 See Los Angeles Times at: http://www.latimes.com/opinion/op-ed/la-oe-muggah-latin-america-violence-20170822-story.html for more on this.
17 There is no universally recognized definition of a gang under international law. In its *Guidance Note*, the UNHCR advises that a gang is: 1. A street-based group of young people for whom crime/violence are integral parts of their identity; 2. An organized criminal group for whom crime is for personal gain; 3. A vigilante type group involved in criminal activities. For more on this and on the manner in which gang related asylum claims are made see UNHCR guidelines at: http://www.unhcr.org/en-us/gang-resources.html. A further UNHCR resource is at: http://www.refworld.org/docid/4bb21fa02.html. Finally Gayla Ruffer, J.D., at The Center for Forced Migration Studies at Northwestern University (g.ruffer@northwestern.edu), is a good resource.
18 Central American gangs are transnational: they were originally formed in the United States by immigrants from Central America, who fled, especially from El Salvador, during the wars that raged there in the twentieth century. As MS-13 and other gangs became more dangerous in California, members were exported to their countries of origin. Gangs are attractive to young men, even to children, who have been brutalized at home and have no opportunity for education. For more on this see: Arana, 2005; Quirk, 2008; Brenneman, (2011). There is an excellent NPR (Fresh Air) podcast on the subject at: https://www.npr.org/2018/02/15/585937834/trump-uses-ms-13-to-sell-draconian-overhauls-of-border-issues-journalist-says. The journalist interviewed on the program, Jonathan Blitzer, believes that 60,000 is a small number, relative to population of El Salvador, and could be dealt with, were the government willing.

19 For a more recent analysis of data in regard to Sagot's report see Bott, Guedes, Goodwin & Mendoza, 2013.
20 Sagot's findings, including the fact that many abused women look outside for help but do not find it, have been more recently (2017) supported by a UN report available at: http://www.unwomen.org/en/news/stories/2017/2/take-five-adriana-quinones-femicide-in-latin-america.
21 According to a recent editorial in the *New York Times*, we too have difficulty enforcing laws related to gender violence. More about this is at: https://www.nytimes.com/2018/02/08/opinion/trump-porter-abuse-women.html?em_pos=small&emc=edit_ty_20180209&nl=opinion-today&nl_art=3&nlid=643 17041&ref=headline&te=1.

For more information on human rights laws which address these issues see: http://www.ijrcenter.org/regional/inter-american-system/#gsc.tab=0. For laws that apply specifically to women, see: https://www.thedialogue.org/blogs/2015/12/protect-womens-rights-hold-latin-american-governments-accountable/.
22 International legal codes are based on law as it is understood in the West. The major difference between Western and Islamic legal codes, as I understand them, is that the former are based on agreements between human beings about the nature of "real" events, as they have happened in the past. In contrast, the latter is based on "revelation" and is generally interpreted in the moment by "experts." My source here is attorney Efrahim Afsah at: https://www.coursera.org/learn/muslim-world).
23 Other groups were also present when the Spanish arrived, including the Cuzcatlecs, the Lanca, and later the Nahua (Aztecs). However, since the Maya civilizations were the major ones, and since, according to Lebrun (2008), six million Maya descendants remain. I am focusing here on them.
24 There are presently 300,000 Garifuna in Central America (information is at: http://globalsherpa.org/garifunas-garifuna/). I am including their numbers here because one of the women I interviewed was Garifuna and was very proud indeed to be so.
25 For more about this see: https://www.nytimes.com/2018/02/03/world/americas/mayan-city-discovery-laser.html.
26 The Aztecs, largely in Mexico, did not have a phonetic script, as did the Maya, and thus they wrote down less. See more at: http://www.mexicolore.co.uk/aztecs/spanish-conquest/the-aztecs-are-back.
27 Lebrun, D (Director). *Breaking the Maya Code.* For more on this at: https://www.amazon.com/Breaking-Maya-Code-David-Lebrun/dp/B01AVJ3L6E/ref=sr_1_1?s=movies-tv&ie=UTF8&qid=1517760837&sr=1-1&keywords=breaking+the+maya+code&dpID=61Pi%252BV5jSBL&preST=_SY300_QL70_&dpSrc=srch.
28 An apparent exception to this was Toniná, a matriarchy, in which a queen ruled after the failure of two male heirs (Bell, 2002).

29 This aspect of culture seems to have continued today. As anthropologist R. K. Callahan points out (2005), life is hard in communities of Maya today and when this is the case (as it certainly was more so a thousand years ago) the care one can extend to others is limited.
30 This tradition still continues, as was made clear to me by the Guatemalan asylee I interviewed, a speaker of Quiché, described in Chapter One.
31 Copan is a very large Maya archeological site, in Honduras, which has been reconstructed.
32 An additional and fascinating example of the continuation of ancient Maya culture is described by anthropologist Daniel Núñez (2018) in an article entitled "Conceptions of shame in Maya law." This article describes an attempt to reinstate shame (*verguenza*), which was an integral part of the earlier Maya system of justice, into Maya culture today, in Santa Cruz del Quiché, among other places. Núñez describes the reconstruction of this apparently judicial norm as a project, which is ongoing and contentious because of disagreement over its implications. In these societies, let me also underscore, the preservation of the family is valued much more than is the preservation of the community (Callahan, 2005).
33 A recent paper on the presence of honor codes in Spain today has been published by the European Union and can be found at: http://hasp-project.eu/wp-content/uploads/2017/05/HRV-in-Spain.pdf.
34 Honor, the word/concept, according to Pitt-Rivers, is present still in the Spanish code of law, whereas it is not in its Anglo-Saxon equivalent. Unfortunately, he does not tell us exactly where they appear.
35 An example of female subjugation in Mexico (also subjected to Spanish invasion and its accompanying patriarchy) is Sor Juana (1651–1695) a brilliant woman who became a nun because she believed that this would allow her access to writing and study, which she desired passionately. However, the prelates of the local church, based on rulings from Spain, forbade her this freedom because she was a woman. Had she continued to write the plays and poetry for which she had become famous, she was promised death by the Spanish Inquisition. A recent online course at edX (at: https://www.edx.org/course/seducciones-de-sor-juana-mexicox-sdsj01x) describes her journey. Under this pressure she renounced her studies in 1694 and died the next year. There is a movie about this woman, *Sor Juana Inés de la Cruz* (available on Netflix in the United States at the time of writing).
36 Designated as such by anthropologist Sonia Montecino (1991/2017).
37 Detailed accounts are available at: http://www.csuchico.edu/~sbrady/355 bananahistory.htm. In addition, there is an excellent account with a fine reference list by C. McCracken (1998) at: http://members.tripod.com/foro_emaus/BanPlantsCA.htm. I have relied on this for most of the information in the section above.
38 One resource reports half to two thirds of the population lives below the poverty line in Central America. See: https://borgenproject.org/poverty-in-

central-america/ More about this is at: http://www.ticotimes.net/2013/06/24/central-america-remains-the-poorest-region-in-latin-america-despite-success-reducing-extreme-poverty.

39 In regard to the effect of losing their land on farmers, a recent article in the New York Times quotes the wife of a farmer in Simpson, Australia, who was about to lose his land and so killed himself, as follows: "When a farmer is looking down the barrel of having to sell his farm . . . or give up the profession he'd done all his life, it's devastating. . . . They just lose their identity." Wife of farmer who killed himself in Simpson Australia. *New York Times*, May 21, 2018 at: https://www.nytimes.com/2018/05/20/world/australia/rural-suicides-farmers-globalization.html.

40 See Booth, Wade, & Walker (2006) for more about this. In addition, reliable chronologies, reports about devastations in each of the countries in the Northern Triangle in regard to war there in the past forty years are available, respectively, at: Guatemala: https://www.pbs.org/newshour/health/latin_america-jan-june11-timeline_03-07. El Salvador: https://cja.org/where-we-work/el-salvador/. Honduras: http://www.bbc.com/news/world-latin-america-18974519.

41 A horrifying example of this is reported by an American nun, Sister Dianna Ortiz. She was picked up in Guatemala, in 1989, by special forces, trained by an American CIA agent (whom she met), and tortured mercilessly for twenty-four hours. Her release came about only because, once she had gone missing, her photo was in all the newspapers. In 2005, she told her tale for a human rights investigation, on video at Democracy Now at: testimony:https://www.democracynow.org/2005/10/12/sister_dianna_ortiz_details_her_abduction. Her book (Ortiz, 2002) is, among other things, a detailed account, not only of the torture to which she was subjected but of the steps she took towards recovery.

42 A less nuanced report is Noam Chomsky's (1985/2015, location 211). "No region of the world has been more subject to US influence over a long period than Central America and the Caribbean," he writes, an "influence," that, according to him, has successively created "horrors" for peasants, which:

> began in the late Carter years, then escalat[ed] sharply under Reaganite brutality . . . The first major massacre of peasants, at Rio Sumpul, took place in May 1980 (145). It was noteworthy not only because of the scale and character of the atrocities, but also because it was a joint operation of two terrorist armies supported by Washington, the armies of Honduras and El Salvador . . . The region is one of the world's most awful horror chambers, with widespread starvation, semi-slave labor, torture and massacre by US clients. Virtually every attempt to bring about some constructive change has been met with a new dose of U.S. violence, even when initiated by Church-based self-help groups.

43 According to one source (Navin, 2004), education continues to be offered largely to light skinned men – the elite – who are presumed to be descendants of the Spanish. It is, she says, "seen as an elite right, more than a human right." (p. 2). The World Bank, in 2017, assessed access to education in Latin America as a whole. Although, according to them, its availability is increasing, there is not a great deal of access still for the poor, in part because early education is inadequate. More about this can be found at: http://blogs.worldbank.org/education/crossroads-higher-education-latin-america-and-caribbean.
44 These are people who fled either dictatorships in the 1980's or earthquakes. More about this is available at: https://www.migrationpolicy.org/article/central-american-immigrants-united-states.
45 More on this is at: http://www.unwomen.org/en/news/stories/2017/2/take-five-adriana-quinones-femicide-in-latin-america.
46 Statistics are at: https://www.indexmundi.com/facts/indicators/SP.POP.GROW/map/central-america.
47 This is a quote from a UN report at: http://www.unwomen.org/en/news/stories/2017/2/take-five-adriana-quinones-femicide-in-latin-america.
48 Serving in the military, in the country from which Elena comes, implies an on-going commitment to the government in charge and thus often to incredibly cruel treatment of any group that threatens/threatened it. It also indicates a probable openness to corruption.
49 To repeat, it is often women without partners who are set upon by gangs.

References

Arana, A. (2005). How street gangs took Central America. In *Foreign Affairs*. Retrieved from: https://www.foreignaffairs.com/articles/central-america-caribbean/2005-05-01/how-street-gangs-took-central-america.

Ardren, T. (Ed.). (2002). *Ancient Maya Women*. New York, NY: Walnut Creek.

Bell, E. E. (2002). Engendering a dynasty: A royal woman in the Margarita Tomb, Copan. In T. Ardren (Ed.), *Ancient Maya Women* (pp. 89–104). Walnut Creek, CA: Altamira Press.

Benedek, T. (1959). Parenthood as a developmental phase: A contribution to libido theory. *JAPA*. 7: 389–417.

Benjamin, J. (1988). *The Bonds of Love*. New York, NY: Pantheon.

Benjamin, J. (2018). How therapy with victims of political trauma repairs the third – Commentary on Gómez and Kovalsky's work in the context of postdictatorship Chile. *Psychoanalytic Dialogues*. 28: 115–121.

Booth, J. A., Wade, C. J. & Walker, T. W. (2014). *Understanding Central America: Global Forces and Change*. 6th edition. New York, NY: Routledge.

Bott, S., Guedes, A., Goodwin, M., & Mendoza, J. A. (2013) Summary report: Violence against women in Latin America and the Caribbean: A comparative analysis of population-based data from 12 countries. Washington, DC: PAHO.

Brady, M. (2017). Afflictions related to "ideals" of masculinity: Gremlins within. *Contemporary Psychoanalysis*. 53: 196–208.

Bragin, M. (2007). Knowing terrible things: Engaging survivors of extreme violence in treatment. *Clinical Social Work Journal*. 35: 229–236.

Brusco, E. (1995). *The Reformation of Machismo: Evangelical Conversion and Gender in Colombia*. Austin, TX: University of Texas Press.

Brenneman, R. (2011). *Homies and Hermanos: God and Gangs in Central America*. New York, NY: Oxford University Press.

Burton, N (2014). The psychology of humiliation. *Psychology Today*. Retrieved from: https://www.psychologytoday.com/blog/hide-and-seek/201408/the-psychology-humiliation.

Campbell, L. (1997). *American Indian Languages*. New York, NY: Oxford.

Callahan, R.K. (2005). Doubt, shame and the Maya self. *Dissertation Abstract*. University of Pennsylvania. AA13197654.

Caravallo, E. (2012). Latin America: A region split by its cultural complexes. In: P. Amezaga; B. Barcellos, A. Capriles, J. Gerson, & D. Ramos (Eds.), *Listening to Latin America: Exploring Cultural Complexes in Brazil, Chile, Colombia, Mexico, Uruguay, and Venezuela*. New Orleans, LA: Spring Journal Books.

Chomsky, N. (1985/2015). *Turning the Tide: U.S. Intervention in Central America*. [Kindle version]. Retrieved from www.amazon.com.

Deere, C. D. & León, M. (2001). *Empowering Women: Land and Property Rights in Latin America*. Pittsburgh, PA: University of Pittsburgh Press.

Dutton, D. G. (2007). *The Abusive Personality*. New York, NY: Guilford.

Feldman, B. K. (2012). The cut skin in Latin America. In P. Amezaga, B. Barcellos, A. Capriles, J. Gerson, & D. Ramos (Eds.), *Listening to Latin America: Exploring Cultural Complexities in Brazil, Chile, Colombia, Mexico, Uruguay and Venezuela*. New Orleans, LA: Spring Journal Books.

Foster, L. (2002). *Handbook to Life in the Ancient Maya World*. New York, NY: Oxford.

Fromm, E. (2006). *The Art of Loving*. New York, NY: Harper.

Gerson, S. (2011). Hysteria and humiliation. *Psychoanalytic Dialogues*. 21: 517–530.

Gilligan, J. (1997). *Violence: A Reflection on a National Epidemic*. New York, NY: Vintage.

Goldner, V. (2004). When love hurts: Treating abusive relationships. *Psychoanalytic Inquiry*. 24: 346–372.

Gustafson, L. & Trevelyan, A. (2002). *Ancient Maya Gender Identity and Relations.* Santa Barbara, CA: Praeger.

Hirst, K. K. (2006). Maya writing got early start. *Science.* Retrieved from: https://www.sciencemag.org/news/2006/01/maya-writing-got-early-start

Jackson, S. E. (2013). *Politics of the Maya Court: Hierarchy and Change in the Late Classical Period.* Norman, OK.: Oklahoma University Press.

Jabr, S. & Berger, E. (2017). Trauma and humiliation in the occupied Palestinian territory. *Arab Journal of Psychiatry.* 28: 154–159. (doi: 10.12816/0041719).

Kellogg, S. (2005). *Weaving the Past.* New York, NY: Oxford University Press.

Kuriloff, E. A. (2013). *Contemporary Psychoanalysis and the Legacy of the Third Reich.* New York, NY: Routledge.

Ladutke, L, (2013). Why does Guatemala have one of the highest rates of feminicide in the world? *Amnesty International Human Rights Now Blog* Retrieved from: https://blog.amnestyusa.org/americas/why-does-guatemala-have-one-of-the-highest-rates-of-femicide-in-the-world/.

Layton, L. (2006). Racial identities, racial enactments and normative unconscious processes. *Psychoanalytic Quarterly.* 75: 237–269.

Lebrun, D. (Director), Guthre, R. (Producer). (2008). *Breaking the Maya Code.* (Documentary). Night Fire Films. Retrieved from www.amazon.com.

McCracken, C. (1998). The impacts of banana plantations on development in Central America. Retrieved from: http://members.tripod.com/foro_emaus/BanPlantsCA.htm.

Marcus, S. J. (2004). Maya commoners: The stereotype and the reality. In J. C. Lohse & F. Valdez Jr. (Eds.), *Ancient Maya Commoners* (pp. 255–284). Austin, TX: University of Texas Press.

Martinez, O. & Anderson, J. L. (2017). *A History of Violence: Living and Dying in Central America.* New York, NY: Penguin Random House.

Mendoza, E. (2009). Machismo literature review. Center for Public Safety Initiatives, Rochester University. Working paper #2009-12. Retrieved from: Rochesterhttps://www.rit.edu/cla/criminaljustice/sites/rit.edu.cla.criminaljustice/files/docs/WorkingPapers/2009/2009-12.pdf .

Mirandé, A. (1997). *Hombres y Machos: Masculinity and Latino Culture.* Boulder, CO: Westview.

Montecino, S. A. (2017). *Madres y Hauchos: Alegorías del Mestizaje Chileno.* Santiago, Chile: Catalonia. (Original work published 1991).

Musalo, K. & Bookey, B. (2013). Crimes without punishment:An update on violence against women and impunity in Guatemala *Hastings Race and Poverty Law Journal.* 10: 265–292. Retrieved from: https://cgrs.uchastings.edu//sites/default/files/

Munévar, M.C. (2012). In the shadow of the Virgin Mary. In P. Amezaga, B. Barcellos, A. Capriles, J. Gerson, & D. Ramos (Eds.), *Listening to Latin America: Exploring Cultural Complexes in Brazil, Chile, Colombia, Mexico, Uruguay, and Venezuela* (pp.153–168). New Orleans, LA: Spring Journal Books.

Nash, J. (2002). Introduction. In Ardren, T. (Ed.), *Ancient Maya Women* (Preface). New York, NY: Walnut Creek.

Navin, C. (2004). Female education in Honduras: The creation of a community of congruence for women. Retrieved from: http://www.macalester.edu/education-reform/reformcomposition/CinthiaSR.pdf.

Nguyen, B. & Martin, S. (2017). Eliminate that seven times statistic: How to stay away for good. BTSADV. Retrieved from: http://www.breakthesilencedv.org/beat-that-seven-times-statistic/.

Núñez, D. (2018). Conceptions of shame in Maya law. *International Sociology.* 33: 151–160.

Ortiz, D. (2002). *In the Blindfold's Eyes: My Journey from Torture to Truth.* New York, NY: Orbis.

Paz, O. (1994). *The Labyrinth of Solitude.* New York, NY: Grove Press. (Original work published 1961).

Pitt-Rivers, J. (1996). Honour and social status . In J. G. Peristiany (Ed.) *Honour and Shame: The Values of Mediterranean Society* (pp. 19–77). Retrieved from: http://home.iscte-iul.pt/~fgvs/Pitt-Rivers_Honour.pdf.

Plumer, H. (2011) Gender in Mesoamerica: Interpreting Gender Roles in Classic Maya Society. *CJA Anthrojournal.* 1. Retrieved from: http://anthrojournal.com/issue/october-2011/article/gender-in-mesoamerica-interpreting-gender-roles-in-classic-maya-society.

Quirk, M. (2008). How to grow a gang. *The Atlantic.* 301: 24–25.

Ramirez, J. (2008). *Against Machismo: Young Adult voices in Mexico City.* New York, NY: Berghahn.

Restall, M. (2003). *Seven Myths of the Spanish Conquest.* New York: Oxford University Press.

Ruhl, K. (2006). Guatemala's feminicides and the ongoing struggle for women's human rights. *Gender and Refugee Studies.* University of California, Hastings College of the Law. Retrieved from: https://cgrs.uchastings.edu/sites/default/files/Guatemalas_femicides_ongoing_struggle_Ruhl_2006_0.pdf.

Sagot, M. (2005). The critical path of women affected by family violence in Latin America. *Violence Against Women.* 11:1292–1318. (2013). El feminicidio como necropolítica en Centroamérica. Labrys, etudes feminists. Retrieved from: http://docplayer.es/69039042-El-femicidio-como-necropolitica-en-centroamerica.html.

Sagot, M. (Ed.). (2017). *Femininismos: Pensamiento Crítico y Propuestas Alternativas en América Latina*. Buenos Aires, Argentina: CLASCO. Retrieved from: www.biblioteca.clasco.edu.air.

Sharer, R. J, & Traxler, L. P. (2006). *The Ancient Maya*. Stanford, CA: Stanford University Press.

Silverblatt, I. (1987). *Moon, Sun and Witches. Gender Ideologies and Class in Inca and Colonial Peru*. Princeton, NJ: Princeton University Press.

Torres, S. (1987). Hispanic-American battered women: Why consider cultural differences? *Response*. 12:113–131.

Tylim, I. (2016). Machismo and the limits of male heterosexuality. In V. P. Pender (Ed.), *Violence and Activism* (pp. 221–235). New York, NY: Karnac.

Volkan, V. D. (1988). *The Need to have Enemies and Allies: From Clinical Practice to International Relationships*. Northvale, NJ: Jason Aronson.

Afterword

As I write these words, (June 2018) we in the United States are reeling from the chaos that our present administration has wrought on immigration. The decision to separate children from their families at the border, a policy that the Trump administration believed would stem the tide of people coming from Central America and Mexico, has just been revoked because the popular response was so negative that Trump had no choice, given his desire to have his party (and himself) remain in power, but to withdraw it. Nevertheless, according to the *New York Times*,[1] 2,300 children are already in a camp somewhere unknown to their parents and the ordeal of separation has possibly caused those children long-term emotional damage. The effects will not be clear for years.

Just before this disastrous event, the Trump administration declared that domestic abuse would no longer be grounds for applying for asylum.

These are two examples of the cruelty of the present-day immigration policy in the United States of America, a country more and more isolated from the world and in defiance of international human rights laws. What the future will hold in this regard is unclear.

To my mind, the most frightening aspect of the immigration crisis worldwide, other than the creation of refugee camps mentioned above, in which families can live for generations, is the growing disrespect for human rights law everywhere and the lack of compassion of individual nations that has accompanied this. Recently this is most apparent not only in our policies, but in Hungary's new "Stop Soros" law, which makes it a crime to give aid to migrants,[2] and in increasing hostility to migrants in Germany,[3] and in other European countries as well.[4] In the previous pages some of the results of this situation have been presented.

How the future will unfold, at this point, in regard to the invention of a widely acceptable design for the integration of immigrants and refugees in countries which have the room to take them in, is presently unclear. Unclear as well is whether the rule of law, in the Western tradition, will hold. Only time will tell.

Notes

1 For more on this see: https://www.nytimes.com/2018/06/20/us/politics/trump-immigration-children-executive-order.html.
2 At: https://www.npr.org/2018/06/20/622045753/hungary-passes-stop-soros-laws-bans-aid-to-undocumented-immigrants.
3 https://www.nytimes.com/2018/06/15/world/europe/germany-merkel-migrants-bavaria-seehofer.html.
4 More about this is at: https://www.theguardian.com/commentisfree/2018/jun/10/sunday-essay-how-we-colluded-in-fortress-europe-immigration.

Appendix 1

Asylum law in brief[1]

Beyond the Geneva Conventions, described briefly and referenced in Chapter One, asylum law requires the following of asylum applicants.

For those who arrive in the United States with valid immigration status (students, for example), formal application for asylum is made by filing form I-589, which must be sent by mail to the United States Citizen and Immigration Services (USCIS). This should be submitted within one year of arrival, unless prevented by "extraordinary" circumstances.[2] Once received, the case will be assigned to an asylum officer. The burden of proof will then be upon the applicant to demonstrate how and why she fears further persecution, should she be forced to return home. Papers in support of her claim may be submitted to her officer, before whom she must also appear for an interview. This is scheduled forty-five days after her application has been submitted. These interviews are stressful for the applicant: in all likelihood, she will be asked for details about her life, including the trauma she has experienced. However, she can bring help to her interview, an attorney or witnesses, for example. Then, within one hundred and eighty days following her original application, based on the "totality of circumstances" she has presented,[3,4] the asylum officer will grant her asylum, or not, in writing, either in person or by mail. If her plea is denied, she will either be deported or her case, when it is inconclusive, will be referred to immigration court (a judge) for a hearing.

In those cases in which asylum is granted, the asylee can apply for a work permit one hundred and fifty days after approval.[5] Thirty days later she can work. She can also travel abroad, and (with the prior consent of the attorney general) sponsor immediate relatives for "derivative asylum" (PHR, 2012, p. 7). A year later she can apply for a green card and then, further along, also for citizenship in the United States.

Should her case be referred to immigration court (the second possibility above) it will eventually be heard by a federally appointed immigration judge. Because of a huge backlog of cases, the wait for these hearings is long, presently two years or more.[6] When, finally, the day of her hearing arrives, the judge will determine her status (again: asylum or not).[7] If she is turned down, she can appeal her case to the Board of Immigration Appeals (BIA). Once again, because these cases are also considerably delayed, she will have to wait for her case to be heard.[8]

For others, those who enter the United States without valid immigration documents, the asylum process is termed a "defensive" one. At present (September 2017) the largest number of people of this kind coming to the United States are entering via our southern borders from Mexico and Central America.[9] There is the likelihood that an individual such as this will be intercepted by an officer from United States Customs and Border Protection. If the individual indicates to Border Patrol that she fears returning home, she is legally entitled to an interview by a representative of USCIS whose job it is to determine whether her fear of returning home is "credible." Recently however, many border protection officers have been illegally refusing such interviews to asylum seekers[10] and sending them back from whence they came.

If and when the credible fear interview has been completed, removal proceedings in "defensive" cases will begin when United States Immigration and Customs Enforcement (ICE) files a Notice to Appear (NTA) document with the immigration court, date, and time assigned, a copy of which the applicant will receive, usually by mail.[11] This appearance will also be before a federal immigration judge. During her appearance, she will have the right to be represented by an attorney of her choice (which will considerably increase her chances of receiving asylum) and to have an interpreter (if she needs one); the fee for the latter will be covered by the United States. An ICE attorney will usually be present at her hearing as well, presumably to argue for her removal. It is the judge, however, who will finally determine her case, discretionarily. If asylum is denied, she can appeal her case to the BIA, as described above.[12]

Beyond simply appealing her case, there are a few alternative "forms of relief from removal," (PHR, 2012, p. 23) which, if her case is denied, she may be able to pursue, based on the details of her case. See footnote below for more about these.[13] None provides quite the same degree of privilege as does asylum.

These days asylum seekers are increasingly being put into (illegal) detention,[14] especially if they are picked up at our border by a patrol officer and are without papers. The Department of Homeland Security uses detention because presumably they want to make sure that such individuals will show up at their removal hearings. In actuality it is used because removal is easier to accomplish from detention, in those cases in which asylum is denied. Because of this, the health professional may be asked to conduct an evaluation inside a prison. See below for more about this.

In addition to asylum there are other routes to residency in the United States, including Cancellation of Removal;[15] hardship waivers (1-601, 1-601 A); U visas; waivers in regard to taking the United States Citizen Exam. When a psychologist is asked to evaluate a client for one of these reasons, the goal is the same as is true for an asylum evaluation, to cover the client's past life, trauma, and present symptoms, but to focus also on the *hardship* potential to both the client and his or her family should the member be sent home.[16]

Notes

1 The entire asylum process is described by the American Immigration Center at: https://www.us-immigration.com/uscis-guide-being-granted-asylum-u-s/.
2 USCIS requirements are at: https://www.uscis.gov/humanitarian/refugees-asylum/asylum. The one year deadline seems arbitrary to many attorneys. There are ongoing attempts to appeal it. For a comprehensive report of this subject see: https://www.humanrightsfirst.org/wp-content/uploads/pdf/1YD-report-FULL.pdf.
3 This legal term refers to all the factors considered by an officer or judge in deciding whether to grant asylum, including ties to the United States, evidence of good moral character, of past persecution, of criminal history or violation of immigration laws, etc. See p. 6 PHR (2012) for more on this.
4 The often devastatingly discretionary nature of this process can be seen in a documentary called *Well-Founded Fear*, available online at various sites. More information about the first steps in asylum application is available at: https://www.uscis.gov/humanitarian/refugees-asylum/asylum/questions-answers-credible-fear-screening.
5 More information about this appears online below. Needless to say, she will need to find some means of support during the period before she has permission to work. Often this is difficult to come by. Sometimes churches provide it. Sometimes trades can be made (e.g., the asylee can baby sit in exchange for room and board, etc. http://www.nolo.com/legal-encyclopedia/asylum-applicants-work-permit-timing-32297.html.

6 Presently half a million asylum-related cases are waiting to be heard. More about this is available at: https://qz.com/771583/a-record-half-million-cases-are-waiting-to-be-heard-by-us-immigration-courts/.
7 A list of grounds for removal is at: http://hrlibrary.umn.edu/immigrationlaw/chapter8.html and includes criminal behavior and threatening health status.
8 More information about this is available at: https://www.uscis.gov/humanitarian/refugees-asylum/asylum/obtaining-asylum-united-states.
9 Under the Trump administration, the number of illegal entries at our southern borders has been diminishing. See for example: http://www.latimes.com/nation/la-na-border-apprehensions-20170309-story.html.
10 See https://www.washingtonpost.com/world/the_americas/us-border-officials-are-illegally-turning-away-asylum-seekers-critics-say/2017/01/16/f7f5c54a-c6d0-11e6-acda-59924caa2450_story.html?utm_term=.53497189ab25 for more on this.
11 Removal proceedings, according to PHR (2012, p. 19) begin for one of three reasons: (1) USCIS has denied an affirmative asylum case and referred it to court; (2) A border patrol person has detained an individual without papers at the border; (3) ICE has charged an individual already living in the United States with an immigration violation, as is happening presently all over the United States.
12 Individual judges vary considerably in the rate at which they grant asylum. More on this can be found at: http://www.wnyc.org/story/seeking-asylum-success-varies-judge/.
  A list of judges and their respective decision rates, state by state, can be found at: http://trac.syr.edu/immigration/reports/judgereports/.
13 Removal can be withheld for the following reasons: (1) Applicant does not meet criteria for asylum, but her life would be threatened if she returned home; her life is protected by the Convention Against Torture (CAT) (see more at: https://www.uscis.gov/ilink/docView/FR/HTML/FR/0-0-0-1/0-0-0-54070/0-0-0-57543/0-0-0-59216/0-0-0-59526.html); (2) she is eligible to be considered under the Violence Against Women Act (VAWA, in 2000 at: http://icwclaw.org/services-available/violence-against-women-act-vawa/); (3) she can procure a U visa or a T visa (information about these is at: https://suhreandassociates.com/immigration/deportation-removal-defense-options/t-and-u-visa-relief/), which can be used by victims of trafficking or violent crimes; and, finally, (4) some have Special Immigrant Juvenile status. (https://www.nilc.org/wp-content/uploads/2015/11/lawfully-residing-imm-categories-CHIPRA-2016-07.pdf). Descriptions of these are also available in PHR guide (2012) pp. 23–29.
14 Use of detention has increased at an astonishing pace as a result of changes in immigration law made first by Bill Clinton, added to by Obama, and increased profoundly by President Trump's executive orders on asylum seekers in particular, according to a paper by a group at Harvard Law School (2017). For more on the situation for prisoners of this kind see Appendix II.

15 See the following sites for more information about these: https://www.lawyers.com/legal-info/immigration/deportation/cancellation-of-removal.html.
16 Resources in regard to these cases can be found at: http://www.appleseednetwork.org/immigrationcollaborative/.

Reference

PHR. (2012). *Examining Asylum Seekers*. Boston: PHR.

Appendix II

Imprisoning asylum seekers

In the United States, asylum seekers are most frequently incarcerated in one of a number of privately run, profit-making prison facilities, owned by organizations such as The Corrections Corporation of America (the largest), The Geo Group, etc.[1] It is largely to these organizations that the 352,850 people detained each year across the United States are sent, pending the outcome of their immigration proceedings, according to a UN human rights panel.[2] Imprisoning asylees is illegal, according to international law (the Geneva Conventions). In addition, often these individuals are imprisoned without due process, which is illegal under United States law. Recently, a group of detainees sued the United States government for violation of their right to due process, claiming that detention also chilled their rights under the First and Fifth Amendments and was specifically designed "to so burden the plaintiff's right to petition for asylum that plaintiffs will simply relinquish their rights and return to their homelands. This constitutes constructive removal and de facto *refoulement* without the full and fair process of law."[3] Refoulement (forcible return of the plaintiff to his or her country of origin) is illegal under international law.

Prison organizations notoriously treat prisoners poorly.[4] They are generally overcrowded, have poor medical facilities and, because of where they are located (e.g., far away from cities) they isolate prisoners from the legal help they need in order to move forward with their appeals. This has been well documented both by Human Rights First and by Harvard Law School.[5] Often asylees remain in these facilities for inordinate lengths of time, months, even years in some cases. In other cases (often in federally operated facilities), asylees are incarcerated alongside hardened criminals of all kinds.

Imprisoning asylum seekers 139

I had a first-hand exposure to the effects of imprisonment on asylees, in the summer of 2015, when I spent a week in a privately run prison facility for women and children, The South Texas Family Residential Center, in Dilley, Texas,[6] as a member of a highly inventive project, The CARA Family Detention Pro-Bono Project, organized by a consortium of four legal groups[7] and still in operation as at September 2017. Each week CARA sent/continues to send a different group of professionals (lawyers, social workers, nurses, doctors, students in all these fields, and others) to evaluate unrepresented detainees.[8] Those incarcerated are citizens of a Central American country or (rarely) of Mexico. They have fled their homes because their lives have been endangered, either by gangs or by brutalizing partners. They have been picked up, once they reached our border, by border patrol operatives and then incarcerated.[9]

Perhaps because of the presence of so many outsiders, the prisoners I encountered were well fed and housed, although health care was poor. Many of the children had pneumonia, according to a nurse practitioner on our team, sleep was difficult to come by, many children were severely depressed, and there was little for the mothers to do. The noise level within the facility was also extraordinarily high and privacy non-existent, which was very difficult for some of the women to bear.

Project volunteers came from all over the country and had a variety of skills, legal ones being the most valuable. A new group of volunteers arrived each week, to be taught the procedures and be supervised by a small on-site team. The goal was to prepare inmates for their defensive hearings as quickly as possible. We interviewed and wrote up our supportive materials at a rapid pace! The hearings themselves took place in front of a judge (streamed in, online) after which, if approved and appropriate passage already secured, the inmate departed, headed to a friend or relative where she would continue the asylum process. The work was unusually collaborative. The stories I heard (some are repeated in Chapter Four) were both informative and, in some cases, bone-chilling. For me it was an extraordinary experience, one perhaps I can repeat soon.

Notes

1 More about this is available at: https://www.nytimes.com/topic/company/corrections-corporation-of-america

2 See Reuters at: https://www.voanews.com/a/un-us-detention-of-immigrants-asylum-seekers/3985987.html for more about this.
3 See: https://www.courthousenews.com/asylum-seekers-sue-ice-prolonged-detention/ for more information here.
4 An excellent documentary on this subject is at: https://www.youtube.com/watch?v=gF12SgkQKKk and : https://www.nytimes.com/2015/02/08/magazine/the-shame-of-americas-family-detention-camps.html.
5 Descriptions of this can be found at: https://www.humanrightsfirst.org/wp-content/uploads/pdf/090429-RP-hrf-asylum-detention-report.pdf and https://today.law.harvard.edu/wp-content/uploads/2017/02/Report-Impact-of-Trump-Executive-Orders-on-Asylum-Seekers.pdf.
6 Described at: http://www.cca.com/facilities/south-texas-family-residential-center.
7 Each letter of CARA stands for the first letter of one of the four organizations that collaborate in sponsoring this project, The Catholic Legal Immigration Network, the American Immigration Council, the Refugee and Immigrant Center for Educational and Legal Services, and the American Immigration Lawyers Association. For more information see: http://www.aila.org/practice/pro-bono/find-your-opportunity/cara-family-detention-pro-bono-project.
8 Some prisoners had already engaged their own attorneys through family connections outside.
9 An excellent documentary, which depicts the nature of this journey for many is *Which Way Home* (Docudrama Film).

Appendix III

Outline[1]
Prospective affidavit of a mental health professional in support of an asylum seeker

Self-identification and related professional credentials

This section, a statement of professional's name, degree, license(s) held, brief account of training related to trauma/court-related matters, and number of years doing the work, presumably legitimizes him/her in the eyes of the court.

Background information

a) Statement of date and place of interview, asylee's name, date of birth, gender, country of origin; referring agency, reason for referral (e.g., to assess the emotional effects of the trauma she experienced when . . ., as a result of . . . etc.); name of interpreter, if there was one. Name of any other individual(s) who were present during interview. Materials reviewed before evaluation took place.
b) Brief description of client's family of origin, educational and/or work-related background, religious/cultural background, dedication of parents to their children, values, client's place in sibling birth order, education, number of languages spoken, professional status, marital status, number of children (if client has any), illnesses (including mental illness, if relevant) and any other detail that describes the applicant, makes her stand out, e.g., was she the parent's favorite, the chosen one in the family, the boss etc; any special recognition of any kind, etc.
c) Brief chronology of the series of traumatic events which the client experienced as a result of persecution and the suffering (s)he endured as a result, including imprisonment, torture, etc. Often there has been a series of these. It is best to include here details about the traumatic

event(s), if imprisoned, in what kind of a facility (light or dark, clean or dirty, etc.), number of people with that person in the cell, manner in which bodily needs (toileting, feeding, sleeping, etc.) were addressed, numbers of individuals who meted out punishment, etc. If threatened by a gang, how many involved, whether they were masked, how they arrived, left etc. Details not only make the case come alive, but make the client's story more believable to the judge. Sometimes, if the attorney does not provide information about the client's country of origin, footnotes that do so may be useful, such as the law in regard to homosexuality, marriage customs, gangs and gang customs, or the political atmosphere and/or degree of protection individuals can expect from the government, etc. If the client's attorney is going to provide this information it will be unnecessary for the mental health professional to do so.

d) Detailed description of escape from home country and events that took place on the way.

Psychosocial functioning

Include mode of assessment (if other than interview), mental health status exam (brief), brief assessment of functioning and cognitive, behavioral, affective symptoms the client has experienced or is presently experiencing (or, if tests have been used, of test results). At this point in the interview, she will already have revealed many of these (terror, hunger, pain, for example) simply in telling her story. The question of their severity, when they first began, as compared to the time of the interview, is often good to include as well.[2]

Conclusion/interpretation

Here the professional summarizes his or her opinion of the client's symptoms/diagnosis, beginning with a description of the manner in which the asylum seeker interacted with the interviewer, for example:

"Ms. X, an appealing, seemingly highly intelligent (or/and, etc.) young woman, established good eye contact and collaborated with me during our interview. At times she seemed overcome with emotion (emotion should be described here). Given the information that she provided, it is my professional opinion that: she suffers from post-traumatic stress disorder (and/or whatever other diagnosis or descriptors the interview has revealed), described in the DSM-V of the American Psychological Association as follows:

Here, an abbreviated list of the DSM criteria, followed by designation of which symptoms she has and how she meets the criteria of the diagnosis can be useful/convincing. For example:

PTSD:

Criteria A: The person must have been exposed, directly or indirectly, to one of the following: death, threatened death, sexual violence, or serious injury. Client was threatened with death when kidnapped at gunpoint by the Mara gang.

Criteria B: Intrusion symptoms: One of the following required:

Recurrent, involuntary, intrusive memories; traumatic nightmares; dissociative reactions (flashbacks); intense stress after traumatic reminders; repeated exposure to aversive details of events, usually during professional duty. Client meets criteria B in two ways: she has terrible nightmares of (describe nightmare content), which occur once/week; she has periodic flashbacks, during which she relives the experience of being pursued and shot at by the police.

And so on for all of the criteria of the respective diagnoses.

Final paragraph

This paragraph is a simple concluding statement about the apparently consistent/credible nature of the asylum seeker's account of her suffering at the hands of others at home, that you, as the evaluating person, have no reason to doubt her, and that you are convinced, therefore, that her fear of returning there is well founded. It is only her well-founded fear, based on the credible experiences she reports, that will determine her right to asylum.

Do not include anything about the law in this conclusion. Your expertise is only in evaluating the client's affect, not in interpreting the law of the United States.

Notes

1 This outline is no more than a suggested one. There is no required form available for these.
2 I use the DSM. In order to assess those DSM-V symptoms (especially PTSD, but also sometimes depression and/or dissociation or anxiety) not already apparent from the interview itself, I ask the client if she experiences each of the symptoms listed for the respective diagnoses by the DSM.

Appendix IV

Female genital mutilation
Facts and figures

The World Health Organization (2013) describes four types of Female Genital Mutilation as follows:[1]

1. "Clitoridectomy:" the removal of the clitoral hood;
2. "Excision:" Removal of the clitoris with part or all of the labia minora (inner vaginal lips), the most widely practiced;
3. "Infibulation:" Removal of part or all of the external genitalia (clitoris, labia minora, and labia majora) and stitching or otherwise narrowing of the vaginal opening, leaving a hole the size of a match stick to allow the flow of urine and/or menstrual blood. When this is done, the woman's legs are often bound together until the wound heals. Later, because of changes in the anatomy, urination becomes a lengthy process and menstruation can last for weeks. This is the most severe form of FGM.
4. "Unclassified:" Any procedure (pricking, making incisions, burning, scraping etc.) that mutilates the woman's genitals.

In general, the procedure can cause extreme health problems, among which are wound infection, sepsis, shock, micturition problems and fractures, infections of the urinary tract, incontinence, infertility, pain, menstruation, dyspareunia, higher risk for prolonged delivery, post-partum blood loss, perinatal death (Utz-Billing & Kentenich, 2008).

No one knows the origin of the practice, but it has existed for more than two thousand years and takes place in over forty countries, many in Africa (Abreu & Abreu, 2013). It is not connected to any specific religion.

Note

1 For more about this see: http://www.who.int/mediacentre/factsheets/fs241/en/.

References

Abreu, W. & Abreu, M. (2013). Community education matters: Representations of female genital mutilation in Guinean immigrant women. *Procedia – Social and Behavioral Sciences*. 171: 620–628.

Utz-Billing, I. & Kentenich, H. (2008). Female genital mutilation: An injury, physical, and mental harm. *Journal of Psychosomatic Obstetrics and Gynecology*. 29: 225–229.

World Health Organization. (2013). Sexual and reproductive health. Retrieved from: http://www.who.int/reproductivehealth/topics/fgm/overview/en/.

Appendix V

Background information: My clients/other women with FGM

My eight clients, described briefly in Table 3.1, (see Chapter 3) came originally from four different African countries: The Gambia, Senegal, Guinea, and Democratic Republic of the Congo. They ranged in age from twenty-two to fifty-six at the time I saw them. Each spoke three to five languages. Two (Ms. A and Ms. G) were, for all intents and purposes, illiterate. All but two (Ms. F & Ms. H) had been working outside the home in the country from which they had come. All but one (Ms. E) had already experienced FGM and had symptoms of some kind (largely physical) as a result.

PsyLIT, the reference guide of the American Psychological Association, lists two hundred and twenty studies of different subsets of women who have undergone FGM, largely from different African communities. I do not intend to review these studies here because they are too superficial to contribute significantly to my discussion. Briefly, they indicate that a woman's psychological reaction to the process varies, depending on her personal trauma history, the extremity of the cutting endured, the ways in which the community/family regarded the procedure, and whether there has been any attempt to repair the damage. (See for example: Utz-Billing & Kentenich, 2008; Dalal, Lawoko, & Jansson, 2010; Patterson, Davis, & Binik, 2012).[1] Not surprisingly, a very common symptom is dyspareunia (Berg & Denison, 2012a & 2012b).

The only study, mentioned in the body of this paper, to which it is minimally possible to compare my clients, included sixty-six women from twenty-nine African countries who were living in the Netherlands (Vloeberghs et al., 2012). In this study, data was collected using both questionnaires and face-to-face interviews. The results indicated lifelong effects from the procedure. One in six subjects, for example, reported PTSD, and one third both depression and anxiety. Symptoms increased during childbirth and were exacerbated by the judgmental attitude of Western medical professionals towards FGM. Three types of overall reaction to FGM are distinguished: "the adaptive, the disempowered and the traumatized." The *"adaptives"* were "overcoming the FGM experience" (p. 689), at different rates, according to these authors. They had often become activists of one kind or another. They were open to discussion of the past, as well as of their day-to-day lives at the time. They tended to ask for and get help when they needed it (medical help especially). Often religion was an extremely important, integral part of their identity; they seemed to rely on it for help always. Religious practice was also a way of relating to other women, Muslim and Christian alike, and was thus useful in finding like-minded communities which they could join. Although distinct sexual problems seemed to plague them, these women kept the details of these problems to themselves.

A second group, the *disempowered* felt "angry and defeated," according to these authors (p.690). They bore their grief, and were fatalistic about the future because they saw no way out. They tended not to talk about what had happened (or was happening) to them and sometimes abused substances or food as a way to contain their despair. They seemed to avoid sex. When that was not possible, they tended to dissociate during the act, according to the authors.

Finally the *traumatized* group (not all diagnosed specifically with PTSD) suffered "a lot of pain and sadness" all the time (p. 690). They felt extreme shame and anger about their bodies and were reproachful of those who injured them. They felt misunderstood, especially by Western health providers. As a consequence, they tended to isolate themselves, which increased their feelings of anxiety and depression.

In the chapter above, I have focused on one woman as an example of others who seemed to have made a good adjustment to life in the west, post immigration.

Note

1 According to the authors listed above, some women who move to the West attempt to undo FGM surgically.

References

Berg, R. C. & Denison, E. (2012a). Does female genital mutilation/cutting affect women's sexual functioning?: A systematic review of the consequences of FMG/C. *Sexuality Research and Social Policy: A Journal of the NSRC*. 9: 41–56.

Berg, R. C. & Denison, E. (2012b). Effectiveness of interventions designed to prevent Female genital mutilation/cutting. A systematic review. *Studies in Family Planning.* 43: 135–146.

Dalal, K., Lawoko, S., & Jansson, B. (2010). Women's attitude toward discontinuation of female genital mutilation in Egypt. *Journal of Injury and Violence Research.* 2: 41–47.

Patterson, L. P. Q., Davis, S. N., & Binik, Y. M. (2012). Female genital mutilation: Cutting and orgasm before and after surgical repair. *Sexologies.* 21: 3–8.

Utz-Billing, I. & Kentenich, H. (2008). Female genital mutilation: An injury, physical and mental harm. *Journal of Psychosomatic Obstetrics & Gynecology.* 29:225–229.

Vloeberghs, E., van der Kwaak, A., Knipscheer, J., & van der Muijsenbergh, M. (2012). Coping and chronic social consequences of female genital mutilation in the Netherlands. *Ethnicity and Health.* 17: 677–695.

Index

abandoned children 3–4, *see also* Special Immigrant Juvenile status
abandonment decisions, heroic asylum seekers 40, 43–44, 50–52, 55–63
acclimation/adjustment patterns, female genital mutilation (FGM) 76–86; feminicide 120–121; heroic asylum seekers 58–64
adaptive reaction group, female genital mutilation (FGM) 148
adolescents, resistance 80, *see also* children
Africa xvii, xxii, 3, 12–13, 18, 26, 40–44, 47–48, 53, 56–59, 61, 63–65, 69–86, 147–148; female genital mutilation (FGM) xvii, 69–86, 147–148; homosexuality 26, 33, *see also* Cameroon; Guinea; Togo
Afsah, Efrahim 123
aftermath, female genital mutilation (FGM) xix–xx, 68–89, 147–148
afterword xii, xx, 131–132
agencies, psychologists 2–3
agency xix, 68–69, 71, 75, 79–86, 100–101, 106–121, 124; definitions 79–80; female genital mutilation (FGM) xix, 68–69, 71, 75, 79–86; neurobiology 79–80; pain 80, 87, 88; submissive roles xix, 81–86, 100–101, 106–121, 124, *see also* attachment theory
agendas, interviews 5–7
Agger, I. 54
Agosta, L. 21
agriculture, Central America 107–108, 112
Akhtar, Salman 78
Akinsulure-Smith, A. M. 68–69
Alaska 64
alcohol 108, 115

Aleinikoff, T. Alexander xiii–xiv
Ali, Aryan Hirsi 87–88
Allah xix, 74, 77, 84–86, *see also* Islam
alternative 'forms of relief from removal', deportation/removal decisions 3, 134–135
American family dream pursuit, heroic asylum seekers 56–59
American Friends Service Committee (AFSC) xx, 25, 31
American Immigration Center 135
American Immigration Lawyers Association (AILA) 140
American Psychiatric Association xxii, 31, 33
American Psychological Association 31, 33, 78, 143, 147
Amnesty International xv, xxi
Andersen, K. 21–22
Andulasia 104–106
anger xx, 22, 33, 85, 112–113, 148
Anna's story, feminicide 92–93
antibiotics 87
anxiety 7, 53, 62, 147–148; diagnosis 7, 147–148
appeals, asylum law 1–2, 6, 134
appendices 1, 133–149
Arden, Tracey 103
Arendt, Hannah xiv–xv
asylum application forms (I-589s) 1, 4, 75, 88, 133–135; deadlines 4, 88, 133, 135
asylum law xv–xvi, 1–4, 9, 25–26, 29, 75–77, 121–122, 133–140, 142, 143–144; appeals 1–2, 6, 134; background xv–xvi, 1–4, 9, 25–26, 29–30, 75–77, 121–122, 131–132, 133–140, 142, 143–144; burden of proof 133; citizenship applications 76–77, 82–83, 133; critique

9, 29–30, 121–122, 131–132; deadlines 4, 11–12, 133–134, 135; decisions 3–4, 7–8, 75–76, 133–135, 136, 138–139; 'defensive' no-valid immigration documents application process 3–4, 134, 136; deportation/removal decisions 3–4, 7, 133, 134–135, 136, 138–139; derivative asylum sponsorship 133; exclusions 9–10; five protected grounds for persecution claims 1–2, 121; green cards 133; historical background xv–xvi; immigration court hearings 1–2, 6, 8, 30, 75–77, 131–132, 133–134, 139; interviews 133–134, 135; supporting papers 1, 2–3, 133–134, 135; witnesses 1, 14–15, 30, 133–134; work permits 133–134, 135, *see also* attorneys
asylum officers 1–2, 5–6, 133, 134, 135–136; roles 1–2, 133; training 1, 30, *see also* United States Citizen and Immigration Services
asylum seekers, afterword xii, xx, 131–132; definitions xiii, xxi, 1–3, 30, 31, 41; overview of the book i, xii–xx; statistics xiii–xiv, xxi, 9, 70, 111, 138–139, *see also individual topics*
atrocities xii
attachment theory 57, 60, 62, 79–81, 85–86, 117–121, *see also* agency
attorney general 133
attorneys 2–4, 7, 11–12, 25–26, 30, 41, 58, 76, 78, 116–117, 133–134, 139, 140–144; asylum law 2–4, 25–26, 30, 78, 116–117, 133–134, 139, 140–144; background 2–4, 11, 25–26, 30, 76, 78; beneficial aspects 2–4, 30, 41, 116–117, 134, 139; negative aspects 26; pro-bono prospects 2–3, 25–26; relationships 25–26, 58; roles 2–4, 11, 25–26, 78, 116–117; students 25–26; types 25–26; vicarious traumatization 26, *see also* asylum law
Australia 125
author biography i, xii–xiii, 6
avoidance 33
Aztec culture 123

backlog of cases, immigration court hearings 134, 136
bananas, Central America 107–108, 112
behavioral assessments 142–143, 148, *see also* psychosocial assessments

Belarus, subject 10 (Belarus) (Ms. B) heroic asylum seeker 44, 45, 48–49, 54–55, 56–57, 59–62, 64
Belize 121
Benedek, Therese 120–121
Benjamin, Jessica xix, xx, 83–85, 99–100, 118
Bionian field theory (BFT) 10–11
Blitzer, Jonathan 122
Board of Immigration Appeals (BIA) 30, 134
Bookey, B. 99
Booth, J. A. 110–111, 121, 125
border killings xvi
Boulanger, Ghislaine 15, 21, 59
Boxer, Philip 121
Brady, M. 117
Bragin, M. 117–118
Breuer, J. 17
bribes, false imprisonment in country of origin xvi, 47–48; police 88, 112
Brusco, Elizabeth 109
Buddhism 43–45
burden of proof, asylum application forms (I-589s) 133

Callahan, R. K. 109, 124
Cameroon, subject 7 (Cameroon) heroic asylum seeker 42, 44, 53, 55–56; subject 8 (Cameroon) heroic asylum seeker 42, 44, 45, 64
campaigns to end FMG 86
Canada 47–48
Cancellation of Removal residency threats 135
CARA Family Detention Pro-Bono Project 139, 140
Cardozo Law School xx, 31
Carens, J. H. 9
Caribbean 111, 125
Carr, E. H. 100
Carter, Jimmy 125
Catholic Charities 30
Catholicism xx, 30, 43, 45, 61, 104–105, 107, 109–110
Central America i, xii, xvi, xx, xxiii, 18–19, 24, 33, 92–126, 131–132, 134, 139; agriculture 107–108, 112; background 92–126; bananas 107–108, 112; Catholicism xx, 104–105, 107, 109–110; class/status 101–107, 109–110, 112–113, 126; coffee 107–108; colonialism xx,

101–102, 104–121, 123; contraception 98; 'defensive' no-valid immigration documents application process 134; demasculinization feelings 100–101, 117–118; detention 139; drug gangs 97, 119, 122, 126; education 106–107, 111, 114–115, 122, 126; honor code history 100–103, 104–109, 112, 124; human rights 99–100, 121; humiliation xx, 94–95, 98–121, 124; law 98–100, 105–106, 121–122; male/female relations today xx, 96–101, 111–121; Mayan culture xx, 99, 100–104, 106–107, 121, 123–124; 'Moral Third' xx, 99–100, 119–120; murder rates 97; negative attitudes towards women xx, 92–96, 97–101; normative unconscious processes xx, 96–99, 101–121; police attitudes 99; population statistics 111; poverty 108, 110–111; rebellions from the twentieth century 110–111, 122, 125; religion xx, 104–105, 107, 114–115; Spanish colonialism xx, 101–102, 104–121, 123–124, 126; statistics 97–99, 111, 121–122; US 107–108, 110–111, 125, *see also* Belize; Costa Rica; El Salvador; feminicide; Guatemala; Honduras; machismo; Nicaragua; Panama

children 3–5, 31, 51–55, 57, 60, 62, 79–81, 94–95, 99, 113–121, 131–132, 139, 141–144; abandoned children 3–4; attachment theory 57, 60, 62, 79–81, 85–86, 117–121; collaborative childcare 88; feminicide 94–95, 99, 113–121; infanticide 5, 41, 46; machismo 95–96, 99, 118–119; as mothers 5; parental rejection 60, 115–121; prisons 94–96, 131–132; resistance 80; secondary traumatization 54–55; sexual abuse 88, 92–93; Special Immigrant Juvenile status 3; US border separation concerns 131–132

China 43, 45, 53–54, 64, *see also* Tibet
Chomsky, Noam 125
Christianity 30, 43–44, 45, 46, 48–49, 61, 70–86, 104–105, 107, 148
CIA xxi, 110–111, 125
Citizen Exam residency threats 135
citizenship applications, asylum law 76–77, 82–83, 133
class/status, Central America 101–107, 109–110, 112–113, 126

client backgrounds xvi, xvii–xx, 2–5, 9–16, 19–21, 22–25, 40–63, 92–126, 147–148; female genital mutilation (FGM) xvi, xvii–xviii, xix–xx, 69–89, 147–148; past histories 6–7, 19–21, 24–25, 40–44, 70–86; relationships 6–7, 9–16, 70–86; truth considerations 22–25, *see also* feminicide; heroic asylum seekers; psychological assessments
climate change xiii
Clinton, Bill 136
clitoridectomy definition, female genital mutilation (FGM) 145
coffee, Central America 107–108
cognition assessments 6–7, 142–143, 148, *see also* psychosocial assessments
cognitive behavioral therapy (CBT) 57
collaborative childcare 88
colonialism, Central America xx, 101–102, 104–121; education 87, 106–107, 111, 114–115, 122, 126; feminicide xx, 101–102, 104–121; Spain xx, 101–102, 104–121, 123–124, 126; US xx, 107–108, 110–111, 125
Communism xv, 110–111
compliance, machismo 96–97, 113–121
confidentiality issues, psychological assessments 25
Congo, Ms. F (Congo) female genital mutilation 70
contraception, Central America 98
Convention Relating to the Status of Refugees 1951 29, *see also* Geneva Conventions
Corrections Corporation of America 138, *see also* prisons
Costa Rica 121
crying clients 5, 13–14, 28–29, 40
crying interpreters 28–29
cultural awareness 18, 23–24, 33, 56–59, 70–71, 76–77, 83–86, 97–121
Customs and Border Protection officers 134; illegal refusal acts 134–135

Dailey, Anne 8
Dalai Lama 45, 64
Danieli, Yael 22, 59
Daubert Standard (1993) 30
deadlines, asylum application forms (I-589s) 4, 88, 133, 135; asylum law 4, 11–12, 133–134, 135

death threats xvi, xvii, xix, 3, 13, 14–15, 19–20, 41–42, 46, 48, 50, 56, 73–74, 92–121, 143, *see also* feminicide; violence
decisions, asylum law 3–4, 7–8, 75–76, 133–135, 136, 138–139; objectivity/rationality goals 8–9; unconscious subjectivity 8–9
'defensive' no-valid immigration documents application process, asylum law 3–4, 134, 136
dehumanization effects 9
Delaney Hall Detention Facility, Newark, New Jersey 92, 113–114
Delbo, C. xii
DeLoach, J. S. 80, 87–88
demasculinization feelings, Central America 100–101, 117–118
Democratic Republic of the Congo 147–148
denial, heroic asylum seekers 52, 54–56
Department of Homeland Security, detention uses 135
deportation/removal decisions, alternative 'forms of relief from removal' 3–4, 134–135; appeals 134; asylum law 3–4, 7, 133, 134–135, 136, 138–139; statistics xiii–xiv; withheld instances 136
depression 7, 41, 42, 53, 54–55, 60–61, 78–86, 139, 141, 144, 147–148; diagnosis 7, 41, 78–79, 144, 147–148
derivative asylum sponsorship, asylum law 133
detachment 33
detention xiii, xvi, 4, 17–18, 24, 92, 94–95, 113–114, 131–132, 135–140; due process rights xvi, 4, 138–139; illegal aspects 4, 24, 94, 135, 138–139; increasing trends xvi, 4, 131–132, 136; statistics xiv, 138–139; UNHCR guidelines 4, *see also* prisons
Dharamsala, Tibet 56
diagnosis xviii, 7, 17–18, 21, 30–33, 41, 60, 68–69, 78–86, 142–144, 147–148; anxiety 7, 147–148; depression 7, 41, 78–79, 144, 147–148; dissociation 33, 41, 77–78, 88, 143, 144, 148; female genital mutilation (FGM) 68–69, 145; post-traumatic stress disorder (PTSD) xviii, 7, 17–18, 21, 30, 32, 41, 60, 143, 144, 147–148

dictators 11–12, 111, 126
disempowered reaction group, female genital mutilation (FGM) 148
displaced persons, definition xiii, xxi; statistics xiii–xiv, 9, 111, *see also* asylum seekers
dissociation, diagnosis 33, 41, 77–78, 88, 143, 144, 148
diversity agenda 18
divorces 76, 82–83, 119
D.K., Ms. C (D.K.) female genital mutilation (FGM) 70
domestic abuse i, xvi, xix, xx, 71–76, 81–86, 92–126, 131, 139, 141–142, 143; restraining orders 76; uncontained abuse i, xvi, xix, xx, 92–126, 139, 141–142, *see also* feminicide; machismo
dowries 75
drug gangs, Central America 97, 119, 122, 126
DSM-V xviii, 7, 32, 143, 144
Duckworth, M. P. 17
due process rights, detention xvi, 4, 138–139
duels, honor code history 105–106
duration, interviews 6–7
Dutton, D. G. 112–113
dyspareunia symptoms, female genital mutilation (FGM) xxiii, 147–148

education, Central America 106–107, 111, 114–115, 122, 126; colonialism 87, 106–107, 111, 114–115, 122, 126; female genital mutilation (FGM) 69–86, 87; heroic asylum seekers 40–65; Spanish colonialism 106–107, 126; statistics 63–65
Ekman, Paul 23
El Salvador 97, 99, 121, 122, 125, *see also* Central America
electric shock torture 49
Elena's story, feminicide 113–121, 126
embassies, refugees 30
emotional assessments xxiii, 3–7, 13–14, 18–20, 22, 53, 80–86, 131, 142–143, 148, *see also* anger; guilt; psychosocial assessments; sadness; shame
empathetic listening 14–15, 18, 21–22, 27–28, 33
endurance xix, 13–14
Engstrom, D. 8, 10, 16

equal opportunities, freedom of movement of people 9
Erpenbeck, Jenny 63
escape routes, heroic asylum seekers 49, 56–57
ethics 9, 15, *see also* morals
ethnic feuds 51
Europe, immigration 131–132; statistics 9
excision definition, female genital mutilation (FGM) 145
exclusions, asylum law 9–10
experience, female genital mutilation shared past experiences 69–71, 78–86; heroic asylum seekers' shared experiences 41–44, 62; the real 14–15, 55–56, *see also* feminicide
eye contact 7, 24, 28, 33, 77–78, 142
eye movement desensitization and reprocessing (EMDR) 57

false imprisonment in country of origin xvi, 11–12, 40–63, 73–74, 141–142, 143
Family Court 76
fantasies 11, 14–15
fasting 74
father concepts xix, 83–86, 115–121, *see also* God
Faulkner, William 92
fear tests xxi, 2–3, 12, 29, 55–63, *see also* persecution
female genital mutilation (FGM) i, xii, xvi, xvii, xix–xx, xxiii, 68–89, 145–146, 147–148; acclimation/adjustment patterns 76–86; adaptive reaction group 148; Africa xvii, 69–86, 147–148; aftermath xix–xx, xxiii, 68–89, 147–148; agency xix, 68–69, 71, 75, 79–86; campaigns to end FMG 86; client backgrounds xvi, xvii–xviii, xix–xx, 69–89, 147–148; conclusions 85–86; definition 72, 86, 145; diagnosis 68–69, 145; discussion 78–86; disempowered reaction group 148; dyspareunia symptoms xxiii, 147–148; education 69–86, 87; Fulani culture 70–72, 76–77, 80–81, 87–88; interviews 69–72, 77–86; love relationships xix, 77–78; Mr. W (husband/stepbrother of Ms. A (Guinea)) 70, 73–86; Ms. A (Guinea) xix, 69–86, 88; Ms. B (Guinea) 70; Ms. C (D.K.) 70; Ms. D (Guinea) 70; Ms. E (Senegal) 70; Ms. F (Congo) 70;
Ms. G (Gambia) 69–71; Ms. H (Senegal) 70, 78–79; origins 69; practising countries xvii, 68–89, 145, 147–148; practitioners/perpetrators 68–69, 72–73, 81, 86; proponents of the procedure 68–69; psychodynamic perspectives 71–72, 77–86; psychological assessments 68–72, 77–89, 147–148; religion 70–86, 87; shared past experiences 69–71, 78–86; statistics 68–69, 86; studies 68–69, 78–81, 147–148; submissive roles xix, xx, 81–86; trauma xvi, xviii, xxiii, 68–89, 145, 147–148; traumatized reaction group xix–xx, 70, 72–73, 78–86, 148; types xix, 68–69, 70, 72–86, 87, 145; undo attempts 148; US incidence 68–69, 86
feminicide i, xii, xvi, xx, 92–126; acclimation/adjustment patterns 120–121; Anna's story 92–93; children 94–95, 99, 113–121; compliance 96–97, 113–121; definition 93–94, 111–113; Elena's story 113–121, 126; interviews xx, 92–93, 111–126; male/female relations today xx, 96–101, 111–121; Maria's story 92–93; normative unconscious processes 94, 96–99, 101–121; psychological assessments xx, 92–126; reasons 112–113; relatives 92–93, 94–96, 99, 113–116; Rosa's story 94–96, 99, 117–121; statistics 99, 121–122, *see also* Central America; machismo
feminine, definitions 83, 105, 109–110
field/space concepts, interviews 10–11, 14
Fifth Amendment 138
First Amendment 138
five protected grounds for persecution claims, asylum law 1–2, 121
flashbacks (dissociative reactions) 6, 18, 31, 33, 41, 58–59, 143
food and drink facilities, interviews 5, 31; prisons 47–49
forced marriages xix, 70, 73–76, 81–82, 85–88
forensic perspectives i, xii, xviii, 2–4, 8–9; background i, xii, xviii, 2–4, 8–9, *see also* attorneys; psychosocial assessments
foreshortened future feelings, post-traumatic stress disorder (PTSD) 60
Franklin, S. 79

freedom of movement of people, equal opportunities 9
Freeman, Walter 79–80
French 70–86
Freud, Sigmund 17, 120
Fromm, E. xx, 113
Frye Rule of Evidence (1923) 30
Fulani culture 70–72, 76–77, 80–81, 87–88
funders of escape, heroic asylum seekers 40, 43–60

Gambia 69–71, 147–148; Ms. G (Gambia) female genital mutilation 69–71
gangs xiii, xvi, 3, 19–21, 24, 31, 33, 92–97, 119–121, 122, 126, 139, 142–143; definitions 122, *see also* Central America
Garifuna culture 101, 121, 123
general set-up/procedures, psychological assessments 4–7
Geneva Conventions 4, 29, 133, 138; definition 29
Geo Group 138, *see also* prisons
Germany, Holocaust survivors 22, 31, 52–53, 54; immigration 131–132
Gerson, S. 32–33, 100
Ghana 41, 44, 46, 49; subject 11 (Ghana) heroic asylum seeker 44, 46, 49
Gilligan, J. 100
God xix, 20, 60, 74, 77, 84–86, 102
Goldner, Virginia 109
Gottlieb, A. 80, 87–88
Graesser, A. 79
green cards, asylum law 133
group therapy 58–59, 63
Guantanamoa Bay 17–18
Guatemala 97, 98–99, 121, 125, *see also* Central America
Gubrish-Simitis, I. 53
guilt 18–20, 22, 53
Guinea 42–44, 47–48, 56–59, 61, 69–86, 147–148; Ms. A (Guinea) female genital mutilation xix, 69–86, 88; Ms. B (Guinea) female genital mutilation 70; Ms. D (Guinea) female genital mutilation 70; subject 3 (Guinea) (Mr. I) heroic asylum seeker 42, 43, 47–48, 56–59, 61; subject 6 (Guinea) heroic asylum seeker 42, 44
Gulf War 54
Guterres, Anthony xx, 93

hardship waivers residency threats 135
Harvard Law School 136, 138
'have a life' wishes xix, 68, 78–86, 148
health assessments/evaluations xii, xiv, xvi, xviii, xix–xx, xxii, 1–33, 41, 68–89, 92–126, 135, 142–148; female genital mutilation (FGM) 147–148; interviews xiii, xvi, 3–29, 142–144; outline prospective asylum-seeker support affidavit of a mental health professional xiv, xvi, 7–9, 29, 141–144; prisons 4, 135, *see also* psychological assessments
hearing voices 84–85, *see also* psychosis
helplessness 53–56
hernia operations 60
heroic asylum seekers i, xii, xviii–xix, 40–65; abandonment decisions 40, 43–44, 50–52, 55–63; acclimation/ adjustment patterns 58–64; American family dream pursuit 56–59; background i, xii, xviii–xix, 40–65; characteristics 41, 49–55; conclusions 62–63; definition 41, 49–52; denial 52, 54–56; discussion 49–63; education 40–65; escape routes 49, 56–57; funders of escape 40, 43–60; how the role unfolds 47–49; interviews 41–63; prisons 40–63; psychodynamic perspectives 51–55; relatives 40–63; religion 43–63; secondary traumatization 54–55; shared past experiences 41–44; subject 1 (Yugoslavia) 42, 43, 45, 56; subject 2 (Togo) 42, 43; subject 3 (Guinea) (Mr. I) 42, 43, 47–48, 56–59, 61; subject 4 (Tibet) 42, 43, 45, 53–54, 56, 64; subject 5 (Tibet) 42, 43, 53–54, 64; subject 6 (Guinea) 42, 44; subject 7 (Cameroon) 42, 44, 53, 55–56; subject 8 (Cameroon) 42, 44, 45, 64; subject 9 (Myanmar) 44, 54–55, 56; subject 10 (Belarus) (Ms. B) 44, 45, 48–49, 54–55, 56–57, 59–62, 64; subject 11 (Ghana) 44, 46, 49; trauma 40–63, *see also* protestors
hijab 11–12
Hill, K. 84
Holmes, Oliver Wendell 8
Holmqvist, R. 21–22
Holocaust survivors 22, 31, 52–53, 54
homosexuality 3, 26, 33, 142
Honduras 97, 121, 124, 125, *see also* Central America

honor code history, Central America 100–103, 104–109, 112, 124
honor-bound machismo *see* machismo
housing 75–77, 82–83
human dignity xv
human rights xii–xx, xxi, 7–8, 29, 99–100, 121, 131–132, 138–139, 140; Central America 99–100, 121; definitions xiv–xv; historical background xiv–xv, xxi; political perspectives xv
Human Rights First (HRF) xx, 25, 30, 31, 138, 140
Human Rights Watch xiv
humiliation, Central America xx, 94–95, 98–121, 124; definition 100, 112, *see also* shame
Hungary 131
hyperarousal 33

ICD xxii
ideals, ruin of the old ideals 109
ideological critique xv
illegal aspects, detention 4, 24, 94, 135, 138–139
Imams 76, 82
immigration court hearings, asylum law 1–2, 6, 8, 30, 75–77, 131–132, 133–134, 139; backlog of cases 134, 136; online-streaming aspects 139
Immigration and Customs Enforcement (ICE), Notice to Appear document (NTA) 134
impotence factors, machismo 113
incest 92–93
inequalities 9, 107 108
infanticide 5, 41, 46
infectious diseases xxiii, 72–86, 87, 104–105, 139, 141, 145
infibulation definition, female genital mutilation (FGM) 145
international legal codes 123
interpersonal and relational psychoanalysis (IRP) 10–11, 15–16
interpreters, crying interpreters 28–29; interviews 5, 7, 19–20, 24, 27–29, 122; negative aspects 27; physical positioning considerations 5, 28; relationships 27–29; training 27; transferential/countertransferential issues 28–29; vicarious traumatization 28–29
interviews xiii, xvi, xx, 3–29, 41–63, 69–72, 77–86, 92–126, 142–144;

agendas 5–7; asylum law 133–134, 135; 'defensive' no-valid immigration documents application process 3–4, 134; duration 6–7; female genital mutilation (FGM) 69–72, 77–86; feminicide xx, 92–93, 111–126; field/space concepts 10–11, 14; food and drink facilities 5, 31; general set-up/procedures 4–7; heroic asylum seekers 41–63; interpreters 5, 7, 19–20, 24, 27–29, 122; locations 4; machismo 97–126; methods 5–7, 28; observation uses 6–7, 77–78; physical positioning considerations 5–6, 19–20, 28; rehearsed narratives 4–5; relationships 6–7, 9–16, 77–86; stress 5–6, 16, 17–18, 133; transferential/countertransferential issues 9–17, 28–29, 31; trust 11–12, 23–25; vicarious traumatization 21–22, 33, *see also* psychological assessments
Iraq, Gulf War 54
Islam xix, xxii, 11–12, 44, 45, 47–48, 63, 70–86, 87, 123, 148, *see also* Allah
Italy 10

Jaranson, J. 57
Jensen, S. B. 54

Kaplan, S. 59
kidnappings 3–4, 143
Kids in Need of Defense (KIND) 25, 30, 31
Kogan, Ilene 54–55
Kuchuck, Steven 18
Kuriloff, Emily 100

Lacan, J. 14
Laub, Dori 14, 59
law xv–xvi, 1, 2–4, 7–9, 25–26, 29, 75–76, 98–99, 131–132, 133–137, 138–140, 142, 143–144; Central America 98–100, 105–106, 121–122; international legal codes 123, *see also* asylum law
Layton, Lynne 94, 96, 110, 112, 117
learning disabilities 28
Lebrun, D. 123
Levinson, Edgar 15–17
Lewin, Kurt 10
life/liberty/happiness mission, US 8
Linden, D. E.-J. 84
listening 14–15, 18, 21–22
litigation, due process rights 138–139, 140

locations, interviews 4; psychological assessments 4
Longdon, Eleanor 84
love relationships, female genital mutilation (FGM) xix, 77–78
Lutz, E. L. 63

Maasi chief 86
McCracken, C. 107
machismo i, xx, 92–121; children 95–96, 99, 118–119; compliance 96–97, 113–121; definition xx, 93–94, 96, 108–109, 112–113, 117–118; impotence factors 113; interviews 97–126; male/female relations today xx, 96–101, 111–121; Mayan culture xx, 99, 100–104, 106–107, 121, 123–124; normative unconscious processes 94, 96–121; origins 108–109, 111–112; personality factors 112–113; studies 108–109, 112–113, *see also* feminicide
male/female relations today, feminicide xx, 96–101, 111–121
Malinke 71–72
Mam culture 101, 121
Mandarin 42, 43
Mandingo/Jola 70
Mara gang 19
marginalization factors 3–4
marianismo, definition 109–110
Maria's story, feminicide 92–93
marriages, divorces 76, 82–83, 119; forced marriages xix, 70, 73–76, 81–82, 85–88; Islam xix, 70, 73–76, 81–82, 85–86, 87
Martinez, Jennifer xxi
Martínez, Oscar 111
masculine, definitions 83, 105, 109, 112–113; demasculinization feelings 100–101, 117–118, *see also* machismo
Mayan culture xx, 99, 100–104, 106–107, 121, 123–124
MEDLINE 78
men on the run 42–63, *see also* heroic asylum seekers; men
Mendoza, E. 108–109
menstruation 103
mental health professionals, definition xxii–xxiii; outline prospective asylum-seeker support affidavit of a mental health professional xiv, 7–9, 29, 141–144, *see also* psychiatrists; psychologists; social workers

Mexico xx, xxiii, 108, 123, 124, 131, 134, 136, 139; 'defensive' no-valid immigration documents application process 134, 136; detention 139; machismo origins 108
Milgram laboratory experiments 50
Mirandé, Alfredo 108
Modell, A. H. 79–80, 85
money donations to her boyfriend, subject 10 (Belarus) (Ms. B) heroic asylum seeker 61–62
'Moral Third', Central America xx, 99–100, 119–120
morals xx, 14–18, *see also* ethics
Moyn, Samuel xii, xv, xxi
Mr. I, subject 3 (Guinea) (Mr. I) heroic asylum seeker 42, 43, 47–48, 56–59, 61
Mr. W (husband/stepbrother of Ms. A (Guinea) female genital mutilation) 70, 73–86
Ms. A (Guinea), female genital mutilation (FGM) xix, 69–86, 88
Ms. B, subject 10 (Belarus) heroic asylum seeker 44, 45, 48–49, 54–55, 56–57, 59–62, 64
Ms. B (Guinea), female genital mutilation (FGM) 70
Ms. C (D.K.), female genital mutilation (FGM) 70
Ms. D (Guinea), female genital mutilation (FGM) 70
Ms. E (Senegal), female genital mutilation (FGM) 70
Ms. F (Congo), female genital mutilation (FGM) 70
Ms. G (Gambia), female genital mutilation (FGM) 69–71
Ms. H (Senegal), female genital mutilation (FGM) 70, 78–79
multi-disciplinary collaborative approaches 27–29
Musalo, K. 99
Myanmar, subject 9 (Myanmar) heroic asylum seeker 44, 54–55, 56

narratives 4–5, 14–15, 57
Nash, June 101, 103, 112
nationalism xxi
nationality, five protected grounds for persecution claims 1–2
natural disasters xiii, 15, 22
nazis 54, *see also* Holocaust survivors

negative attitudes towards women, Central America xx, 92–96, 97–101
Netherlands 78, 88, 147
neurobiology, agency 79–80
New York Declaration for Refugees and Migrants xiii
New York Times 131
Nguyen, Leanh 7, 8–9, 14, 18, 32, 113
Nicaragua 121
nightmares 6–7, 18–19, 21–22, 31, 33, 58–59, 143
Nobel Peace Prize xxi
non-refoulement principle, definition 1–2, *see also* refoulement
non-Western cultures, trauma recall differences 23–24
normative unconscious processes 94, 96–121; definition 94, 96, 112–113, 117
Notice to Appear document (NTA), Immigration and Customs Enforcement (ICE) 134
NPR xxi, 122, 132
Núñez, Daniel 124
nurses 46–47, 64

Obama, Barack xxi
objectivity/rationality goals, psychological assessments 8–9
observation uses, interviews 6–7, 77–78
Oklahoma bombings in 1996 xvi
Oliner, P. 50
Oliner, S. P. 50
online access, immigration court hearings 139; truth considerations 23
The Origins of Totalitarianism (Arendt) xiv–xv
Ortiz, Dianna 125
outline prospective asylum-seeker support affidavit of a mental health professional xiv, 7–9, 29, 141–144
overview of the book i, xii–xx

pain, agency 80, 87, 88
Panama 121
paranoia 53
parental rejection 60, 115–121
Paz, Octavio 108, 117
persecution 1–4, 5–7, 8–9, 29, 40–63, 141–142; definitions 29; five protected grounds for persecution claims 1–2, *see also* fear tests; torture
personality factors, machismo 112–113

pesticides 108
Peuhl/Muslims 70
Pew National Trust 64–65
physical positioning considerations, interpreters 5, 28; interviews 5–6, 19–20, 28
Physicians for Human Rights (PHR) xx, 2, 29, 31
Pitt-Rivers, J. 103–105
pneumonia 139
Poland, Warren 14
police 45–46, 49, 75–76, 88, 99, 112
political opinions 1–3, 13–14, 21–22, 40–63; five protected grounds for persecution claims 1–3
political perspectives i, xii–xiii, xv, xviii, 1–2, 7–9, 21–22; human rights xv; psychological assessments 7–9, *see also* psychosocial assessments
population statistics, Central America 111
post-traumatic stress disorder (PTSD) xviii, 7, 17–18, 21, 30, 32, 41, 43–44, 58–59, 60–61, 77, 143, 144, 147–148; criteria 7, 21, 33, 143, 144, 147–148; diagnosis xviii, 7, 17–18, 21, 30, 32, 41, 60, 143, 144, 147–148; foreshortened future feelings 60; remission 77; rules of evidence 30; treatments 58–59, 61, *see also* trauma
poverty, Central America 108, 110–111
power xix, 68–69, 71, 75, 79–86, 87, 112–121, *see also* agency
practitioners/perpetrators, female genital mutilation (FGM) 68–69, 72–73, 81, 86
Prilleltensky, I. 18
prisons xiii, xxii, 4, 11–12, 17–19, 24, 28–29, 40–63, 95, 113–114, 135, 136, 138–140, 141–142; children 94–96, 131–132; false imprisonment in country of origin xvi, 11–12, 40–63, 73–74, 141–142, 143; food and drink facilities 47–49; health assessments/evaluations 4, 135; heroic asylum seekers 40–63; poor conditions 12, 138–139, 141–142; profits 138; statistics xiv, 138–139, *see also* detention
profits, prisons 138
The Program for Survivors of Torture at Bellevue Hospital 8–9, 58–59, 61
proponents of the procedure, female genital mutilation (FGM) 68–69
prostitution 108

Index   159

protestors i, xii, xvii, xviii–xix, 13, 40–65; American family dream pursuit 56–59; background i, xii, xvii, xviii–xix, 13, 40–65; characteristics 41, 49–55; conclusions 62–63; denial 52, 54–56; discussion 49–63; heroic asylum seekers 54–55; how the role unfolds 47–49; Milgram laboratory experiments 50; psychodynamic perspectives 51–55; World War II 50, 52–53, *see also* heroic asylum seekers
psychiatrists xxii–xxiii
psychoanalysis 10–11, 14, 52–53, 69–72, 79–86, 99–100, 120–121
psychodynamic perspectives i, xii–xiii, 6–7, 51–55, 71–72, 77–86, 148; female genital mutilation (FGM) 71–72, 77–86; heroic asylum seekers 51–55, *see also* psychosocial assessments
psychological assessments xii, xiv, xviii, xix–xx, xxii, 1–33, 41, 68–89, 92–126, 142–144, 147–148; attorney relationships 25–26, 58; confidentiality issues 25; female genital mutilation (FGM) 68–72, 77–89, 147–148; feminicide xx, 92–126; general set-up/procedures 4–7; goals 2–4, 7–8, 10–11; interpreter relationships 27–29; locations 4; methods 5–7, 28; objectivity/rationality goals 8–9; political perspectives 7–9; processes 2–29; tests/questionnaires 6–7, 32; transferential/countertransferential issues 9–17, 28–29, 31; truth considerations 22–25, 98–99, *see also* diagnosis; interviews
psychologists xvi, xx–xxi, xxii–xxiii, 2–3; agencies 2–3; health assessments/evaluations xii, xiv, xvi, xviii, xix–xx, xxii–xxiii, 1–33, 41, 68–89, 92–126, 135, 141–148; outline prospective asylum-seeker support affidavit of a mental health professional xiv, 7–9, 29, 141–144; qualities/characteristics 14–15, 18, 21; relationships with clients 9–16, 19–22; roles xvi, xx–xxi, xxii–xxiii, 2–4, 7–9, 10–11, 15–16, 25–26; self-care support groups 22; training 18, 27, 30; vicarious traumatization 21–22, 26, 33, *see also* mental health professionals
psychosis 4, 84–85

psychosocial assessments i, xii, xiv, xviii, xix–xx, 1–33, 120, 139, 142–144; processes 2–29, *see also* behavioral assessments; cognition assessments; emotional assessments; forensic perspectives; political perspectives; psychodynamic perspectives; psychological assessments
psychosomatic complaints 53
psychotherapy xii–xiii, xiv, 14–15, 22, 27–29, 57–63, 116–117
PsycINFO 78
PsyLIT 147

qualities/characteristics, heroic asylum seekers 41, 49–55; psychologists 14–15, 18, 21
Quiché culture 24, 101, 121, 124
Quiroga, J. 57

racial profiling xvi
Randall, G. R. 63
rape xvii, xxii, 5, 19, 22, 24–25, 40–41, 44, 46, 48–49, 54, 60, 77–78, 83, 86, 88, 92–93, 104, 115
Reagan, Ronald 125
the real, experience 14–15, 55–56
rebellions from the twentieth century, Central America 110–111, 122, 125
recall difficulties, trauma 23–24
refoulement (forcible return to country of origin) 1–2, 138; definition 1, 138, *see also* non-refoulement principle
refugees, definition xiii, xxi, 29, 30; embassies 30; statistics xiii, xiv, xxi, 9, 111, 138–139, *see also* asylum seekers
rehearsed narratives, interviews 4–5
relationships, with attorneys 25–26, 58; client backgrounds 6–7, 9–16, 70–86; with interpreters 27–29; interviews 6–7, 9–16, 77–86; torturers 6–7, 21, 31
relatives, heroic asylum seekers 40–63
religion xix, xx, 1–2, 20, 23, 30, 43–63, 70–87, 104–105, 107, 114–115, 141, 145, 148; Central America xx, 104–105, 107, 114–115; female genital mutilation (FGM) 70–87; five protected grounds for persecution claims 1–2; heroic asylum seekers 43–63; international legal codes 123, *see also* Buddhism; Christianity; Islam; Mayan culture

remission, post-traumatic stress disorder (PTSD) 77
resilience xix, 10, 16–17, 71–86
resistance xviii–xix, 40–63, 80–81; adolescents 80; ethnic feuds 51; how the role unfolds 47–49; World War II 50, 52–53, *see also* heroic asylum seekers; protestors
respect 18
restraining orders, domestic abuse 76
retraumatization issues, advantages 18–21; definitions 16–17
Reuters xiv
Riesman, P. 81, 87–88
Rio Sumpul massacre 125
rituals, violence 5, 46, 86, 101–104
Roosevelt, Franklin xv
Rosa's story, feminicide 94–96, 99, 117–121
Roth, Ken xiv
ruin of the old ideals 109
rules of evidence, post-traumatic stress disorder (PTSD) 30
Russia 59–61

sadness 148
Sagot, M. 97–99, 120, 122–123
sanctions against refugees xiv, xvi
Schoen, S. 17–18
secondary traumatization, definition 54–55
self-care considerations, vicarious traumatization 22
self-esteem 18, 118–119
self-understanding 11–12, 15, 52, 55–57, 59–60, 62–65, 79–82
Sembène, Ousmane 86
Senegal xxiii, 70, 86, 147–148; Ms. E (Senegal) female genital mutilation (FGM) 70; Ms. H (Senegal) female genital mutilation 70, 78–79
sepsis 145
Sesotho 72
sex traffickers 6–7, 30
sexual intercourse 6–7, 61, 73–77, 81–82, 88, 98, 148
sexual violence xvii, xxii, 5–7, 19, 22–29, 40–49, 54, 60–61, 73–75, 77–78, 88, 98–121, 143; rape xvii, xxii, 5, 19, 22, 24–25, 40–41, 44, 46, 48–49, 54, 60, 77–78, 83, 86, 88, 92–93, 98, 104, 115
sexuality 3, 26, 33, 142
Shadera-Kevorkian, Nadera 92
shame 6–7, 13–14, 19–20, 22, 76, 82, 87, 95, 98–121, 124, 148, *see also* honor; machismo
Shapiro, Fran Geteles 32
Shatan, C. 22
Shock, K. 17
Sicalides, E. L. 68–69
Sierra Leone 18, 71
singsonging/rhythmic narrative of a client 4–5
Slavin, J. H. 79–80, 85
social group membership, five protected grounds for persecution claims 1–2, 31
social workers xxiii
Somalia 63
Sor Juana 124
South America 10–11, 97, 100, 111–112, 122, *see also* Central America
South Texas Family Residential Center, Dilley, Texas 24, 92, 94, 122, 139, 140
Spanish colonialism, Central America xx, 101–102, 104–121, 123–124, 126
Spanish Inquisition 124
Spanish language xx, 24, 92–121
Special Immigrant Juvenile status 3
Stern, Donald 10, 14–16, 52, 59
'Stop Soros' law, Hungary 131
stress, interviews 5–6, 16, 17–18, 133
students 1, 25–26, 59–60, 133; law students 25–26
subject 1 (Yugoslavia), heroic asylum seekers 42, 43, 45, 56
subject 2 (Togo), heroic asylum seekers 42, 43
subject 3 (Guinea) (Mr. I), heroic asylum seekers 42, 43, 47–48, 56–59, 61
subject 4 (Tibet), heroic asylum seekers 42, 43, 45, 53–54, 56, 64
subject 5 (Tibet), heroic asylum seekers 42, 43, 53–54, 64
subject 6 (Guinea), heroic asylum seekers 42, 44
subject 7 (Cameroon), heroic asylum seekers 42, 44, 53, 55–56
subject 8 (Cameroon), heroic asylum seekers 42, 44, 45, 64
subject 9 (Myanmar), heroic asylum seekers 44, 54–55, 56
subject 10 (Belarus) (Ms. B), heroic asylum seekers 44, 45, 48–49, 54–55, 56–57, 59–62, 64

subject 11 (Ghana), heroic asylum seekers 44, 46, 49
submissive roles xix, xx, 81–86, 96–121, 124; agency xix, 81–86, 100–101, 106–121, 124
suicide attempts 19, 125
Sullivan, Harry Stack 62
support groups 22, 63, 113; vicarious traumatization 22
supporting papers, asylum law 1, 2–3, 133–134, 135
Supreme Court 29
Symonds, M. 10
Syria 63

terrorism xvi
tests/questionnaires 6–7, 32
Therese's story 19–21
third individuation process, definition 78
Tibet 42, 43, 45, 53–54, 56, 64; Dharamsala 56; subject 4 (Tibet) heroic asylum seeker 42, 43, 45, 53–54, 56, 64; subject 5 (Tibet) heroic asylum seeker 42, 43, 53–54, 64
Togo, subject 2 (Togo) heroic asylum seeker 42, 43
Toniná 123
torture xix, 2–9, 11–12, 21, 30, 31, 40–63, 110–111, 125, 141–142; CIA 110–111, 125; The Program for Survivors of Torture at Bellevue Hospital 8–9, 58–59, 61; relationships 6–7, 21, 31; studies 57; symptoms 57–58; treatments 8–9, 57–59, 61, *see also* persecution
tourist visas 40, 70–71
training 1, 18, 27, 30, 46–47; asylum officers 1, 30; interpreters 27; psychologists 18, 27, 30
transferential/countertransferential issues 9–17, 28–29, 31; interpreters 28–29; psychological assessments 9–17, 28–29, 31
trauma xvi, xviii–xix, 2–4, 6–7, 15–17, 18–29, 33, 40–63, 145, 147–148; female genital mutilation (FGM) xvi, xviii, xxiii, 68–89, 145, 147–148; heroic asylum seekers 40–63; recall difficulties 23–24; retraumatization issues 16–17, 18–21; secondary traumatization 54–55; vicarious traumatization 21–22, 33, *see also* post-traumatic stress disorder; violence

traumatized reaction group, female genital mutilation (FGM) xix–xx, 70, 72–73, 78–86, 148
treatments, cognitive behavioral therapy (CBT) 57; eye movement desensitization and reprocessing (EMDR) 57; group therapy 58–59, 63; narrative therapy 57; post-traumatic stress disorder (PTSD) 58–59, 61; The Program for Survivors of Torture at Bellevue Hospital 8–9, 58–59, 61; torture 8–9, 57–59, 61
Trump, Donald xxi, 131–132, 136, 140
trust 11–12, 23–25, 61
truth considerations, psychological assessments 22–25, 98–99

U visas residency threats 135
Ullman, Chana 15, 33
unconscious subjectivity 8–9, 94, 96
uncontained abuse i, xix, xx, 92–126, 139, 141–142
undo attempts, female genital mutilation (FGM) 148
UNICEF 68
United Nations xiii–xv, xx, xxi–xxiii, 4, 31, 32, 93, 113, 121–123; High Commissioner for Refugees (UNHCR) xiii–xiv, xx, xxi–xxiii, 4, 31, 93, 122
United States Citizen and Immigration Services (USCIS) 133, 134, 135–136, *see also* asylum officers
Universal Declaration of Human Rights, historical background xv
US, Central America 107–108, 110–111, 125; CIA xxi, 110–111, 125; colonialism xx, 107–108, 110–111, 125; critique 9, 29–30, 121–122, 131–132; feminicide xvi; FGM incidence 68–69, 86; life/liberty/happiness mission 8; parent/child border separation concerns 131–132; statistics xiii–xiv, xxi, 9, 68–69, 86, 111, 138–139, *see also individual topics*

Vaisman-Tzachor, R. 2, 29
valid immigration status 133
vicarious resilience, definition 10, 16
vicarious traumatization, attorneys 26; definition 21–22; interpreters 28–29; positive effects 22; psychologists 21–22, 26, 33; self-care considerations 22

Vioeberghs, E. 78, 85, 88
violence i, xvi, xvii, xviii, xix–xx, xxii, 5–7, 12, 19–31, 40–63, 71–76, 81–86, 92–126, 131, 139, 141–142, 143; domestic abuse i, xvi, xviii, xix–xx, 71–76, 81–86, 92–126, 131, 139, 141–142, 143; feminicide i, xii, xvi, xx, 92–126; heroic asylum seekers 40–63; machismo i, xx, 92–121; rape xvii, xxii, 5, 19, 22, 24–25, 40–41, 44, 46, 48–49, 54, 60, 77–78, 83, 86, 88, 92–93, 104, 115; rituals 5, 46, 86, 101–104; sexual violence xvii, xxii, 5–7, 19, 22–29, 40–49, 54, 60–61, 73–75, 77–78, 88, 98–121, 143, *see also* Central America; female genital mutilation; trauma
Virgin Mary xx, 107, 109–110
voice-hearers 84–85, *see also* psychosis
Volkan, Vamik 50–51, 56, 103
volunteers xiii, xx–xxi, 2–3, 25–26, 30, 139

Wade, C. J. 110–111, 121, 125
Walker, T. W. 110–111, 121, 125
wars xiv, xvi, 12–13, 18, 22, 31, 50, 52–53, 54, 63–64, 111, 114, 126; Holocaust survivors 22, 31, 52–53, 54, *see also* World War

weaving skills, Mayan culture 102
well-being assessments 3–4, 32, 53, 87, 110
Well-Founded Fear documentary 30, 135
Which Way Home documentary 140
the will to survive i, xvi–xviii
Wilson, John 21
Winnicott, D. W. 79
witnesses, asylum law 1, 14–15, 30, 133–134; heroic asylum seekers 40–63
women on the run xix, xx, 40–63, 92–126, 139, 142–143; studies 93–94, *see also* female; feminicide; heroic asylum seekers; machismo
work permits, asylum law 133–134, 135
World Bank 126
World Health Organization (WHO) 86, 145
World War I xiv
World War II xxi, xxii, 22, 50–51, 52–53; Holocaust survivors 22, 31, 52–53, 54; protestors 50, 52–53

Yacouba/Evangelical Christians 70
Yugoslavia, subject 1 (Yugoslavia) heroic asylum seeker 42, 43, 45, 56